PATTON
AND THE BATTLE FOR
SICILY

Map 0.1 ▪ American forces landed between Licata and Scoglitti, while the British forces landed at the southeastern corner of Sicily. They all had over a month of hard fighting before they reached their goal: Messina.

EA
Messina
Reggio di Calabria
Brolo
Sant'Agata
Santo Stefano
Strait of Messina
Taormina
Troina
Nicosia
Mt. Etna
Enna
Catania
tanissetta
Primosole Bridge
Caltagirone
Augusta
Gela
82nd Airborne
Vittoria
Syracuse
Vittoria
Comiso
Ragusa
Noto
Scoglitti
5th Brit Div
50th Brit Div
51st Brit Div
Pachino
n Inf Div
cent Force"
1st Can Div
Malta Channel
BRITISH 8th ARMY
(Montgomery)

Permissions

Excerpts from *Crusade in Europe* by Dwight D. Eisenhower, © 1948 by Penguin Random House LLC. Used by permission of Doubleday, an imprint of the Knopf Doubleday Publishing Group, a division of Penguin Random House LLC. All rights reserved.

Excerpt(s) from *Darby's Rangers: We Led the Way* by William O. Darby with William H. Baumer, © 1980 by Penguin Random House LLC. Used by permission of Presidio Press, an imprint of Random House, a division of Penguin Random House LLC. All rights reserved.

Excerpts from *Doctor Danger Forward: A World War II Memoir of a Combat Medical Aidman, First Infantry Division* © 2000 Allen N. Towne by permission of McFarland & Company, Inc. Box 611, Jefferson, NC 28640 www.mcfarlandbooks.com

Excerpts from *Drive* by Charles Codman, © 1957. Reprinted by permission of Little, Brown, an imprint of Hachette Book Group, Inc.

Excerpts from *My Three Years with Eisenhower: The Personal Diary of Captain Harry C. Butcher, USNR*, by Harry C. Butcher. © 1946 by Harry C. Butcher. Copyright renewed 1974 by Harry C. Butcher. Reprinted with the permission of Simon & Schuster LLC. All rights reserved.

Excerpts reproduced with the permission of the Second World War Experience Centre, www .war-experience.org, from the donated papers of Mr. Arthur Royall, reference LEEWW.2001.1238

Excerpts from *A Soldier's Story* by Omar N. Bradley used with permission from Publishing Holdco, Inc. d/b/a Rand McNally Publishing.

PATTON AND THE BATTLE FOR SICILY

THE GENERAL, THE NAVY, AND OPERATION HUSKY

FLINT WHITLOCK

Naval Institute Press
Annapolis, Maryland

Naval Institute Press
291 Wood Road
Annapolis, MD 21402

ISBN: 978-1-61251-691-2 (hardcover)
ISBN: 978-1-61251-711-7 (ebook)

Library of Congress Cataloging-in-Publication data is available.

♾ Print editions meet the requirements of ANSI/NISO z39.48–1992 (Permanence of Paper).
Printed in the United States of America.

33 32 31 30 29 28 27 26 25 9 8 7 6 5 4 3 2 1
First printing

All maps created by the author.

CONTENTS

MAPS

INTRODUCTION

I am the best there is.
—George S. Patton Jr.

As he stood in the darkness at the chain railing of the *Crescent City*–class attack transport USS *Monrovia*, his floating headquarters for the invasion of Sicily, fifty-six-year-old three-star general George Smith Patton Jr. peered outward, trying in vain to see the vast armada that he could only hear and smell and feel.

It was just past midnight on Saturday, 10 July 1943. Before dawn he would witness the armada's mighty power unleashed. He knew that somewhere out there on that darkened island there were hundreds of thousands of German and Italian soldiers equipped with deadly weapons that could make hash out of his invasion force, but he felt no fear. It was the enemy who would soon be shaking in their boots, pissing in their pants. They had no idea what was about to hit them—the greatest air and sea invasion up to that moment of the war.

Out there in the blackness were 945 American ships and landing craft transporting one armored and three infantry divisions, along with three Ranger battalions—some 87,000 American soldiers—rushing toward death or destiny, charging forward at full speed like a line of cavalry horses. Overhead, 226 C-47 and C-53 transport planes were about to deliver 2,781 American paratroopers to drop onto the enemy's island. Another

670 bombers and fighters were already aloft, carrying out escort duties, making diversionary runs on targets in various locales to keep the enemy guessing, or preparing to bomb ground targets in the one-hundred-mile-wide invasion area.[1]

Patton also knew that far off to the east at that very moment were 1,645 vessels of the British Royal Navy carrying some 94,000 soldiers of the Eighth British Army, commanded by his counterpart and nemesis, General Bernard Law Montgomery. The coming battle, just hours away, would not only be the biggest battle yet between the Allies and Axis; it would also be a test to see if his Yanks were equal to—or better than—Monty's battle-hardened Brits. He had had quite enough of British disparagements of the fighting quality of the American soldier. His personal and professional reputation—and the vindication of Gen. Dwight Eisenhower's trust in him—was riding on the backs of his own soldiers.

He felt a surge of pride course through his body. "All my life I have wanted to lead a lot of men in a desperate battle," he recalled having written in his diary just prior to Operation Torch, the invasion of North Africa; now he was again doing it. He also recalled writing in his last letter to his wife Beatrice, who was waiting out the war back in their handsome white Colonial home on Asbury Street in Hamilton, Massachusetts, "If I win, I can't be stopped! If I lose, I shall be dead."[2]

Yes, the coming battle would be the supreme test for him—and for his men. In the days previous, he had given a plethora of pep talks to the soldiers who were about to bring the fight to the enemy, many of them for the first time. He had done all he could do to instill in them a fighting spirit, a lust for battle, a thirst for blood. Soon, control of the battle would slip out of his grasp and be turned over to the lower-ranking generals, the colonels, the captains, the lieutenants, the sergeants, the corporals, the privates—many of them frightened, fresh-faced teenagers who had never before even killed so much as a rabbit. The outcome of the battle would be decided by them. God, he hoped they were ready for the challenge. Like a truly great coach or commander, he had done all he could to make them so.

Patton was flesh and blood, a leader full of contradictions, simultaneously brash and contrite, pious and profane, vainglorious and humble, personally courageous and situationally fearful, overconfident and self-doubting—a hard-charging commander with a soft side who earned the love and loyalty of his troops, and also their hatred.

He was dressed splendidly for the occasion: an olive-drab tanker's jacket over his beribboned khaki shirt; a khaki tie; a pair of jodhpurs with the flared thighs; gleaming knee-high brown leather cavalry boots; an ivory-handled pistol strapped to his right hip; a pair of binoculars and a 35-millimeter camera slung around his neck; a steel helmet with three silver stars soldered to it; and a riding crop/swagger stick in one hand. It was as close as he could get to the gleaming panoply of a *legatus*—a Roman general.

Unlike some other American generals—he thought briefly of Lloyd Fredendall, who preferred to lead from the safety of the rear—he planned to come ashore as soon as practical to direct operations on the ground, to be there so that his men could see him, marvel at him, and gain strength and courage from him as he stood on the shore—or rode into battle—with his "war face" on, a face designed to frighten the enemy, and perhaps even his own troops.

His stern countenance was not only a device to frighten; it was also a reflection of his feelings at being handed a plan that was not his and with which he did not agree, and of his anger at the fact that Harold Alexander and Montgomery and others within the British military hierarchy were still dismissive of the American soldier's fighting abilities.

Standing at his shoulder on that deck, also dressed for battle and straining to see in the darkness, was the commander of the American armada, the old salt Vice Adm. H. Kent Hewitt, in charge of the Western Naval Task Force (TF 34). Patton's feelings toward Hewitt ran hot and cold. He prayed that Hewitt would live up to his expectations and deliver the greatest invasion fleet yet assembled to its appointed shores and at the appointed time, but he had his doubts. Two months earlier, after a contentious meeting, he had written that Hewitt "as usual, cannot decide anything and is full of querulous reasons for failure." He also worried that the U.S. Army Air Forces could not be relied upon.[3]

As the minutes to H-hour—the scheduled start of the assault—ticked away, and as the fleet bounded over storm-driven waves, Patton remembered what he had once told the 2nd Armored Division troops during the 1941 Carolina

Maneuvers: "Battle is not a terrifying ordeal to be endured. It is a magnificent experience wherein all the elements that have made man superior to the beasts are present: courage, self-sacrifice, loyalty, help to others, devotion to duty." He hoped his men also remembered those words.[4]

The moment was all so wondrous, so glorious. He had never been so exhilarated. To him, war was mankind's highest calling, the ultimate test of courage, the epitome of manhood itself. To him, cowards and shirkers were the lowest forms of life, unworthy of breathing the same air as brave men who had proven themselves in combat. Anyone who did not do his duty, no matter how arduous and hazardous, did not deserve to call himself a man. Battle had always thrilled him—from the moment that he had, as a young lieutenant, engaged in firefights with Pancho Villa's Mexican *banditos* in May 1916 on the dusty plains of northern Mexico.[5]

Patton deeply admired the pantheon of past military heroes—Hannibal, Julius Caesar, Horatio Nelson, Napoleon Bonaparte, William Sherman, Stonewall Jackson, John J. Pershing—and hoped that one day he would be included in their exalted ranks. He had a strong belief in divine destiny and trusted that he had been prepared by some cosmic force—call it God—to accomplish great things.

He had sent a stirring message to all those about to participate in the upcoming operation:

> We are indeed honored in having been selected [for], this new and greater attack against the Axis. . . . When we land we will meet German and Italian soldiers whom it is our honor and privilege to attack and destroy. . . . During the last year we Americans have met and defeated the best troops [our enemies] possess. Many of us have shared in those glorious victories. Those of you who have not been so fortunate now have your opportunity to gain equal fame.
>
> In landing operations, retreat is impossible. To surrender is as ignoble as it is foolish. . . . Keep punching. No man is beaten until he thinks he is. . . . Civilians who have the stupidity to fight us we will kill. Those who remain passive will not be harmed. . . .

> The glory of American arms, the honor of our country, the future of the whole world rests in your individual hands. See to it that you are worthy of this great trust.[6]

He had inscribed a little prayer in his diary the night before the invasion: "God, help me and see to it that I do my duty, but I must have Your help. I am the best there is, but of myself I am not enough."[7]

■ ■ ■

In a short while, one of the naval officers on the bridge notified Patton and Hewitt that the armada had reached its destination in the Gulf of Gela and that the bombardment, airborne invasion, and amphibious assault were about to begin. Suddenly, at H-hour—0245 hours on 10 July—all around the *Monrovia* great flashes belched from the muzzles of the unseen warships, hurling shells as big around as a fullback's thighs into the predawn blackness and punching the eardrums with painful blows. Moments later, bright bursts of light appeared on shore, followed by *boom, boom, boom* but sounding like *doom, doom, doom*—a drumroll letting the recipients know that George Patton and the Seventh Army had arrived and that Operation Husky had begun.

BACKSTORY

THE DECISION FOR SICILY

Behold Sicily—the largest island in the Mediterranean Sea. At almost ten thousand square miles, about the size of the state of Massachusetts, it is one of the most beautiful places on Earth. Clear azure waters teeming with life surround its white sand beaches. Jagged peaks reach into the sky. Olive groves and cactus patches add an emerald cast to the undulating, khaki-colored hills. Europe's largest active volcano—Mount Etna—dominates the northeast landscape. Traces of human settlements date back thousands of years before the Egyptian pyramids. Remnants of ancient Greece and Rome are everywhere. The place is rich with history.[1]

Despite—or perhaps because of—its beauty, Sicily is no stranger to war and conquest. Over the centuries it has been invaded, occupied, fought over, and ruled by the ancient Greeks, Romans, Carthaginians, Vandals, Ostrogoths, Byzantines, Saracens, Normans, French, Spanish, Austrians, and the Bourbon Kingdom of the Two Sicilies. Now the criminal society known as the Mafia, along with Italian Prime Minister Benito Mussolini's Fascists, controlled every aspect of life on the island.

In the early 1940s Sicily swarmed with the soldiers of Mussolini's armies and those of his German partner, Adolf Hitler. Sicily was a strategic fortress that dominated the strait between Tunisia—site of Rome's old rival Carthage—and southern Italy: the gateway to Egypt, the Suez Canal, Greece, the Balkan countries, and the oil-rich Middle East. During the two decades of Italian fascism (*Ventennio Fascista*), Mussolini borrowed two words from the ancient Roman vocabulary and declared the Mediterranean to be *Mare Nostrum*—Our Sea.[2]

It is no mystery, then, why both the Axis and Allied powers paid special attention to Sicily, for whoever possessed it held the key to the gateway.

■ ■ ■

Operation Torch—the invasion of North Africa in November 1942—was the first time American troops had faced German and Italian forces in ground warfare. Even while that campaign was rolling toward a successful conclusion for the Allies by May 1943, the United States and Great Britain were trying to decide where to go next in the march toward victory in Europe. The choices were limited.

A full-scale invasion of the European continent in 1943 or even early 1944 seemed out of the question. The soldiers and supplies necessary to mount such an invasion were still trickling into Britain from the United States, while the number of trained American troops needed to storm the beaches of Europe was still too small to turn the tide of war in favor of the Allies. A further build-up and period of training were essential to crack Hitler's *Festung Europa*—Fortress Europe.[3]

■ ■ ■

In the meantime, as an Allied victory along the southern shores of the Mediterranean Sea was imminent, the logic of starting the invasion of the European continent from the south seemed unassailable—at least to the British. The troops were there, the ships were there, the warplanes were there—why not start the invasion from there? After all, British Prime Minister Winston S. Churchill had declared that this area was "the soft underbelly of Europe," so it must be true.[4]

Except that it wasn't. A glance at a map shows that most of southern Europe's Mediterranean coast is ringed with formidable mountains. And in wartime, mountains are incredibly difficult places in which to maneuver and fight—as U.S. Lt. Gen. Mark W. Clark would later discover to his dismay while his Fifth Army was battling for every foot of ground in Italy. He said that instead of being a soft underbelly, the area was "a tough, old gut."[5]

Another glance at that same map also shows that Sicily is the stepping stone from North Africa to Italy. With the Italian army having performed so poorly in Africa, Germany's chancellor and warlord Adolf Hitler realized that he would need to keep considerable forces in the region to bolster his defenses on his southern front—forces that he would rather have battling the Red Army in the Soviet Union, or performing occupation duties in the countries he had conquered, or manning the coastline of what he claimed was an impregnable "Atlantic Wall" guarding his Fortress Europe from an Allied invasion. But Hitler's finite resources were stretched thin; only minimal numbers of men, tanks, and planes were available to keep the Allies out of Italy and southern Europe.[6]

In spite of this, the Americans were not enamored of the idea of risking their own finite resources on a protracted campaign in the Mediterranean. Gen. George C. Marshall, U.S. Army chief of staff, was eager to get on with invading France and was unhappy to see the war's direction heading toward more fighting in the Mediterranean.[7]

If the war in the Mediterranean had to be fought—at least until an invasion of France became feasible—Sardinia, the island north of Sicily, initially seemed more attractive. In fact, Hitler believed that Sardinia made more sense; he sent his 90th Panzer Grenadier Division to reinforce the four Italian divisions already there.[8] A significant meeting in January 1943 would solidify the Allies' decision for Sicily.

Under swaying Moroccan palms, much was accomplished at the Casablanca Conference, held from 12–24 January 1943 at the Anfa Hotel and code-named Symbol. Although confined to a wheelchair because polio had left him a paraplegic in 1921, President Franklin D. Roosevelt made a long and arduous flight across the Atlantic to meet with Churchill and Free French forces leader Gen. Charles de Gaulle to hammer out a broad strategy for the coming months and years of the war. Soviet Premier Joseph Stalin had been invited but was unable to attend due to pressing war matters at home.

Despite his absence, Stalin's voice could be heard pleading—even demanding—that the Western Allies do something immediately to open a "second front" and take the German pressure off the Soviet Union. It was also at this conference that Roosevelt made his startling declaration that the Allies would accept only unconditional surrender from the Axis powers—a declaration that Churchill thought was too extreme, though he said nothing.[9]

Also in attendance were General Marshall, commander in chief of allied forces in the Mediterranean Lt. Gen. Dwight D. Eisenhower, Maj. Gen. George Patton, Lt. Gen. Mark Clark, and other high-ranking American and British officers. Roosevelt and Churchill and their advisors resolved to concentrate their efforts against Germany in the hopes of drawing German forces away from the Eastern Front, and to increase shipments of war supplies to the Soviet Union. They also agreed to strengthen their strategic bombing campaign against Germany. Invading Italy, the weakest of the Axis partners, was also seen as a worthy goal and could lead to Italy's capitulation. But what was the next step?

The British wanted to expand combat operations in the Mediterranean, but Marshall argued that the Allies should not squander resources there but instead concentrate on the much-discussed eventual invasion of the European continent. It was Churchill who won out—just as he had earlier when he advocated for Torch. With huge military assets already in the Mediterranean, he argued, did it not make more sense for the Allies to employ them to defeat Italy and perhaps keep considerable German assets tied down in the region, far from the gates of Moscow and the beaches of northern France? Without a better plan, the Americans had no choice but to go along with it.[10]

The logic seemed unassailable, and so it was decided to launch the "second front" from the Mediterranean while still building up forces in Britain for the eventual leap across the English Channel into Normandy—an operation that would be code-named Overlord. Marshall reluctantly agreed to continue striking Axis positions in the Mediterranean by first invading Sicily. It would receive the code name Operation Husky.[11]

But who would lead the campaign? General Eisenhower, fresh from Operation Torch, seemed the right choice. Although he had never personally led troops in battle, he had proven his ability to coordinate the myriad tasks needed for a large-scale military operation and to work well with his sometimes-contentious British partners. Except for a few setbacks between Morocco and Tunisia, Ike, as everyone called him, and his forces had done a reasonably competent job; he was retained as Supreme Allied Commander for Husky.

It was also decided that General Sir Harold R. L. G. Alexander would be Ike's deputy commander while Bernard Law Montgomery, Britain's "Hero of El Alamein," would command half of the invading force—the Eighth Army; George S. Patton Jr. would command a yet-to-be-named American army that would comprise the other half.[12]

■ ■ ■

During a break in the conference, Patton had a chance to renew his acquaintance with President Roosevelt and lunch with him and his trusted advisor Harry Hopkins. Although the mood was salubrious, Patton was worried. His diary entry of 21 January reads, "The country [U.S.] and the army are in a hell of a fix and nothing is being done about it. People speak of Germany and Japan as being defeated, [but] we have never attacked them with more than a division."[13]

After Patton learned that Sicily was the next objective for American and British forces once the North Africa campaign was concluded—and that he would command the American forces—he wrote in his diary, "My luck will have to be pretty good and the Lord on the job to put it over. . . . I guess destiny is still on the job." But he was not pleased about the idea of sharing glory for a presumed victory in Sicily with Montgomery, nor being under the command of another British general, Harold Alexander.[14]

The British, of course, had been fighting since 1940 and thus had gained considerable combat experience; the Yanks were new to the game and were still finding their way on the modern battlefield. An invasion of Sicily would prove whether the Yanks could fight as well as the Tommies.

■ ■ ■

And so the build-up for Husky began. Any German or Italian spy near Oran would have had to be blind not to notice the growing assemblage of vessels, vehicles, troops, and supplies—there was no disguising that a major operation was in its preliminary stages. But maybe the enemy could be deceived into thinking it was not intended for Sicily.

Since the island was seen by the Germans and Italians as the probable—even obvious—next step, a deception plan was needed to fool them into thinking it wasn't. That deception plan received the code name Operation Mincemeat but would forever be known as "the man who never was."

Mincemeat was born when two British intelligence officers convinced their superiors that a dead body in a British military uniform washing up on a Spanish shore and carrying faked "top secret" documents indicating that an invasion would come not at Sicily or Sardinia, but at German-occupied Greece, would fool the enemy.

In London, operatives obtained the corpse of a recently deceased homeless Welshman named Glyndwr Michael, dressed him in a Royal Marines uniform, gave him the fictional identity of Maj. William Martin, chained a briefcase full of authentic-looking fake documents to his wrist, and sent him on a submarine voyage to southern Spain where, on 30 April 1943, he was released overboard and allowed to drift into shore.

Picked up by fishermen and turned over to pro-German Spanish authorities, the corpse eventually made its way into the custody of German Abwehr agents, who diligently examined every aspect of the corpse and its documents—and declared them authentic. The elaborate ruse worked to perfection; Hitler was so convinced that Greece and not Sicily was the Allies' objective that he transferred the 1st Panzer Division there to augment his four infantry divisions and the Italian Eleventh Army—despite Mussolini's and the Italian high command's belief that Sicily was the real target.[15]

Undoubtedly Eisenhower and Alexander were informed of Mincemeat and its impact on Husky, but was Patton? If he had been, he did not write about it.

■ ■ ■

There was one other pre-Husky matter that demanded attention. Lying one hundred miles off the coast of Tunisia was the fortified island of Pantelleria that Mussolini had turned into a stationary aircraft carrier. The island's presence posed a grave danger to invasion plans and would need to be neutralized before Husky could proceed.

The thirty-two-square-mile island was bristling with anti-aircraft defenses and a five-thousand-foot-long runway with a bomb-proof underground hangar carved out of solid rock. This hangar was one thousand feet in length, eighty-five feet wide, and sixty feet high and could hold six bombers and sixty fighters. Tiny Pantelleria was also home to 10,000 civilians, 11,000 Italian soldiers and airmen, and 600 German specialists who operated key radar installations. Any Allied air or naval traffic that came near the island would be spotted and reported by the radar operators and intercepted by the fighters and bombers based there. If Pantelleria could be neutralized, the Italian and German forces in Sicily would essentially be blind to the Allies' air and sea movements.

Not wanting to risk the Husky invasion forces, on 18 May 1943 Eisenhower decided to unleash what has been described as the heaviest and most prolonged naval and aerial bombardment against any target up to that point in the war. The British and Americans plastered Pantelleria night and day for thirty-five days with 5,285 bombing sorties that dropped 6,313 tons of explosives (including four-thousand-pound "Blockbusters"). Finally, on 11 June British troops on a British ship entered the shattered harbor and accepted the surrender of the dazed garrison. The passage from North Africa to Sicily was now clear.[16]

■ ■ ■

When George Patton discovered that the admiral in command of the ships that brought American forces to North Africa for Operation Torch—Vice Adm. H. Kent Hewitt—would also be in command of the American half of Husky, he was not happy.

The two men had gotten off to a rocky start months earlier. In August 1942 Patton was working on the plans for Torch and his Western Task Force (3rd and 9th Infantry Divisions and elements of the 1st and 2nd Armored Divisions) that would sail from Virginia and land near Casablanca in French Morocco. The Central Task Force, under Major Gen. Lloyd Fredendall, would land at Oran, while Major Gen. Charles Ryder's Eastern Task Force would come ashore at Algiers.[17]

Torch was a bold and daring operation, one fraught with danger and uncertainty—especially since the American ground troops had not yet been in combat. In a letter to his brother-in-law Frederick Ayers, Patton expressed his own dark thoughts: "The job I am going on is about as desperate a venture as has ever been undertaken by any force in the world's history. We will have to meet and defeat superior numbers on a coast where one can only land sixty percent of the time. . . . However, I have a convinced belief that I will succeed."[18] But Patton was also convinced that Hewitt and the U.S. Navy were "very pessimistic as to the possibility of effecting a landing at Casablanca [but] I feel that in spite of all, we will succeed there."[19]

A few weeks later Patton and Hewitt were at Solomon's Island, Maryland, observing an infantry landing rehearsal—a rehearsal that was not to Patton's liking. "The timing of the landing by the Navy was very bad, over forty minutes late to start with, but all we can hope is that they do better next time," he confided to his diary.

During the joint planning for Torch, Patton also clashed with Hewitt and his staff, especially around the concept of how to combat-load a ship so that the items loaded last would be the first out, contrary to Navy practice.[20] The profanity-laced meetings became so contentious that the exasperated Hewitt requested that Marshall replace Patton with someone easier to work with.[21] Eisenhower noted that Patton "had become embroiled in such a distressing argument with the Navy Department that serious thought was being given to his relief from command." Only Ike's intercession on Patton's behalf prevented Patton from being sacked even before he could take command.[22]

Perhaps as a way of keeping his distance from Hewitt, who he complained was "unenthusiastic" and "less than helpful," Patton set up his office in the War Department's mammoth Munitions Building on Washington's Constitution Avenue, while Hewitt's headquarters were in Norfolk, Virginia, from where the fleet would set sail.[23] Patton's unexplained antipathy toward Hewitt continued. According to the general, Hewitt was "in a haze as usual"[24] and "the perfect fool."[25] Luckily, the two men buried the hatchet—at least long enough to establish a sufficient working relationship to manage the overwhelming tasks at hand.[26]

To say that Patton was full of strong opinions is to state the obvious. Truth be told, Patton found it difficult to work with a wide variety of people. As he rose in rank, Patton could look down from his lofty perch and privately comment in his diary on the flaws of his fellow officers—and even kings and prime ministers—with barely a kind word for anyone. In his opinion, Supreme Allied Commander Eisenhower was "timid," "querulous," showed a "great lack of decision," and had "no knowledge of men or war." On one occasion, he journaled that Ike "has an inferiority complex," and another time said Ike was "an ass."[27]

Walter Bedell "Beetle" Smith, Ike's chief of staff, was "a typical s.o.b." who "takes delight in smearing the character of everyone."[28] Mark Wayne Clark, destined to command the Fifth U.S. Army in Italy after Sicily, was just as bad: "Too damned slick. . . . it makes my flesh crawl to be with him."[29] Lloyd Fredendall, whom he relieved as commander of II Corps in North Africa after the Kasserine debacle, was "either a little nuts or badly scared."[30] His old friend Omar Bradley, with whom he would have a falling out and who would one day become the last of only five men to achieve five-star General of the Army rank, was "a man of great mediocrity."[31]

Patton didn't spare his British allies, either. He noted that Lord Louis Mountbatten was "charming but not impressive."[32] General Alan Brooke (chief of Britain's Imperial General Staff) was "nothing but a clerk,"[33] and Winston Churchill was "cunning rather than brilliant but with great tenacity."[34] Britain's King George VI, whom he met in June 1943, was "just a grade above a moron. Poor little fellow."[35] And yet, Bernard Law Montgomery, with whom he would clash many times, was "small, very alert, wonderfully conceited, and the best soldier—or so it seems—I have met in this war."[36]

Of his American subordinates, Patton was most impressed with Troy Middleton (45th Infantry Division), Ernest J. "Mike" Dawley (36th Division),[37] and William O. Darby (commander of the Rangers), who was "really a great soldier."[38]

But, as with all of Patton's feelings about his fellow officers, his opinions could turn on a dime. For example, at their first meeting, he said General Sir Harold Alexander was "quiet and good-looking," "impressive," and "I liked him a lot."[39] But later he said that Alexander "cut a very sorry figure at times; he is a fence walker."[40]

■ ■ ■

Shortly before departing the United States for Operation Torch, Patton stopped in to see John J. "Black Jack" Pershing, his old commander from his days pursuing Pancho Villa on the Mexican border. Although suffering from the disabilities of old age, Pershing sent Patton off with some inspirational words: "I can always pick a fighting man and God knows there are few of them. I am happy they are sending you to the front at once. I like generals so bold that they are dangerous. I hope they give you a free hand. God bless and keep you and give you victory."[41]

Following this bracing visit, Patton and Hewitt reported to the White House for a rousing send-off from President Roosevelt, who greeted the two men with, "Come in, Skipper and Old Cavalryman, and give me the good news."

Patton recalled, "I had fixed up the meeting [with the president] with the hope that he would put some heat on Hewitt about the necessity of landing [no matter what the sea conditions]. As nothing came of it, I said, 'The Admiral and I feel that we must get ashore regardless of cost, as the fate of the war hinges on our success.' [Roosevelt] said, 'Certainly you must,' and that was that. A great politician is not necessarily a great military leader."[42]

In his diary Patton boasted to himself, "When I think of the greatness of my job [as commander of the Western Task Force] and realize that I am what I am, I am amazed, but on reflection, who is as good as I am? I know of no one."[43]

His feelings toward Hewitt also softened temporarily. He noted, "All elements of the convoy . . . will have over 100 vessels. Admiral Hewitt impresses me better. [Rear] Admiral [John L.] Hall [who would command one of the task forces] is great." It would not be long, however, before Patton once more became less enamored of Hewitt.[44]

On 23 October, the day before departing the United States for Torch, Patton wrote in his diary, "Today Captain [Robert] Emmett [the commander of the troop transports] talked [to the troops] for three hours and said nothing. I talked blood and guts for five minutes and got an ovation. . . . Now it is up to the Navy."[45]

■ ■ ■

Fortunately, the Western Naval Task Force's (Task Force 34) voyage across the Atlantic and through the Strait of Gibraltar went well, with little interference by German submarines. Hewitt would soon show his steely resolve during the decisive battle of Casablanca that crippled the French fleet and knocked out the shore batteries there, causing them to cease fire.[46]

Operation Torch was successful, although Patton had to take over command of II Corps after he relieved Fredendall due to a lack of leadership that resulted in the setback at Kasserine Pass.[47] And Patton's aide-de-camp Capt. Richard Jenson was killed during a German bombing raid at El Guettar, Tunisia.[48] Patton also became raging mad at the British for not supplying the air cover his troops needed.[49]

■ ■ ■

The massive battles that Patton had hoped would harden his soldiers did not materialize; the II Corps' role in the closing weeks of the North Africa campaign was mostly just of supporting Montgomery. Alexander and the entire British high command had been keenly disappointed by the performance of the American troops at Kasserine and decided they were only good in a subordinate role.[50]

Omar Bradley, described as Eisenhower's "troubleshooter," was acutely aware of the strained relationships between the Americans and the British. "At the outset of the North African war," he wrote in his memoirs, "there were some British officers . . . who regarded the American army with ill-concealed amusement. Their longer experience in the war caused them to look on us as country cousins, unlettered in the intricate arts of combat. And while they cheerfully conceded the superiority of American equipment, they jibed us for having too much of it."[51]

Patton knew that the next battle—Sicily—would be a make-or-break moment for the reputation of the American soldier, and he was determined that his men would succeed—even if he had to lead them onto the beaches himself.[52]

I

GETTING READY

There will be no prisoners taken.

—George S. Patton Jr.

On 15 April Eisenhower relieved Patton of command of II Corps and installed Omar Bradley in that position, naming Patton head of the I U.S. Armored Corps—the name of a unit that he had commanded earlier at the Desert Training Center in California and then again when it was designated the Western Task Force for Operation Torch. Ike was not unhappy with Patton. On the contrary, the temporary change was made so that the I Armored Corps could be redesignated the Seventh U.S. Army as soon as the invasion fleet left Tunisia for Sicily. Patton would now get to command the army he had been craving.[1]

■ ■ ■

The month of April was filled with meetings, visits, and rehearsals by both the Army and Navy in preparation for Husky. Patton established his headquarters in Mostaganem, about two hundred miles west of Algiers, and regularly monitored practice landings. Admiral Hewitt, who would command all of the U.S. Navy vessels taking part in Husky, urged Patton to relocate to Algiers so that their staffs could be in close contact in order to facilitate the detailed planning for Husky. "For some reason, in spite of their pre-Torch experience, [Patton] did not feel this to be practicable," Hewitt said.[2]

■ ■ ■

Heated arguments and debates about how best to conquer Sicily continued to swirl around Allied Forces headquarters. Plan after plan was discussed, dissected, and discarded because no single plan satisfied everyone. The Americans favored splitting up the attacking forces into a pincer maneuver, with U.S. forces hitting Palermo on the northern side of the island and then driving east toward Messina, while the British landed in the southeast corner and pushed rapidly northward, also toward Messina, to trap the bulk of the Axis forces and prevent them from escaping to mainland Italy. But Montgomery didn't like that idea, and Alexander gave him carte blanche to come up with a scheme that satisfied him.

On 2 May Monty cornered Walter Bedell Smith, Ike's chief of staff, in a lavatory at Allied Forces headquarters at the Hôtel Saint-George in Algiers and drew with his finger on a steamed-up mirror his concept for the invasion of Sicily: Montgomery's Eighth Army would land on the southeastern corner of the island and drive northward along the east coast while Patton's Seventh Army would land on the beaches just to the west and move northward, guarding the Eighth Army's left flank as it advanced. Eisenhower approved it; Patton was not consulted.[3]

The revised plan had Monty's men landing and capturing the port cities of Syracuse and Augusta and the Pachino airfields. Once this had been accomplished, Eighth Army would advance speedily northward toward Catania and Messina beyond, thereby cutting off any chance of escape by the Axis forces to Reggio di Calabria on the toe of the Italian boot. Patton's Seventh Army, after landing on the southern shore, would act as a "shield" to protect Montgomery's left flank.[4]

The Eighth Army was given the lion's share of the operation—and would receive the lion's share of the glory if it succeeded, Patton growled. "Either [Eisenhower] is nuts or else he is under wraps," he wrote to his wife Beatrice.[5] Concerned that Eisenhower was being too passive as supreme commander, he noted, "I think [Ike] sees the light a little but he fears for his head if he stands on his feet."[6]

■ ■ ■

Patton was in one of his periodic blue moods, believing that all the British officers thought that Monty could walk on water; Air Chief Marshal Arthur Tedder disabused him of that notion. Being surprisingly critical of the Eighth Army commander, Tedder confided, "He is a little fellow of average ability who has had such a build-up that he thinks of himself as Napoleon—he is not."[7]

Patton met with Ike the next day in a fury, complaining to his superior that Monty "refused to play ball" with the Americans and that his plan was deemed by the supply services as "logistically impossible."[8] But Eisenhower still declined to assert his authority in the matter. Patton was dumbfounded when Bedell Smith told him that Monty was Britain's national war hero because of his victory over the Germans at El Alamein and was so respected by Churchill that if Eisenhower spoke up, "Ike might get canned."[9]

■ ■ ■

The final surrender of the German army in North Africa took place on 13 May 1943. Eisenhower noted that the number of enemy prisoners taken during the last week of the campaign alone reached 240,000, of which approximately 125,000 were German.[10]

As May progressed, so did the practice landings for the upcoming invasion, but Patton had worries about Hewitt's indecisiveness.[11] Patton noted in his diary that one day after training, "Admiral Hewitt came to spend the night. He did all the things we asked him after a little patting on the back. All you have to do . . . is to tell him how great he is."[12]

It was decided after studying tide tables and phases of the moon that D-Day for Husky would be 10 July. As that date drew nearer, a vast chain of American ships began stretching its way from ports along the U.S. East Coast across the Atlantic toward the Mediterranean, fortunately unhindered by the German U-boat wolf packs.[13]

■ ■ ■

In late May 1943, while the bombardment of Pantelleria was still ongoing, another high-level meeting took place. Eisenhower was visited in Algiers by Prime Minister Churchill, Generals Marshall, Alexander, Montgomery, Tedder, Carl Spaatz, and Adm. Andrew B. Cunningham, commander of Allied naval forces under Ike, plus the chief of the Imperial General Staff, Sir Alan Brooke, to discuss the upcoming Sicily operation—and to continue the discussion of what to do and where to go once Sicily had fallen.

One proposal still favored by Marshall was for the Allies to shut down offensive operations in the Mediterranean and concentrate on a build-up of forces in Britain for the cross-Channel invasion. But doing so would allow the Axis forces free rein in the Mediterranean and even threaten the naval passage through the Suez Canal, the Red Sea, and the route to Britain's interests in India and the Pacific.

Such an abandonment of the Mediterranean, the British stressed, would also allow the Germans to diminish their presence in Italy and Greece, strengthen their attacks against the Soviet Union, and add even more weight to Hitler's fortified "Atlantic Wall" that guarded the 1,800-mile coastline from northern Norway to the France-Spain border. It would also give Nazi Germany a year of respite from attacks by Allied ground forces—from summer 1943 to summer 1944—while preparations for an invasion of northwest Europe were being finalized.

According to Eisenhower, "We badly wanted the fine airfields of southern Italy. Finally, we wanted to keep up the pressure in the belief that Italy would soon crack and quit. Such an outcome would denude the Balkans of Italian garrisons and so force Germany to extend her forces still further."

There was also some talk of abandoning any possible Normandy operation altogether in favor of a thrust northward through Italy or across the Mediterranean coast, but Eisenhower and Marshall quickly disabused their British visitors of that notion. Thus, it was firmly decided that Italy would be the next target once Sicily fell.

After the conference ended, Ike did something extraordinary: In order to maintain the secret that Sicily was about to be invaded, he called in a group of war correspondents—and told them about top-secret Operation Husky! "Because of the confidence I had acquired in the integrity of newsmen in my Theater," he explained, "I decided to take them into my confidence."

The risky move worked. "Mouths fell open as I began the conference by telling the reporters that we would assault Sicily in early July," he said. "From that moment onward, until after the attack was launched, nothing speculative came out of the [Mediterranean] Theater and no representative of the press attempted to send out anything that could possibly be of any value to the enemy."[14]

■ ■ ■

Eisenhower, Alexander, and Cunningham departed Algiers a few days before Husky was launched and set up their forward headquarters in the bomb-ravaged city of Valletta, Malta, in the series of tunnels beneath the Lascaris Battery—tunnels that had been used as an underground command center since before the island came under almost continuous attack starting on 10 June 1940. "Malta had taken a fearful beating but the spirit of the defenders had never been shaken," Ike said. "Its airfields were in excellent condition and its garrison was burning to get into the fight."

As Malta would be one of the key locations from which Allied warplanes would operate during Husky, a new airfield was built on Gozo, a small island northwest of Malta. "On Malta itself," wrote Ike, "was stationed every aircraft that its fields could possibly absorb."[15]

■ ■ ■

Had he not been an army commander, Patton probably could have been a great thespian, or a college football coach, a motivational speaker, or perhaps even a fire-and-brimstone preacher. He was the epitome of the "hands-on," micromanaging type of leader for whom no detail was too small to generate a good, old-fashioned ass-chewing.

One of Husky's invading units—the 1st Infantry Division—was practicing amphibious landings at Arzew, a drill viewed by Patton, Eisenhower, Marshall, and Bradley. As a group of soggy soldiers was wading ashore from their landing craft, Patton charged at them. "Where in hell are your goddamned bayonets?" he roared in his high-pitched voice.

Omar Bradley recalled, "George blistered them with his oaths. Eisenhower stood there in embarrassed silence. Major General Harold R. Bull, an officer on Eisenhower's staff, nodded toward General Marshall and whispered to me, 'Well, there goes George's chance for a crack at higher command. That temper of his is going to finish him yet.'

"George rejoined us a few minutes later having already dismissed the incident from his mind. Those outbursts were characteristic of him. 'Chew them out and they'll remember it,' he would say in speaking of the GIs."[16]

■ ■ ■

What would become the Seventh U.S. Army was composed of the 1st, 3rd, and 9th U.S. Infantry Divisions (the latter kept in reserve), and the 2nd Armored Division—veterans of Torch and the Tunisian campaign. Also added was the unblooded 45th Infantry Division, which had undergone amphibious training in the Hampton Roads area and was brought across the Atlantic to North Africa by Rear Adm. Alan Kirk's Task Force 85 in assault transports.

Carrying Patton's 66,000 ground troops from North Africa to Sicily and then supporting them with offshore naval gunfire was the job of Admiral Hewitt and his Western Naval Task Force, which was divided into three task forces, each charged with establishing a beachhead.

The plan called for Rear Adm. Richard Conolly's Task Force 86, composed entirely of the new landing ship, tanks (LSTs), landing craft, tanks (LCTs), and landing craft, infantry (LCIs) to land Maj. Gen. Lucian K. Truscott's 3rd Division at Licata ("Joss" Beach, on the left flank of the invasion area). Hewitt said, "These LSTs were equipped with davits to carry small personnel landing craft [LCPs] like the assault transports, so that an assault wave could be embarked and sent ahead prior to beaching the mother craft.

"During this May-June period, reinforcements for the Eighth Fleet continued to arrive in ever-increasing numbers: cruisers, destroyers, mine craft, patrol craft, and the LSTs, LCTs, and LCIs, which were to be used and prove their worth for the first time in a major operation. One most welcome unit was my old Cruiser Division [CruDiv] Eight, under the distinguished officer who had relieved me of that command, Rear Admiral Lyal A. Davidson, who was to continue with me throughout the Mediterranean campaign and become an expert on naval gunfire support of landings." CruDiv 8 was composed of the *Philadelphia* (CL 41), *Savannah* (CL 42), and *Boise* (CL 42).

Another arrival was CruDiv 13 under Rear Adm. Laurance T. Dubose with the *Birmingham* (CL 62) and *Brooklyn* (CL 40). "These fine cruisers with their fifteen-gun 6-inch batteries were to prove their effectiveness," said Hewitt. "Admiral [Alan] Kirk himself, with the 45th Division loaded in some eighteen assault transports, and with his necessary screening and other supporting units, arrived in Oran in mid-June." They became the heart of Kirk's Task Force 85 that was scheduled to strike "Cent" Beach at Scoglitti.

Rear Adm. John L. Hall's "Dime" attack force—Task Force 81—which included Rear Adm. Lyal Davidson's Cruiser Division 8 (the cruisers *Boise* and *Savannah*, eleven destroyers, two LSTs, six transports, thirty-three landing craft, eight minesweepers, and ten PT boats), would land the 1st Infantry Division at Gela.[17]

Three new inventions would also make their debut during Husky: the amphibious DUKW, the LST, and the pontoon causeway. In 1940, seeing the signs that the United States would probably be dragged into the war whether it liked it or not, the National Defense Research Committee and the Office of Scientific Research and Development felt it was prudent to begin creating some tools with which to fight that war.

One of their bright ideas was to inspire the creation of a large amphibious truck, which would become known as the DUKW ("duck").[18] It was initially designed in 1941 by yacht designer Rod Stephen Jr., Dennis Puleston, a British deep-water sailor, and Frank W. Speir, a Naval Reserve officer who had been at the Massachusetts Institute of Technology, and was then turned over to the General Motors Corporation (GMC) for testing and production.

Basing it on the existing six-wheel-drive vehicle commonly called the "deuce-and-a-half," GMC sheathed the DUKW in sheet steel to create a boat-like hull and added a couple of propellers at the rear. The engine, a 270-cubic-inch straight six, produced sixty-four horsepower and took up the front third of the vehicle's thirty-one-foot length. It could travel at 6.4 miles per hour on water and 50–55 miles per hour on land. After much testing and modification, the DUKW was ready for its combat debut—during Operation Husky. Eventually, 21,137 units were built by GMC and its subcontractors.[19]

Even before the United States became involved in the war, Winston Churchill had requested that it embark on a crash program to develop a flat-bottomed transport ship that was large enough to carry armored vehicles across the sea and deliver them to a hostile foreign shore. American industry got to work, and during the course of the war, 1,051 of them were built. These LSTs—sometimes called a "large, slow target" by its crewmembers—were 328 feet long and could carry armored vehicles in the tank deck and non-armored vehicles on the main deck. The cargo capacity was 2,100 tons, and the ship could hold approximately two hundred soldiers—a rifle company.[20]

Many of the LSTs were also fitted with the third new invention—pontoon causeways—that allowed them to discharge their tanks and trucks directly onto the beach when the depth of the water offshore did not allow for the ships to be beached.

The pontoon causeway, used since ancient Persian and Roman times, was perfected in the early 1940s by U.S. Navy Cdr. John N. Laycock. It was basically a portable floating pier that enabled ships, while anchored offshore, to offload vehicles. No longer did a port need to be captured before heavy equipment could be brought ashore.[21]

Said Hewitt, "Pontoons, which had been developed by the Navy Bureau of Yards and Docks for the construction of floating docks, bridges, etc., were placed together to form causeway sections wide enough to accommodate tanks and trucks. A section was attached to each side of the LST by an ingenious hinge device and then [hoisted] up so that it would be carried clear of the water."[22] These pontoon causeways would be particularly valuable because the Sicilian coastline was known to be fronted with false beaches—shallow, underwater reefs—that would preclude landing ships from discharging their troops and equipment in shallow water.[23]

■ ■ ■

Even with the fall of Pantelleria, the waters off Tunisia were dangerous. With the Germans and Italians in possession of the northern shore of the

Mediterranean, Hewitt noted that Allied convoys passing along the coast of North Africa were constantly subjected to bombing, torpedo, and floating-mine attacks. He reported, "During June, in spite of all precautions, the U.S. Navy lost two LSTs (with heavy losses of life), a minesweeper, and a patrol boat to torpedoes and mines."[24]

■ ■ ■

On 20 June 1943 Vice Admiral Hewitt and his staff moved aboard the 491-foot, 8,900-ton *Monrovia*, an attack transport docked at Algiers that would serve as the flagship for the Western Naval Task Force—the American half of Husky. Ten days later General Patton would come on board and also make it his floating headquarters.[25]

The accommodations were tight. British Capt. S. W. C. Pack, who served on the planning staff for Husky, noted that *Monrovia* was severely overcrowded: "Embarked were the Admiral and his staff, together with a fighter control group of the Army Air Force, and General Patton . . . with his staff. Three separate code rooms had to be provided, and *Monrovia* had to accommodate 126 officers and 670 men over and above her normal complement of forty-eight officers and 566 men."[26]

■ ■ ■

In mid-June, Patton had flown to Bou Sfer, Algeria, site of the temporary training camp of the 9th U.S. Infantry Division and its crusty commander, Maj. Gen. Manton S. Eddy, a veteran of World War I.[27] The 9th had taken part in Operation Torch, and Patton regarded Eddy as an outstanding combat leader. Observing a 9th Division practice landing, Patton was much impressed with the soldiers but complained, "The Navy was forty-five minutes late, but hit the beach exactly."

He then addressed the division's officers: "I told them that I had come to tell them how to fight, but after seeing them, I knew I had nothing to tell them. I then stressed shooting and killing, and the use of the bayonet, and that Americans are the pick of the more adventurous people of all races."[28]

Lt. Charles Scheffel, one of the 9th Division officers in attendance, recalled that Patton also delivered an unfortunate choice of words shortly before the Sicily invasion:

Patton began an amazingly bellicose and agitated tirade about what we were going to do to the enemy when we got to Sicily. Then he said, "And gentlemen, when we land on the beaches of Sicily, there will be no prisoners taken."

I sat stunned in the first row of officers, not ten feet away from the pompous man. His words made my skin crawl. Nobody said anything for a long moment. General Eddy stepped forward and tugged gently at Patton's shirtsleeve. "General," he said so softly I could barely hear him, "you might want to rethink your last statement."

Patton looked out over the group of officers sitting on the sand before him. Then he wagged his hand toward us. "Forget what I just said."[29]

■ ■ ■

Lt. Col. Charles Codman, Patton's aide, watched his boss observing a division's bayonet training session. When it was over, the general gathered the men around him. "Good, very good, but not good enough." Pointing at a shredded dummy, he said, "That's a German. You don't hate him enough. You're all too gentlemanly. Just because you've been brought up not to kick your grandmother in the ass, don't think *he* hasn't, because he has—they *all* have. They are the lowest so-and-so's [Patton used a different expletive] that crawl the earth, except perhaps the Japs, but we won't have to worry about them until next year. For the present, just keep hating Germans. They are all [expletive deleted by Codman] and damn fine soldiers. Get mad and keep mad all the time."

On the way back to headquarters following this little pep talk, Patton saw a truck driver without a necktie on. Patton yelled "Stop!" to his driver and directed Codman to "go up there and find out why he has no necktie. Get his name. Have him court-martialed." Despite the general's often-explosive temper, Codman said, "I can't get over how much I like my boss. Have never seen anything to equal him."[30]

■ ■ ■

Col. Homer W. Jones, the Seventh Army's judge advocate general, recalled that Patton also gave a rousing speech on 27 June to officers of the recently arrived 45th Infantry Division. Jones said that the general "told of some of the experiences he had had in Tunisia that he had known of where Germans had indicated they were offering to surrender and when our troops arrived [to take them prisoner] the Germans immediately shot them down. He did indicate that in a situation of this sort, if the enemy waited until our troops were about to capture them, and then immediately offered to surrender, that the American soldiers could not afford to take the chance—that it was too late, and they should kill them."[31] It was a lesson that several 45th Division members would take to heart—with horrific results.

■ ■ ■

Historians who write about invasions and battles invariably speak of the thousands of men taking part as nameless, faceless, monolithic hordes, so it is easy for them to forget that each one of those men was a living, sentient being—a person with a name, a family, a lover; someone with a wife, a mother, a father, and children; someone who had interests and desires and fears; someone who wanted nothing more than to have the war come to a quick and victorious conclusion so that he could return home and resume the regularity of life. And yet this war had become all-consuming, and he was caught up in it like a fly in a spider's web, unable to escape or alter his fate.

One of those young men caught in the web was nineteen-year-old Harley Reynolds, a 1st Infantry Division sergeant from Virginia full of strong opinions. "It didn't seem to me that we were ready and trained for the invasion of Sicily so soon after the North African campaign," he groused. "We had only made a couple of small-unit practice landings and the shoreline didn't in any way resemble the shoreline we landed on."

Reynolds had already participated in Torch, coming ashore at Arzew, Algeria, and fighting his way through Tunisia, and he had already formed a negative opinion of General Patton: "I didn't like Patton worth a damn. 'Old blood and guts—our blood, his guts.' He was a 'strange duck,' as the Brits used to say. In North Africa, they tried to instill in us the wearing of neckties in the 'rear areas,' just as General Patton had tried to do on the front lines. That was what Patton had ordered as soon as he took over our II Corps.

"Can you imagine neckties in combat? It didn't look that bad on Patton or Bradley with their cleaned, pressed uniforms that they always wore for the benefit of the photographers, but not with our dirty, muddy, and many times bloody clothes we had been wearing for weeks without change. Only an idiot would wish that on a soldier."

As the date for Husky grew closer, Reynolds sensed a growing tension among the veterans who had already been under fire. He noted, "We now had the new LCVPs [landing craft vehicle/personnel], otherwise known as Higgins Boats, with the ramps on the front that lowered for us to run off, not jump off as we did in North Africa. In a short time we were back on board a troopship again; this time an American ship, the *Samuel F. Chase* [APA 26]."[32]

What lay in store for Reynolds and the other 66,000 Americans? They would soon find out, for it was now time for the launch of Operation Husky. But the vital cooperation between the U.S. Army and the U.S. Navy was still an unanswered question.

·2·

THE AIRBORNE

FIRST TO FIGHT

All were shaken up by the heavy landings on trees,
buildings, and rocky hillsides.

—James M. Gavin

It had never been tried before. No army had ever attempted to make a large-scale combat parachute drop at night. But 3,405 men from the 505th and 504th Parachute Infantry Regiments of Maj. Gen. Matthew B. Ridgway's 82nd "All-American" Airborne Division were eager to leap into history and become the first American troops to set boots on Sicily.[1]

Their mission was complex: to grab as many enemy airfields as they could, gain control over vital road intersections, secure important bridges, prevent enemy troops from attacking the beachheads, and generally create havoc and confusion in the Axis ranks.[2] To accomplish those missions, they would need to be dropped at just the right spot; there was no room for error.

There were to be two American jumps, one right after the other, a day apart. The first one, dubbed Husky I, would involve thirty-six-year-old Col. James M. "Jumping Jim" Gavin and three battalions of his 505th Parachute Infantry Regiment (PIR) on the night of 9–10 July flying from a base in North Africa. Attached to the 505th was the 3rd Battalion of the 504th PIR, Company B of the 307th Engineers, and the 456th Parachute Artillery Battalion. This would be followed twenty-four hours later by the 504th PIR's jump, Husky II, to be led by Col. Reuben H. Tucker commanding the 1st and 2nd Battalions of his 504th PIR, minus the 3rd that had been attached to the 505th.[3]

■ ■ ■

The preparations for the upcoming battle were about as meticulous as they could be. At the 82nd Airborne's departure point, the Tunisian city of Kairouan, the men were reintroduced to tough physical and mental conditioning. Long runs under the blistering desert sun were followed by hours of calisthenics. During their off-duty hours, the paratroopers cleaned their weapons, sharpened fighting knives, checked their equipment over and over, and studied the detailed "sand tables"—scale models of the terrain into which they would be dropping. Each company's mission was gone over in great detail. During breaks, some men found time to write home to parents, wives, sweethearts. No one knew if they would ever have the chance to write again.[4]

The responsibility for transporting the 505th to their drop zones belonged to the 61st Troop Carrier Squadron of the 315th Troop Carrier Group, 52nd Troop Carrier Wing, XII Air Force, which had been absorbed by Lt. Gen. Carl Spaatz's Northwest African Air Force in February 1943.[5]

Gavin's men would make their journey in 226 Douglas C-47 Skytrain transport aircraft of the 315th Troop Carrier Group flying in formation in groups of three *V*s. Only the leading plane in each group of nine carried a trained navigator; the rest followed the leader. Unlike during the later parachute drops over Normandy, no American pathfinder parties were pre-dropped into enemy territory where they could use colored panels, light markers, or radio beacons to show the drop zones to the main body. The drop zones were to be identified by eye from aerial photographs—an almost impossible task in the dark.[6]

The 505th's primary objective was the Ponte Olivo bridge north of Gela. Gavin recalled the convoluted route his paratroopers were to take: "Taking off from Tunisia in a long column of aircraft, we were to fly [directly east] to the island of Linosa [then] to Malta. There we were to dog-leg to the left, coming in on Sicily's southwestern shore. This was an important point—the island was to come into sight on the right side of the approaching aircraft. The orders were that every man would jump even though there might be some uncertainty in his mind as to his whereabouts." Gavin made it clear that it was a one-way trip—only the pilots and crews would be returning to North Africa.[7]

The troops were also briefed that, in the likely event that they were scattered upon landing, the call sign upon meeting an unknown person in the dark was "George"; the countersign was "Marshall."[8]

What did the troops scheduled to invade the island know about the opposition they could expect? After the war Gavin wrote, "Two German panzer divisions* were on Sicily, a fact known to General Eisenhower and the Allied high command in advance through Ultra [the top-secret system that intercepted and deciphered German messages]. But to protect the secret of Ultra for use in future campaigns, the invading troops were not informed of this. On the contrary, they were told that only a few German technicians were on Sicily."[9]

■ ■ ■

In war, the slack times eventually end, and then the bloody business begins. So it was on the night of 9 July 1943 at the 52nd Troop Carrier Wing's jam-packed airfield at Kairouan. There was little boisterousness on the flight line as the "sticks" of paratroopers, about eighteen or twenty men to a plane, stood in lines outside their Douglas C-47 Skytrains—known to the Commonwealth forces as Dakotas and nicknamed "Gooney Birds" by U.S. troops—before laboriously climbing into the machines that would drop them over enemy territory.

Each paratrooper was encumbered with plenty of equipment: his main parachute and a reserve, an M-1 Garand rifle or carbine, combat knife strapped to a leg, grenades, rations, water, and compass. Some men also carried radios and a bazooka and several rounds for it in a pouch. "The bazookas," Gavin said, "were important, since they were the only weapons the troopers were carrying that would enable them to engage the German armor on reasonable terms."

---

* In actuality, there was one panzer division and one panzer grenadier division, the 15th, at this time. Such a unit was the equivalent of a U.S. Army mechanized infantry division.

The straps of the parachute, musette bag, rifle, and cartridge belt dug into each man's shoulders, waist, and groin. And although the sun had set, the heat in the enclosed fuselages was oppressive, and each man was drenched in sweat. Even the stiff wind blowing across the airfield brought no cooling relief.

The paratroopers still had no idea if this was just another training exercise or the real thing. If real, where were they heading—Sicily? Greece? Sardinia? Italy? Gavin noted that "because of security restrictions, it had not been possible to inform every trooper of our destination until just before takeoff."[10] He had prepared a printed sheet that read,

> Soldiers of the 505th Parachute Combat Team:
>
> Tonight you embark upon a combat mission for which our people and the free people of the world have been waiting for two years.
>
> You will spearhead the landing of an American Force upon the island of SICILY. Every preparation has been made to eliminate the element of chance. You have been given the means to do the job and you are backed by the largest assemblage of air power in the world's history.
>
> The eyes of the world are upon you. The hopes and prayers of every American go with you.
>
> Since it is our first fight at night you must use the countersign and avoid firing on each other. The bayonet is the night fighter's best weapon. Conserve your water and ammunition.
>
> The term "American Parachutist" has become synonymous with courage of a high order. Let us carry the fight to the enemy and make the American Parachutist feared and respected through all his ranks. Attack violently. Destroy him wherever found.
>
> I know you will do your job.
>
> Good landing, good fight, and good luck.[11]

Gavin had many worries that evening, but the most immediate one was the wind. A gale blowing through the strait between Tunisia and Sicily would undoubtedly play havoc with the transport planes, glider tugs, and timetables. Training jumps had normally been canceled when the wind reached about fifteen miles an hour or more in order to minimize injuries. As the men waited for takeoff, an airman from the weather station at Kairouan came running up with a message for Gavin: "I was told to tell you that the wind is going to be thirty-five miles an hour, west to east."

It was troubling news but there was nothing Gavin could do about it. "Few of us had ever jumped with winds more than twenty-five miles an hour. But we couldn't change plans now. Besides," Gavin reflected, "there were many other hazards of greater danger in prospect than the thirty-five-mile-an-hour wind."

Just before the fuselage door to Gavin's plane, dubbed "Mister Period," was closed, another man came running up with a large barracks bag on his shoulder, saying that the bag contained prisoner-of-war tags. "You're supposed to put one on every prisoner you capture, and be sure to fill it out properly," the soldier directed. About an hour after departure, Gavin had his personnel officer throw the bag into the Mediterranean.

After each plane was filled, the fuselage doors were slammed shut and dogged down. As each man sat listening to his own sweat dripping, no doubt each was lost in a flurry of thoughts: *Sicily! The first Americans on the enemy's home soil! That would be a tale to tell my kids—if I live to have kids. What will the drop be like? Will we land together or be scattered like in practice? Will this windstorm cause Patton to call off the drop? The whole operation? Will the enemy run away or stand and fight? Do I have all my ammo? What was that challenge sign again—"George" something? And the countersign—"Marshall" or something? Will I chicken out under fire and let my buddies down? Will I be killed or wounded?*

The introspections were cut short as the twin engines of each plane whined, coughed, then caught. The roar of the 226 planes—452 engines—rose to a deafening crescendo. One by one the planes began moving toward their places in the takeoff sequence. At 2030 hours a green flare was fired from the control tower and the first C-47, carrying Colonel Gavin, revved its engines, slowly rolled down the runway, gained speed, and lifted off into the gathering dusk. There was no turning back now. In three hours they would meet either glory or defeat.

The paratroopers were packed and strapped tightly into their C-47s, ten seated on either side of the near-dark fuselage. Conversation was impossible because of the throbbing, almost-painful noise of the two Pratt and Whitney R-1830 1,200-horsepower engines outside each plane's thin aluminum walls beating against each trooper's eardrums, a sound that seemed solid, impenetrable. Any commands that had to be given—stand up, hook up, check equipment, move to the door, *GO!*—would be given by the jumpmaster using hand signals. A small box with two colored lights—red and green—was mounted near the single door at the rear of the fuselage. All eyes would be focused on the light that would be red until it was time to jump, when the green light would be switched on.

Gavin recalled, "My own flight with the Regimental Headquarters group was uneventful until Linosa was due. It was not to be seen. Malta, which was to be well-lighted to assist our navigators, could not be seen either."[12]

The first two hours of the flight were bumpy but unremarkable; airsick men threw up their dinners. The plans called for the aerial armada to head east until reaching Malta, when it would make a sharp left turn to the north, but the high winds pushed the planes past Malta. When the error was detected, some planes made a reverse-angle turn to the northwest, eventually coming over the southeastern corner of Sicily, where the British were due to land. A heavy concentration of bombing by B-24s and B-17s was to precede the jump.[13]

■ ■ ■

The night of 9 July was nerve-wracking. In Valletta, Malta, Ike and the other officers on the planning staffs stayed up late and left their underground command center below the Lascaris Battery platform to watch the aerial armada pass overhead on its way to Sicily. Ike lit up a Camel, said a prayer, and rubbed together the seven "lucky" coins—an American silver dollar, a British five-guinea coin, and five others—that he always kept in his pocket as a talisman.

"A number of us went out on the hilltops to watch them pass," Ike wrote. "In the wind and storm it was difficult for them to keep direction. Our plotting board in the air operations room showed that many planes . . . were blown far off course, but generally the columns kept on target and when the one we were watching had passed overhead, we returned to headquarters to await reports. Most of us turned in to catch a few hours of sleep."[14] Aboard the planes, no one was catching any sleep.

■ ■ ■

Gavin noticed the white wakes of hundreds of ships below, all spearing toward Sicily. He said, "Obviously, we were off course, since our plan called for us to fly between the American fleet on the left and the British [fleet] on the right. In fact, the Americans told us that we would probably be shot down if we flew over them."

Gavin knew that if everything were going according to plan, Darby's Rangers and Maj. Gen. Terry de la Mesa Allen's 1st Infantry Division would soon be hitting the beach at Gela, while Middleton's 45th Infantry Division would be arriving at Scoglitti about four hours after the 505th's drop. If the amphibious troops could punch through the coastal defenses, they would be able to help bolster his paratroopers, and the Navy's warships would be on call to lend their firepower in the event things really became difficult.

At least so he hoped. On a complex operation like this, so many things could go badly wrong—the Navy could show up late, or land their troops at the wrong beaches, or run into floating minefields, or the enemy response could be stiffer than expected. *Or, or, or.* Gavin pushed the negative possibilities out of his mind. They *had* to succeed—failure was not an option.[15]

The planes continued on to Malta, finally making a forty-five-degree dog-leg turn to the left. Suddenly the flash of gunfire and explosions could be seen through the dust and haze caused by the pre-invasion bombing. To soften up the enemy on Sicily, the Allied air forces combined to deliver heavy aerial bombardments before Husky that matched or exceeded anything else that had come before. On 9 July a fleet of B-24 Liberator bombers of the Ninth U.S. Air Force plastered the beautiful resort city of Taormina— where the San Dominico Palace was used as the headquarters of the German Wehrmacht in Italy—on Sicily's east coast and left it a smoldering ruin.[16] But that was far from the 505th's drop zone.

Finally the coast itself came into view. "Unfortunately, many of the planes overflew the Malta dog-leg," Gavin said, "and the island first became visible on the left, thus causing confusion and widespread dispersion of

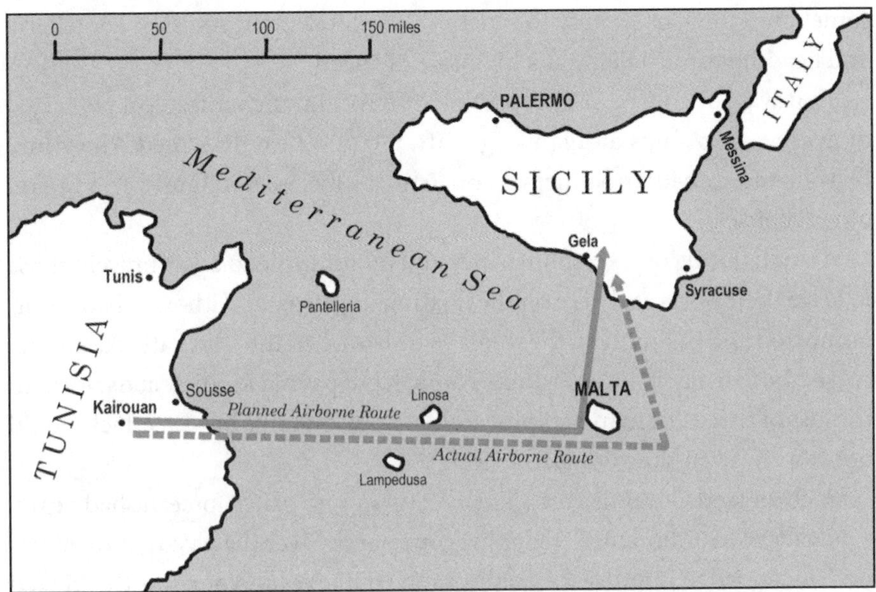

Map 2.1 ▪ The planned route of the 82nd Airborne's 505th Parachute Infantry Regiment, shown alongside the route as it was actually flown

the troopers."[17] Across darkened Sicily all was quiet, but the Italian night watch was awake; earlier that evening reports filtered down that Axis aerial reconnaissance had spotted the vast armada and General Alfredo Guzzoni, the sixty-six-year-old commanding general of Italian Sixth Army, had put all units on full alert. The troops scanned the black skies brightened by a first-quarter moon and speckled with brilliant stars. On the southern shore, whitecaps were foaming in the wind, and the gunners on the beach and the men manning the searchlights resorted to wearing goggles to keep the flying sand out of their eyes.

On 5 July Guzzoni, at his palatial headquarters at Enna near the center of the island, had learned that the number of Allied hospital ships in North African ports had increased from five to sixteen. Reports from Axis reconnaissance planes and from agents on the ground, too, noticed a build-up of ships, supplies, and soldiers. Submarines also were detected off Sicily's southern shore. The most concerning report came on 9 July when the Allied fleet was at sea;

somehow a force of seventy to ninety ships was spotted south of Pantelleria and heading toward Sicily at a high rate of speed.[18]

That was, of course, only a partial accounting; the entire fleet consisted of nearly 3,000 ships and landing craft, 160,000 heavily armed American, British, and Canadian soldiers, 1,800 artillery pieces, 600 tanks, and 14,000 other vehicles.

A small flotilla of Axis submarines and motor torpedo boats bravely chose to leave their ports and take on the floating juggernaut. Although badly outnumbered and outgunned, the small boats launched into their attack, sinking two LSTs, five merchant ships, and a tanker, but paying for their audacity with the loss of three German and nine Italian craft. But this brazen attack would not stop, or even slow down, the fleet.[19]

Back on land Guzzoni's own Sixth Army was no paltry force; he had nearly a quarter of a million men under his command. Over the past month efforts were increased to improve the quality of the pillboxes and bunkers that ringed the island, and new, more powerful artillery was shipped in from Germany. More mines were laid on the beaches thought most likely for an amphibious landing.

But reports from the field, and his own inspection tours, fed Guzzoni's worst fears—his men were poorly equipped, poorly trained, poorly led, and poorly motivated. Would they fight with the patriotic fervor of Giuseppe Garibaldi's Red Shirt revolutionaries a century earlier during the civil war for Italy's unification? Or would they throw down their weapons and throw up their hands? Guzzoni hoped for the former but feared the latter.[20]

One of Guzzoni's ablest officers was Lieutenant Colonel Dante Leonardi, the commander of the 3rd Battalion, 34th Infantry Regiment of the 4th "Livorno" Division that was headquartered north of Gela. The Livorno was nearly at full strength, and its artillery, engineers, and four of its six infantry battalions were fully motorized. It was considered the best Italian division in Sicily, as it had been trained for the eventual invasion of Malta—an invasion that never happened. The untested Livorno, commanded by Giandomenico Chirieleison, would receive its baptism of fire on D-Day morning—a baptism that it would not survive.[21]

■ ■ ■

Albert Kesselring, that wily Luftwaffe field marshal and overall commander of German forces in Italy and Sicily, made certain that Sicily was well-guarded by his air force units. Every one of the more than thirty Axis air bases on Sicily was within range chock-full of German and Italian fighters and bombers, including Catania (home to *Jagdgeschwader* [fighter wing] 53 with a *Staffel*, or squadron, of Messerschmitt BF 109 fighters); Gerbini (home to two *Staffeln* of *Schnellkampfgeschwader* [fast bomber wing] 10 with Focke-Wulf 190 bombers); Castelvetrano (home to two *Staffeln* of *Schlachtgeschwader* [dive bomber wing] 2 and their Focke-Wulf 190 ground attack fighter-bombers); Trapani (two *Staffeln* of *Jagdgeschwader* 77's BF 109 fighters); and Sciacca (another *Staffeln* of *Schlachtgeschwader* 77 BF 109s). In addition, Junkers Ju 88 and Savoia-Marchetti SM 79 medium bombers stood by at bases in Italy that were also within range of Gela.[22]

Kesselring, dubbed "Smiling Albert" by the Allies for his perpetual grin, was one of Germany's most accomplished and decorated soldiers. He had seen action in World War I as an artillery officer and received the Iron Cross, First Class. Between the wars he joined the Luftwaffe—a branch of service that the Treaty of Versailles prohibited Germany from possessing. He learned to fly at age forty-eight and became instrumental in secretly reestablishing Germany's military aviation industry and the expansion of the air force. In 1936 he became chief of staff of the Luftwaffe.

His star continued to rise as Hitler prepared for war. During the 1939 German invasion of Poland, Kesselring was in charge of air operations over that country and successfully supported the Wehrmacht's ground assaults, as well as directing a bombing campaign that flattened Warsaw and other Polish cities.

When Germany's campaign switched to the Western Front in 1940, Kesselring's fliers contributed to the fall of Belgium and the Netherlands, including dropping paratroopers and bombs on Rotterdam. Kesselring was also ordered by Luftwaffe chief Hermann Göring to use his aerial forces to stop the British cross-Channel evacuation from Dunkirk, France. Despite protesting that his forces were depleted, Kesselring obeyed—but failed.

In June 1940 Kesselring's aviators managed to gain air superiority over much of France until that nation begged for an armistice and was swiftly conquered by Germany. Then it was Britain's turn to feel the weight of German bombs as Kesselring's air fleet mercilessly hit London and other British cities before the Royal Air Force was able to win the Battle of Britain.

Unable to subdue the British, in June 1941 Hitler turned his attention eastward and launched Operation Barbarossa, his nearly four-million-man invasion of the Soviet Union; Kesselring's Second Air Fleet was a part of the support for Army Group Center, devastating the cities of Minsk and Smolensk. With the war in the Soviet Union seemingly won, Kesselring's air fleet was transferred to the Mediterranean in late 1941—a fatal mistake. The Soviets renewed their counteroffensive, but Kesselring and his machines were no longer available to resist it.

In November 1941 Kesselring was appointed commander-in-chief of the Wehrmacht in Italy and began a two-year campaign to eliminate Malta as a British base and to supply General Erwin Rommel's Afrika Korps, which was battling Lieutenant General Neil Ritchie's Eighth British Army in North Africa. In October 1942 Kesselring was placed in command of all German land and air forces in North Africa except for Rommel's German-Italian Panzer army.

Despite the injection of Eisenhower's 65,000-man U.S. Army in November, months of bitter fighting lay ahead in North Africa. After the German defeat in May 1943, Kesselring correctly anticipated that the Allies' next target was Sicily despite the deception campaign designed to convince the Germans otherwise.[23]

Kesselring wrote in his memoirs, "At the time of the [German] capitulation in Tunis the outlook in Sicily, as everywhere, was very black. I counted on the enemy's following up his victory, if not immediately, at least after the shortest possible breather. . . . Every day the enemy gave us was a day gained, however, and gradually a striking force was organized. Field-Marshal [Wolfram] von Richthofen, the new C-in-C of Air Fleet 2, quickly made himself acquainted with the special problems of this theatre of war."[24]

■ ■ ■

Gavin's paratroopers, twisting in their seats to get a glimpse out of the planes' small windows, would have seen just blackness below them, striped with tiny streaks of white—the wakes of hundreds of U.S. Navy warships on their way to Sicily. It was a heartening—and frightening—sight.

As the planes approached the coast, the red "stand-by" light in each plane came on; the men were ordered to stand up and hook up. Suddenly the red light switched to green, and paratroopers began shuffling for the exits.

The 505th's jump was a chaotic mess with paratroopers blown across Sicily like dandelion seeds. Gavin and the rest of the regiment jumped into darkness that was alive with tracer rounds. Despite the high winds and intense ground fire, Gavin said, "Undaunted, our paratroopers jumped on schedule. Out we went. The reception was mixed. Some of us met heavy fighting at once, others were unopposed for some time, but all were shaken up by the heavy landings on trees, buildings, and rocky hillsides." Gavin was the first man out of the first C-47 over Sicily and the first to hit the ground—which he did with a terrific force on the rocky ground. It was one of the roughest landings he had ever experienced, and he sprained his ankle.[25]

On schedule they might have been, but off target they definitely were. Doug Bailey of Battery B, 456th Parachute Field Artillery Battalion, recalled, "Anti-aircraft fire got us as we came over the coast of Sicily. Red light came on, then green light. The pilot missed our drop zone by about twenty miles and gave us the green light over an area of pillboxes, rock walls, and trees. Door load partly stuck in door. I went out head first, could see flashes and tracers from ground fire before my chute opened. I don't think we were over 250 to 300 feet when we jumped. When chute opened, grabbed front risers and slid most the way to ground, hit very hard. We jumped with our guns unloaded and had little tin crickets* for identification. Lots of firing going on. Loaded gun and got grenades ready."

Once on the ground, Bailey tried to figure out where he was. "We had hard time getting oriented; every time we moved, machine-gun bullets whizzed over our heads. Joined a group of troopers and started looking for my gun crew. Came across paratrooper with broken leg. He had crashed into a tree

---

* Paratroopers were issued small brass clicking devices commonly called crickets as a way of distinguishing friend from foe in the dark. When encountering an unknown person, one click was supposed to be answered by two clicks.

stump. He was on the wrong side of a brick wall about five feet high. When some of the firing let up, about four of us jumped over the wall and lifted him over on the safe side."[26]

■ ■ ■

In several of the noisy C-47s being violently jolted on the air currents, machine-gun bullets suddenly began bursting through the floors of the fuselages. Anti-aircraft guns also opened up, and explosions outside sent shrapnel tearing through the planes' thin aluminum skins. Some of the pilots instinctively began bobbing and weaving their planes left and right, up and down, like a boxer trying to dodge the punches of his opponent, but it was no use; there was no way to anticipate where the next shot was coming from.[27]

Not every paratrooper made it out safely from his C-47. In one, a captain was standing in the open doorway watching the black sea pass six hundred feet beneath him when suddenly he was struck dead by a piece of anti-aircraft shrapnel. At that moment, the green jump light came on, even though the plane was a minute from the coast. As the captain fell out of the plane, the second and third man behind him jumped but drowned when they landed in the water. The rest of the stick, given a few seconds' more grace, jumped and landed in a complex of Italian pillboxes where they engaged in a fierce firefight, eventually winning out.[28]

■ ■ ■

In another of the leading planes was Pvt. John H. Allen, carrying a bazooka. "We jumped out; the sky was a mass of tracer bullets," he recalled. "I landed on a pile of rocks, my carbine smacked into my mouth, so I was spitting blood for half an hour. In the meantime a real shooting war was going on; I was a bit confused as we had been told to only use our knives that night. With everyone shooting and yelling in Italian, I got so mixed up I decided to wait until a flare was fired."

Separated from the rest of his squad, Private Allen spent the next three days hiding out, not knowing which way to go or which side was winning or losing. He finally met up with a Canadian soldier and discovered that he had been dropped sixty miles from his intended drop zone (DZ). "I didn't feel too bad about being missing for three days, as a colonel came in thirty minutes after me," he said.[29]

■ ■ ■

Sgt. Otis Sampson, a paratrooper in Company E, was shuffling with the others in his eighteen-man stick toward the open door at the rear of his C-47's fuselage. In a moment, he said, "I was in space, falling, with perfect control of my mind, judging the time for opening. A sudden jerk with a hammer-like blow on my steel helmet; my helmet was well down over my face. I had the feeling I'd been poured into the bottom of my harness. I took stock of the darkness below; a searchlight was raking the sky and the sound of rifle and machine-gun fire drifted up."

Sampson was hanging high up in an olive tree and was all alone. With his razor-sharp combat knife he cut himself out of his harness, lowered himself to the ground, jammed a thirty-round magazine into his Thompson submachine gun, and set off to find any fellow Americans who might have dropped nearby. "We are definitely in the wrong area," he thought to himself. "This isn't anything like the sand table that Sergeant Bly made up from the photos of our DZ." He didn't know what to do. "As a sergeant, I'm a complete flop," he mused.

He moved off and after what seemed like forever finally ran into another paratrooper; they almost shot each other in the dark because neither had given the correct challenge and password. Gradually Sampson met more men from his company. It felt good to be among friends, even if none of them knew where they were or where they should be going.[30]

■ ■ ■

Ten paratroopers and a two-ton 75-millimeter howitzer were being hauled in C-47 number 42–32922, piloted by 2nd Lt. George C. Merz. It had been a long, boring flight until, on the approach to Scoglitti, anti-aircraft fire began streaking into the formation, causing many of the pilots to begin swerving. Suddenly, there was a shudder and a loud metallic crunching sound as Merz's C-47 collided with another, piloted by his flight leader, Robert Trimble. C-47 42–32922 was crippled and going down.

Flying at an elevation of only about 400 feet above the waves and at a speed of 120 miles per hour, Merz had no choice but to ditch in the sea. The landing was jarring. Merz said, "One paratrooper came crashing through to the cockpit [and landed on the control console]. The airplane settled—slightly nose low—so the door in the back was fairly high above the water.

"I looked back to see if everybody was okay. . . . the ditching here was smooth; it was one of my better landings." Luckily, the howitzer that probably would have broken its mooring straps and crashed through the cockpit had somehow been jettisoned into the sea by the paratroopers just prior to the crash. "I went back to these guys. They were all in a mess trying to get their parachutes off. A big job—the best way to put it."

The aircraft remained afloat long enough for the men to free up a couple of life rafts and deploy them into the water. After paddling toward shore for a considerable length of time, they finally reached land shortly before 0200 hours. But Merz felt no relief; from the pre-invasion briefing he knew that when the clock struck three a terrific naval bombardment would begin that would saturate the beachhead.

As the ranking officer in the group, Merz quickly led the ten paratroopers and three additional C-47 crewmembers inland a short way, where they dug in to await the firestorm of naval shells. "At three o'clock, I looked at my watch because I knew what was coming," Merz said. "Sure enough, at three o'clock on the nose, we could see orange flashes out over the water, and then we saw the smoke and these little blue lights coming up, like a nine-plane formation. Three, three, three; the Navy fired broadsides from a cruiser—right on time.

"All nine guns, *boom*, *boom*, *boom*, and then the shells came up, up, up. It looked like they were climbing up the sky, and all of a sudden they'd get to whistling. Then they'd go *tchoom*, and they'd go *schh, schh, schh, tchoom*—something like that," Merz said, "then the crash, and then the ground would shake, even though they weren't firing at our location. We just happened to be in a good spot—between Gela and Scoglitti—and the shells were flying in the area toward Gela.

"That went on for a little while, and then it stopped. At dawn, we heard these Italians coming down the beach and they were talking loud, you know, like Italians do. Then I said 'Sshh.' Somebody else said, 'Yeah, sshh—that's the enemy down there.' And here they came. They saw the life rafts, Mae Wests [life jackets], footprints, several footprints. you know. They went into a huddle—and then everything was quiet talk.

"One of our paratroopers held a grenade, and I said, 'If they come up the hill, throw it, but not unless they come up the hill.' They didn't even try; they turned back down the beach, and that was the end of it." Merz and his crew-members made it back to the shoreline, where they were later picked up and taken back to North Africa from where they would later fly more missions.[31]

■ ■ ■

Out of his 2,700-man unit, Gavin initially gathered only twenty paratroopers—one planeload's worth—and some of them were injured. The rest of his regiment and their equipment was scattered far and wide; some troopers were dropped in the British zone, some sixty miles to the east. One of Gavin's missions was to block any roads leading toward the landing beaches that the enemy might use to attack the invasion force. Knowing he had to perform that mission no matter how many or how few men he had, Gavin decided to press on. As he limped toward Gela in the morning light, more and more paratroopers, some of whom had landed in olive trees, appeared.[32]

Unknown to Gavin, eight of the 61st Troop Carrier Squadron's C-47s had been shot out of the sky by enemy gunfire, and another ten were badly damaged. The pilots of the stricken planes, though, were able to reach land and release their paratroopers, even if they were nowhere near their DZs.[33]

■ ■ ■

After assembling more men and using compasses, maps, and flashlights, Gavin began trying to figure out where they were. "Soon we came face to face with our enemy," he said. "It happened about an hour after we landed. I was moving ahead with about twenty troopers. I was leading and [Captain Ben] Vandervoort [the 505th PIR's operations officer] was alongside. I had been picking up troopers as I moved along through the shadows in the olive groves, over stone walls, darting across moonlit roads, going in what I hoped was the direction of our objective.

"There had been occasional bursts of small-arms fire, sometimes quite close, but so far we had not seen an actual enemy. . . . We crawled into the night. Although some men were suffering from jump injuries, they drove themselves toward the cascading flame and white phosphorous of bursting shells that could be seen on the distant horizon. . . . We were 'moving toward the sound of the guns.'"

Lost and wandering in the dark, at about 0230 hours on 10 July Gavin's men ran into a machine-gun position manned by troops from the U.S. 45th Division's 180th Regimental Combat Team; he then learned that he was near Vittoria, about twenty miles southeast of Gela. Gavin borrowed a jeep from the 45th and set out to round up more paratroopers; he found about 250 of them—members of Lt. Col. Ed "Cannonball" Krause's 3rd Battalion of the 505th—a few miles away, just waking up after a night in a tomato field. Rousting the men out of their foxholes, and finding a platoon of the 307th Combat Engineers, Gavin and Krause headed for Gela.

It wasn't long before a German motorcycle, with a German medical officer in the sidecar, roared up; the officer was taken prisoner. "He was the first live German we had ever seen in combat," Gavin said, commandeering the motorcycle and sending the two Germans to the rear under armed guard.

Gavin merged his small group with Krause's men, and off they went toward "the sound of the guns."

■ ■ ■

Another of Gavin's parachute battalions—Maj. Mark Alexander's 2nd—had been perfectly dropped almost intact in one place. Unfortunately, that place was south of Santa Croce Camerina, nearly seven miles southeast of Scoglitti and in the middle of a group of pillboxes that would require the battalion's attention all of D-Day.

The first rays of the morning sun were beginning to illuminate the landscape. "We headed down the hillside through open pastureland bearing right to keep out of sight of a pillbox below us," said paratrooper Otis Sampson. Mortar shells began splattering nearby and Sampson figured they were American. "About 200 feet to our right we saw an Italian soldier running downhill parallel with us on the other side of a chest-high stone wall. I yelled for him to stop but he didn't."

The enemy soldier continued running to a complex of pillboxes, and soon Italians were streaming out of the pillboxes and buildings with their hands in the air. After directing the surrendering soldiers to the rear, Sampson and the small group moved through an olive grove and came upon a gruesome sight—hanging from the branches were dead paratroopers. A lieutenant from his company was stretched out on the ground, also dead. An Italian machine gun began chattering, and some of the men in his platoon fell dead and wounded. Sampson decided to go after the deadly weapon. "My first thought was of revenge," he said, flushed with anger. "No one is killing any of my men and getting away with it."

Approaching a pillbox concealed by a haystack, Sampson spotted a machine-gun barrel sticking out and carefully crawled forward. When the enemy gun again opened up on some approaching paratroopers, Sampson lobbed a grenade into the haystack, silencing the gun. He then stood and sprayed the mound with his Thompson and followed up with another grenade through the pillbox's embrasure.

Entering the pillbox, Sampson found a young Italian dying on the floor, "his shirt blown open revealing shrapnel-made holes in his chest; he was breathing his last. A coating of dust had settled on him from the grenade's blast. I put my foot on his chest and pushed to see if he was playing possum. I had the feeling of being the victor. 'I have killed my first,' I thought, 'and balanced the score.'"[34]

Luckily, Alexander's battalion signal officer was able to radio a British cruiser and request fire on enemy positions. Alexander reported, "The cruiser immediately laid in two salvos. The first must have come in about seventy-five feet over our heads, and you can believe me when I say that the whole slope went up in flames. . . . we received no more harassment from snipers the rest of the night." The next day 2nd Battalion captured Santa Croce Camarina and Vittoria.[35]

The battalion that landed closest to the assigned drop zone was Lt. Col. Arthur "Hardnose" Gorman's 1st Battalion, which came to earth between Gela and Niscemi around 0200 hours on D-Day. Like Gavin, Gorham spent valuable time rounding up as many paratroopers as he could find, then advanced in the dark. He encountered a large farmhouse near a broad, treeless plain east of Ponte Olivo known as Piano Lupo that was surrounded by barbed wire, trenches, and six dome-shaped pillboxes; he would soon discover that the farmhouse held sixty Italian soldiers with ten machine guns. The twenty-eight-year-old Brooklyn native decided to delay his unit's attack on the position until dawn, by which time he had been joined by fifty more paratroopers.[36]

At that moment, unknown to the American paratroopers, hundreds of British glider troops off to the east were having their own appointment with destiny.

-3-

LADBROKE

RISKY BET

The pilot said, "Equipment off. Prepare for ditching."
—Lieutenant Arthur Royall, British Army

Since 1886 Britain has had a chain of sports betting shops known as Ladbrokes. To code-name a very risky military operation "Ladbroke" seems like a curious choice, for many of the British soldiers scheduled to take part in it no doubt felt the operation was a risky bet.

Ladbroke, the British glider operation, was the opening phase of Bernard Montgomery's Eighth British Army's multipronged invasion of the southeastern corner of the island. The mission was to seize and hold the Ponte Grande bridge over the Anapo River south of Syracuse until seaborne forces could land and capture the city.

Just as the American airborne assault was divided into two separate operations—Husky I and Husky II—the British also had a two-part aerial invasion, under the command of Brigadier Philip Hicks, head of the 1st British Airlanding Brigade. The first part, on the night of 9 July—simultaneously with Husky I—involved hundreds of American C-47s towing 136 CG-4A gliders (dubbed Hadrians by the British) and eight equipment-carrying British Airspeed Horsa gliders to landing zones near Syracuse. The second part, on 13 July, was Operation Fustian and would involve 135 aircraft delivering both gliders and parachutists from the 1st Parachute Brigade.[1]

Carrying Monty's amphibious invaders—the 5th, 50th Northumbrian, and 51st Highland Divisions, and the 1st Canadian Division—was the British Eastern Naval Task Force, commanded by Admiral Sir Bertram Ramsey and, like the Americans, divided into three attack forces: Force A (under Rear Admiral Ernest C. T. Troubridge), scheduled to deliver XIII Corps (5th and 50th Divisions) to Syracuse and Avola (and later Augusta); Force B (under Rear Admiral Rhoderick R. McGrigor), carrying XXX Corps (51st Highland Division) to Marzamemi, fifteen miles south of Avola; and Force V (under Rear Admiral Philip L. Vian), whose objective for the 1st Canadian Division was Pachino.[2]

These divisions would be augmented by a tank battalion, an armored regiment, and three commando units. Number 3 Commando and the South African Squadron of the Special Air Service would come ashore near Syracuse, while Numbers 40 and 41 Royal Marine Commandos (under Robert E. Laycock) would precede the Canadians at Pachino.[3]

Unfortunately, the mission began to unravel weeks before the actual invasion. First, while the tow planes would be flown by American pilots, the American-built gliders would be operated by British pilots. Second, not enough time was allotted for training; consequently, the glider pilots had only a few hours in the cockpits. And third, the mission involved the gliders being towed at night from Kairouan to their release point off the east coast of Sicily—a distance of nearly four hundred miles.

Since the British had not operated American gliders before, the U.S. Army sent 110 of their own glider pilots to Egypt in February 1943 with the mission of supervising the assembly of the engineless machines (they came disassembled like kits in huge crates) and then teaching British pilots how to fly them.

■ ■ ■

The glider concept was sound enough: Surprise the enemy by swooping down on him in silent, engineless aircraft as the Germans had done earlier at Fortress Eben Emael during the May 1940 invasion of Belgium and their April 1941 attack on Crete. But those had been well-thought-out daylight actions with plenty of well-trained personnel.

There was also a debate at the highest levels: a daylight operation versus one under the cover of darkness. Both had their strong points and deficiencies. In a daylight operation the pilots could better pick out their landing zones, but gunners on the ground could better pick them out, too. A night operation allowed for greater stealth, but the risks of collision and becoming lost rose exponentially. General Montgomery, who had opted for gliders rather than paratroopers, made the final decision: night.[4]

The commander of the British 1st Battalion Glider Pilot Regiment was Lieutenant Colonel George Chatterton, and he was horrified by what he and his battalion were being ordered to do. Instead of British glider pilots being trained to fly British Horsa gliders, his battalion was trained by American glider pilots to fly American CG-4As. This might have been fine had there been sufficient time for training, but it was a rushed, hurried affair.[5]

In addition, the American pilots were not seasoned combat veterans; many, if not most, of them had just graduated from glider-pilot school themselves. And because of the shortage of British glider pilots, many of the Operation Ladbroke copilots would be American. The men flying the C-47 tow planes also had had very little experience towing gliders; the 51st Air Wing had never done such a thing before.[6]

■ ■ ■

If Ladbroke seemed like a jury-rigged, last-minute, ill-conceived operation, that's because it was. Montgomery had created serious problems in May during the planning stages of Ladbroke when he switched the roles of the 51st and 52nd Troop Carrier Wings. Originally the 51st was to have operated with the U.S. 82nd Airborne Division while the 52nd would carry the British 1st Airborne Division. The switch meant that the 51st would now be towing gliders—something for which it had little experience. The troops scheduled to pilot and ride in the gliders were equally inexperienced.

A disaster of major proportions was brewing. As one historian put it, "As long as the airborne mission called for commando tactics against beach defenses, the gliders had been destined for follow-up operations or transport of key air personnel to Sicily. Now that the British airborne forces were to fight it out with enemy troops on the approaches to Syracuse, the firepower and concentration possible in a glider landing came to seem of paramount value.

"Thus about the last week in May, Montgomery's parachute mission turned into a midnight glider assault. The decision is said to have been made by Montgomery himself. In vain did the British Airborne Forces advisor, Group Capt. T. B. Cooper, RAF, protest that a glider assault on a dark night with inexperienced crews was not practicable. The decision stood."[7] The reason behind the switch of the 51st and 52nd Troop Carrier Wings has never been explained.

■ ■ ■

Adding to the overall sense of a monumental, impending catastrophe was the fact that five hundred CG-4A Waco gliders themselves had only arrived by ship in North Africa in April and May. Most were still in their shipping crates and needed to be assembled; each glider required a week's work by six men. By June, with just over a month to go before Husky, only 30 of 240 gliders had been assembled.

Suddenly, though, the Army lit a fire under the situation, and the manpower was found to begin a crash course in glider construction. Three weeks before Husky, there were finally enough Wacos—350 of them—so that training could proceed. By the time the operation was set to launch, however, British glider pilots had received less than five hours of practice flying—and only one of those hours at night. Nineteen American glider pilots volunteered for the mission, but it was not nearly enough.[8]

■ ■ ■

There was also a parachute component to Ladbroke. In this two-phased operation, pathfinders from Britain's 21st Independent Parachute Company, brought in from Tunisia by the 51st Troop Carrier Wing, would drop before dawn on 10 July in phase one—Operation Marston—and mark the drop zones with colored panels and signal lights.

Following right behind, the paratroopers of Major General George F. Hopkinson's British 1st Airborne Division—the "Red Devils"—would land and seize the Ponte Grande bridge over the Anapo River, just south of

Syracuse. They were to hold it until the British 5th Division, coming ashore by landing craft at Cassibile, some seven miles to the south, could reach and relieve them.

While this was to take place, the glider-borne infantry of Brigadier Hicks' 1st Airlanding Brigade, being towed in from Tunisia, would land near Syracuse. Their mission was to seize the harbor and knock out Italian guns guarding it so that it could be used as a port to bring in supplies and reinforcements.

In addition, the 2nd Parachute Brigade was supposed to drop and seize the port of Augusta, twenty miles north of Syracuse, while simultaneously the 1st Parachute Brigade would grab the Primosole Bridge over the River Simento and hold it until reinforcements arrived.

Prepared or not, on the night of 9 July the Ladbroke aerial force departed from six airfields around Kairouan. It was made up of the 51st Troop Carrier Wing's 109 C-47s and the 38th Wing's 28 Albemarles and 7 Halifax bombers that would tow 6 British Horsa gliders and 127 American CG-4A Waco gliders.[9]

■ ■ ■

Probably unknown by the men who would be flying and riding in the Waco gliders was the craft's checkered history. The U.S. government had handed out contracts to all kinds of manufacturing companies that had never built a single flying machine before. Delays, cost overruns, and slipshod construction were the norm.[10]

The final straw was that the gliders would have to be towed from their bases on the evening of 9 July for almost four hundred miles—over five agonizing hours—while being severely buffeted by winds just a few feet above the cresting waves to avoid German radar. Practically every man in every glider would be stricken with motion sickness.

One of the British soldiers taking part was Lieut. Arthur Royall, a platoon commander with Company B, 1st Battalion, 1st Border Regiment, 1st Airlanding Brigade. He recalled,

> The glider pilots were newly trained and had no experience of landing at night. Our pilot was Sergeant Smith of the Glider Pilot Regiment, with Flight Officer Guy Hunter of the U.S. Army flying as copilot.

> The first of 1st Border's gliders took off at 1905 hours. . . . Once we were airborne we had, barring accidents, a five-hour flight ahead of us. None of us, I think, were unduly worried, but we were all going to feel a great deal better when we had completed and hopefully made a safe journey. However, I must confess that I was not particularly happy about the type of landing zone on which we were to descend. As far as I could tell from the information given at our briefing, they were small, strewn with rocks, and bounded by stone walls.
>
> The journey was noisy and bumpy. The Waco was very noisy in flight as the canvas [sides] drummed against the steel frame. We had, of course, an issue of brown paper bags into which we could be sick, and many of us were—we soon discovered that the bottom seam of the bag gave way after only the minimum of use! During the flight, the wind increased at times to forty-five miles per hour.[11]

Shortly before 2300 hours the aerial formations approached the coast of southeast Sicily. The towplane pilots were frantically trying to find the landing zones in the dark while at the same time avoiding the mass of other tow planes and gliders bucking like wild horses around them. In the gliders, the pilots' arms were cramping after trying to hold their kite-like aircraft steady after such a long, stressful ride. The wind was stronger than anyone had expected and many of the pilots had badly miscalculated it; many dropped out of formation and, lost in the dark, flew on alone. Fuel was approaching the halfway mark; the tow planes would have to release their gliders and turn back soon if they hoped to make it back to their North African bases.

The tight formation had been scrambled. A dozen gliders remained in flight long enough to reach the coast and make safe landings, while forty-seven others crashed into the sea; the other seventy-five crash-landed onto the island. Casualties were heavy. The only good part was that the scattered drops confused the enemy and caused them to believe that the air assault was larger and more widespread than it actually was.

■ ■ ■

At last the C-47 pilots announced to the glider pilots over the intercom line: "Get ready to release," even though they were miles from their release point.

Then the tow planes flashed their navigation lights—the signal for the glider pilots to pull the release handle. The glider pilots, perhaps knowing they were still far from land and now catching the first bursts of anti-aircraft fire from below, told the men behind them to discard all their combat gear and prepare to ditch into the sea.

Panic! The 134 gliders, made of fabric wrapped around plywood framing and metal tubing, and packed with 1,600 troopers, cracked apart or flipped as they collided with the waves, and men began frantically clawing their way to the emergency exits and out into the cold, dark water, inflating their lifebelts as they went. Some of the gliders floated for a few minutes; others sank like bricks, taking their human cargo with them. Few life rafts appeared. Men in boots and waterlogged clothing clung to floating bits of gliders while others began struggling in the long swim for shore; most never made it. Searchlights scanned the water; bullets and shells followed.[12]

Arthur Royall recalled his own ordeal: "As we approached Sicily, ack-ack* fire was to be seen some distance ahead of us and the glider rocked badly. I felt the glider being released and, although I could not see clearly, we were over the sea and there was no sight of land. In what seemed a very short time the call came down from the pilot: 'Equipment off. Prepare for ditching.' We hit the water with a tremendous thump."

Royall's glider quickly sank to wing level and he was briefly knocked unconscious. "When I came to, the water was up to my shoulder. I was alone, it was dark, and I still had my equipment on. How to get out?" He suddenly remembered the commando dagger on his belt and cut his way through the canvas top. "My appearance was greeted with: 'Here he is.' I was hauled out through the hole, leaving my equipment behind."

Royall and most of the other troopers stayed with the floating wreckage through the night. "We paddled from one portion to the other, changing position when the portion we were on, or holding on to, sank deeper in the water than what was comfortable. There was a heavy swell and it was much colder than I ever imagined the Mediterranean could be. I am

---

* The term "ack-ack" is slang for anti-aircraft guns or fire and likely derives from *acht-acht*, the German spelling for "eight-eight" or "eighty-eight," the millimeter size of a standard type of German anti-aircraft gun.

sure that we believed that if we could hold on until daylight we would be rescued."

Two men asked him for permission to swim for the shore, "which was clearly some distance away—at least five or six miles was my estimate. I was reluctant to give permission, but I felt that they should have the chance to swim for the shore if they felt they could make it." They didn't have far to swim; an assault landing craft came in and pulled them aboard.

Royall was worried: "When daylight came, those of us still with the wreckage, including our American glider pilot, could see ships and crafts of all sorts passing by, but they couldn't or didn't see us. As we were low in the water this was understandable, but it was frustrating and began to dent our morale. To have survived a night in the sea and then not be rescued was an awful thought."

At daylight a Greek destroyer, part of the assault force, spotted the floating wreckage and the thirteen men; the ship came alongside and rescued them. "Scrambling nets were lowered and we pulled ourselves aboard. Some of the chaps just couldn't manage and the Greek sailors dived into the sea and helped them to and up the nets." Unfortunately, three of the men, including Sergeant Smith, the British glider pilot, drowned.

A few hours later the thirteen were transferred to an empty troopship that had deposited Canadian troops at Pachino. Three days later Royall and his mates reached Algiers a bit worse for wear but grateful to be alive.

He noted, "Of the seventy-two Waco gliders that carried men of the Border Regiment on Operation Ladbroke, one landed in Malta, seven in Africa, forty-four in the sea, and only twenty-three in Sicily—and these were widely scattered. Only eleven officers and 191 ORs [other ranks] actually landed in Sicily. Casualties for the Airlanding Brigade and Glider Pilot Regiment were 605 officers and men, of whom some 300 were drowned without ever getting the opportunity to fight." After being treated for his injuries (a cut on his forehead had become infected) in military hospitals, Royall rejoined his unit at the beginning of August.[13]

It was one of the worst disasters of the war. Glider historian Scott McGaugh reported, "More than 600 officers and men died" in Operation Ladbroke, "more than half of them by drowning. Of the seventy-three gliders that were released farther out than the 3,000-yard release point, only one in sixteen made it ashore. Of those released inside 3,000 yards, about eight in ten made it ashore." Every C-47 tow plane made it back to North Africa, however.[14]

Omar Bradley reflected on the British disaster: "Only twelve of those gliders reached their objective, the [Ponte Grande] bridge over the [Anapo River] south of Syracuse. Forty-seven others pancaked into the sea and the remainder were scattered wildly inland. Of the eight officers and sixty-five men who struggled to the bridge, four officers and fifteen men were still holding to that position when the vanguards of Montgomery's invasion force relieved them on the afternoon of D-Day. This decimated British platoon had stood off an enemy infantry battalion reinforced with artillery and mortars."[15]

The brave Brits held the bridge until 1530 hours on 10 July when overwhelming enemy strength took it away from them. The 17th Infantry Brigade of the 5th Infantry Division, marching from the south, arrived and recaptured it.[16]

Casualties weren't limited to the lower ranks. Admiral Lord Ashbourne recalled, "We were stopped in the *Keren* off the beaches. I saw a body floating in the sea, almost alongside and evidently alive. I told the captain of the *Keren* to pick him up. . . . He turned out to be Major-General G. F. Hopkinson, commanding the 1 British Airborne Division. . . . We wrung out his clothes, gave him a plate of eggs and bacon, and then sent him ashore to catch up to the rest of his soldiers.

"Poor chap, he was later killed near Taranto [Italy] 10 September 1943. He was a splendid man and must have been a great loss to his airborne troops."[17]

■ ■ ■

As terrible as the Ladbroke disaster was, the second American airborne drop the next night added to the Allies' unnecessary casualty toll. That was still in the future; now the amphibious forces were coming ashore to an uncertain reception.

4

RANGERS LEAD THE WAY

Naval gunfire had given us a convincing demonstration.

—William O. Darby

Scheduled to be the first American amphibious troops to reach the beach at Gela was Lt. Col. William Orlando Darby's 2,400-man Ranger Force. The Arkansas native said, "One hundred and thirty warships were included in the gigantic ship concentration while 324 vessels were employed for the transportation of the assault troops and their equipment. The ships rendezvoused in the Tunisian channel and then moved eastward toward Sicily via Cape Bon, south of Pantelleria."

The 1st and 4th Ranger Battalions were loaded aboard three landing ships and were attached to Terry Allen's 1st Infantry Division that would be landing on Dime Beach at Gela, while the 3rd Ranger Battalion was attached to Truscott's 3rd Infantry Division landing simultaneously at Joss Beach, near Licata.[1]

The coastal city of Gela has a long history. Although people had lived in the area for thousands of years, the city counts its official birth at around 688 BCE when colonists from Rhodes and Crete established a settlement there at the mouth of the muddy Gela River; archeologists consider Gela the second-oldest city in Sicily, after Syracuse.

In 405 BCE the city was sacked by Carthage, struggled back to life, and was nearly abandoned in 282 BCE during Roman times. The later city was founded in 1233 CE by Frederick II and given the name Terranova di Sicilia until 1928, when it was changed back to Gela. By 1943 shabby three- and four-story buildings made up the central core of the city that was dominated by several careworn churches dating from the seventeenth century. The population was about 32,000.

Now, Mussolini's fascist minions were manning the guns, as well as two divisions of battle-experienced Germans—some 60,000 men—who stood nearby to defend the towns and beaches and fly recon missions overhead, trying to get a glimpse of the expected Allied invasion.[2]

Gela sits atop a hill about 150 feet above the water. On another hill about four miles to the northeast is a sturdy old fortress known as Castel di Lucio (or Castelluccio) dating from the sixteenth century. It commands the intersection of roads leading to Piazza Armerina, Butera, and Mazzarino—all early objectives of the invasion. Ancient Greek ruins cover a hill known as Capo Soprano. Jutting out from the center of town was a pier some two thousand feet long; concrete bunkers guarded the approaches from the sea.

Darby's mission was to secure the town and neutralize Castel di Lucio before the 1st Division came ashore and then move inland to assist Gavin's paratroopers who would have landed somewhere north of the city. Darby recalled, "As the first convoys moved out of the harbors, General Patton issued his first order of the day addressed to the 'Soldiers of the Seventh Army.' He exhorted the Americans to feel pride in their selection to fight by the side of the famous British Eighth Army and pointed out, 'In landing operations, retreat is impossible. We must retain this tremendous advantage by always attacking, rapidly, ruthlessly, viciously, and without rest.'"[3]

■ ■ ■

The Rangers have an interesting genesis. Arriving in Belfast, Northern Ireland, in January 1942, the 34th Infantry Division was one of the first American units to go overseas. According to William Baumer, who coauthored Darby's autobiography, "General George C. Marshall, chief of staff of the U.S. Army, was anxious for American forces to get combat experience before the invasion of Europe. The best opportunity seemed to be with Lord Louis Mountbatten, chief of Combined Operations, the headquarters of the British Commandos.

Colonel Lucian K. Truscott Jr. was called upon to implement this project, and on 1 June he wrote instructions to General [Russell P.] Hartle to organize a commando-type American unit.

"On 8 June, Bill Darby's hopes were realized: he was assigned to this new unit, to be called the Rangers. Thus does lighting strike in wartime. Darby has the requisite training; he was on the spot; and he knew how to react to his good fortune."[4]

Sgt. Ralph G. Martin, a reporter for *Yank, The Army Weekly*, noted while on a transport sitting in an unnamed port that morning, "We know we are headed somewhere, for something big. We know we are headed for trouble, but except for the shortage of women and deck chairs, this has been like a peacetime Mediterranean cruise, at least until a few days ago. Then things changed and today's latrine rumor says we're finally shoving off tomorrow. The captain put teeth in the rumor when he announced we couldn't use the ship's radio to monitor the news any more."[5]

■ ■ ■

"There is nothing in warfare, or perhaps even in life, to be compared with the hushed mystery of the final approach in a night landing," wrote naval historian Adm. Samuel E. Morison. "Everything ahead is uncertain. There is no sound but the rush of waters, the throbbing of your ship's engines and of your own heart. You cannot see your friends on either flank, nor anything but the ship ahead and the ship astern. The shore, if dimly visible, is shrouded in darkness . . . There can be no drawn battle, no half-success, in an amphibious landing; it is win all splendidly or lose all miserably."[6]

Committed to winning all splendidly was Lt. Col. Bill Darby, one of the great American soldiers of the war. Born at Fort Smith, Arkansas, on 9 February 1911, Darby graduated from West Point in 1933 with a commission in field artillery. After the United States entered World War II, he served as aide-de-camp to Major General Hartle, commanding the 34th Infantry Division. Arriving in Belfast, Northern Ireland, in January 1942, the 34th was one of the first American units to go overseas, but a smaller, commando-type unit was needed to conduct raids on a hostile shore. And so the Rangers were born.

After intensive training in Scotland alongside British commandos, the Rangers went off to combat. Participating with Canadian forces in the abortive Dieppe, France, invasion in August 1942, Darby's men enjoyed more success during Operation Torch and the drive across North Africa, where they were attached to Terry Allen's 1st Infantry Division and were usually either the spearhead of an attack or in the thick of the fighting.

For Husky, Darby put himself in command of the 1st Battalion while Maj. Roy Murray commanded the accompanying 4th Battalion; the 3rd Battalion, under Maj. Herman Dammer, was attached to the 3rd Infantry Division that would attack Joss Beach at Licata.[7]

But now, on the rough crossing from Algiers, Darby reflected on how little control he had over the outcome of the pending battle—and especially the weather. During the voyage a storm had roared into the sea between Tunisia and Sicily and rocked their ships and landing craft. Darby noted that many—if not most—of his rough, tough Rangers were terribly seasick: "Holding their heads in their hands, they moaned, they vomited."

The 1st and 4th Ranger Battalions were sailing on three transports: the USS *Joseph T. Dickman* (APA 13) and former passenger ships HMT *Prince Albert* and HMT *Prince Charles*, converted to small landing ship troop transports. Sailing with them were two engineer battalions whose job it would be to clear land mines, demolitions, and obstacles, and to fight as infantry if the going got sticky. General Allen had dubbed this group "Force X."[8]

At about 0115 hours Rear Adm. John Hall's Task Force 81, carrying the first assault wave for Dime Beach, reached their station a few miles off the coast of Gela. As the very seasick men were transferring from the transports into landing craft, someone aboard the *Dickman* played a recording of Glenn Miller's "American Patrol" over the loudspeakers. The jazzy piece picked up spirits at a time when it was most needed. At 0220 hours the 4th Ranger Battalion's Companies A, B, and C reached shore, followed by D and E.[9]

At 0335 hours—two-and-a-half hours later—they were approaching the beach. "There were some forty-eight boats in all," Darby said, "and because of the rough sea off Gela, the boats began milling around in the water." The seasick men were aching to go ashore—enemy or no enemy.[10]

■ ■ ■

Southern Sicily was home to some of the Axis forces' strongest units in the Mediterranean—at least on paper. Gela's beaches were guarded by the men and guns of the Italian XVIII Coastal Brigade and 429th Coastal Battalion. The highway to the north—Highway 117—led to the Ponte Olivo airfield where the tanks of the Italian Mobile Gruppo E were stationed. Beyond was the city of Niscemi, where the Italian 4th "Livorno" Infantry Division, commanded by Giandomenico Chirieleison, and elements of German Luftwaffe Lt. Gen. Paul Conrath's "Hermann Göring" Panzer Division were known to be stationed. But ground forces weren't the only enemy the Yanks had to contend with. Hundreds of warplanes were ready to pounce.[11]

As the Americans would quickly find out, the landing at Gela was about to become the military equivalent of whacking a very large hornet's nest.

The predawn hours were pitch black, but the guide boats that were supposed to help direct the landing craft toward the shore were nowhere to be seen. "It was intended that the amphibious units would be met by two guide boats," said Darby. "Orders were shouted back and forth: 'Follow me! Over here!' Sorting out the landing craft was a difficult job while the storm was still in progress and forty-mile winds were whipping up the waves. When the boats were almost collected, the guide boat appeared. I called to its skipper, 'Are you on course?'

"The answer came back, 'Sure, I'm on course.'

"That was all I wanted to know, so we followed the guide boat to the beach. As we got closer, six searchlights on shore turned on us and, as one of the Rangers later said, 'The Jerries on the flanks began to tune up, and the show was on.'"

Behind them, big guns boomed, and hundreds of shells from the Navy's warships screamed over the landing craft, bursting with bright flashes against the shore and in the city. Parched fields inland of Gela caught fire, and the rising flames and smoke silhouetted the city's buildings. With the oncoming flotilla spotlighted like a herd of deer caught in a car's headlights, the enemy on shore opened up with everything they had.

"Blue streaks of fire flew toward and among the boats," Darby recalled. "Near shore, the gunboat guides showed their lights and hailed the first assault wave, shouting: 'Go straight ahead! You'll see the light on your right! Look out for mines ashore! Good luck!' Going toward shore we could see blue tracers cutting across the beach. It looked as if nobody could possibly live through all the stuff the Italians were shooting out across the beach."

There were also plenty of mines in the surf, ready to blast landing craft out of the water, and mines on the beach ready to rip apart the men disembarking from them. Two battalions of combat engineers that accompanied the Rangers would have their hands full trying to neutralize the buried explosive devices—if they made it to shore alive.

Darby was aboard a rocket-firing landing craft support ship that carried twelve rockets in two banks, each shell about the size of a 105-millimeter artillery round. "When the rockets went off, it seemed as if the boat had blown up," he said. "The rockets hit an ammunition dump in the town, blowing everything sky high and knocking out the defenses on that side of the beach. An entire block and a half of buildings was leveled. It was a lucky hit."

It was now H-hour—0245 hours. The charging flotilla of landing craft packed with Rangers was now approaching the two-thousand-foot-long cement pier that the Rangers were tasked with capturing for the future offloading of vehicles from LSTs. But the 1st Infantry Division's intelligence officer had warned Darby that it might be packed with explosives and rigged for demolition. "He was right," Darby said.[12] As the 1st Battalion's boats fanned out to the east of the pier and the 4th Battalion's went to the west, and as the Rangers' boats ran parallel to it, the whole center section of the pier exploded. Miraculously, no one was hurt—except for some ringing eardrums.[13]

The 1st Battalion's landing craft now scraped the sand and came to an abrupt halt that shoved everyone forward; the ramps dropped with a mighty splat, and the Rangers came pouring out in a jumble, stumbling through the water, expecting enemy fire to tear through them at any moment.

Darby said,

> Searchlights spotlighted the men as they jumped out of their boats, but as the ships out at sea ranged on them, the lights went out one by one. . . .

> Red and blue streaks of fire plunged across [the Rangers'] path. Naval guns spouting black smoke and bursts of flame made direct hits on an annoying battery of guns.
>
> The flotilla commander had boasted that he would put my boat high and dry on the beach, which he did; many of the boats were sticking on a sandbar several hundred yards off shore. We splashed through a few yards of surf, went rapidly across the beach, and hugged the sea wall. The town was dead ahead. Behind us the 83rd Chemical Mortar Battalion swung ashore in LCIs, landing just to the right of the pier.[14]

The Rangers also had the mission of knocking out a coastal gun battery on the western edge of Gela. While still in Algeria, the Rangers had practiced countless times attacking a mock-up of the position. Now it was about to become reality.

After watching the duel between shore batteries and the Navy's ships, Darby pulled the commanders of Companies A and B aside shortly before midnight on 9 July and spoke to them. Capt. James B. Lyle, head of Company A, 1st Ranger Battalion, recalled that Darby said,

> You have observed the fireworks ashore, and you can see that we are not going to have an easy time tonight. You were selected for the gun battery mission because you are one of the "old timers" of the outfit, and I have confidence you will find some method of destroying that gun position. As you well know, we have a great number of officers who have not had any combat experience. I expect you, and the enlisted men who we can class as "old timers," to guide the green officers and men along.
>
> It has been reported that the gun battery will be a hard nut to crack. . . . During the landing and capture of the battery you will probably lose a great number of personnel. You must expect this. The Rangers, as you know, have never lost very many officers or men during any one operation. Tonight you must expect to lose from one to seventy-five percent of both companies. But don't forget—that gun battery must be destroyed!
>
> If casualties are high, it will not be a reflection on your leadership abilities, and if you find need of assistance, contact me promptly and I will try to fulfill your request. May God be with you, young feller![15]

The plan called for the first wave of Rangers—made up of Companies C, D, E, and F—to hit the beach first, followed by Companies A and B in the second wave. The third wave was made up of 1st Battalion of the 39th Combat Engineers, and the fourth would be the 83rd Chemical Mortar Battalion. By neutralizing the beach defenses, the 1st Infantry Division would be able to land with greater ease.

While Darby's 1st Ranger Battalion easily made it to the first line of buildings rimming the beach, Maj. Roy Murray's 4th, to the west of the pier, was briefly delayed as barbed wire and buried mines took their toll on the men charging inland in the dark. Also waiting for them were the guns of the 429th Coastal Battalion.

Landing Craft, Assault 712 was carrying a platoon of men from Capt. Ralph A. Colby's Company D. Once the boats crunched sand in the darkness, the Rangers dashed out toward their objective—right into a minefield and the crossfire from two Italian concrete pillboxes that nearly wiped out an entire forty-man platoon.

Second Lt. Walter Wojcik yelled "Follow me!" to his men, ran forward, and triggered a "Bouncing Betty" mine that popped up to waist height and ripped his chest apart with steel fragments. As he lay bleeding to death in the arms of 1st Sgt. Randall "Harry" Harris, his last words were, "I've had it, Harry." The blast had also wounded Harris; other mines killed four more men.[16]

A wounded first sergeant from Company D bravely led his men toward the fortifications and put them out of action. The rest of the platoon dashed up the twenty-foot-high dunes behind the position.[17]

On the beach, Darby glanced back out to sea and saw a large infantry transport stuck on a sandbar—the perfect sitting target. The Italian gunners changed their focus from the Rangers to this large craft, slamming round after round into it. "Their hard luck was a break for the Rangers," Darby said. "The firing on the beach dropped off considerably, allowing us to advance into the town with our own mortars in support."[18]

Captain Lyle recalled, "From a study of the scale model the following information was gained: the height of buildings, width of the beach, and distances to various parts of the town. This model was so realistic and complete in detail that one quickly became thoroughly familiar with the town plan, obstacles, and probable enemy positions."[19]

To hide the Rangers during their exit from the boats, the destroyer USS *Shubrick*'s (DD 639) gunners blew out two XVIII Coastal Brigade searchlights and took several of the brigade's artillery positions under fire, neutralizing them.[20]

At last overcoming the obstacles, Murray's 4th Ranger Battalion entered the town and dashed to the right as Darby's 1st Battalion swung to the left in a pincer movement; the engineer battalion, which was also trained to fight as infantry, occupied the center of the line. Small-arms fire and hand grenades cleared the darkened buildings of snipers as the men moved farther forward; the force then advanced toward the hilltop fort. As dawn gradually lightened the sky, the Rangers could see that the approaches to the fort were blocked by rows of barbed wire, pillboxes, machine guns, and artillery pieces of different calibers. It was time to call on the Navy's big guns.

Darby noted that the prearranged plan of attack provided for the Army commanders, once on shore, to call for naval gunfire.

> Through an accompanying naval officer, I asked for fire on the fort from the cruiser *Savannah*. [The *Savannah* and the *Boise* of Rear Adm. John L. Hall's Task Force 81, plus eleven destroyers and other craft, were assigned to provide fire support at Gela.] In a few minutes a salvo of big shells landed on the fort, throwing up debris. Hitting in a steady stream, the shells defenders silenced many of the guns. My men ran forward at the first lull in the' fire, asking the cruiser to lift fire. Just as we got close to the fort's walls, several projectiles hit inside the fort. The concussion was terrifying, and the fort surrendered. Naval gunfire had given us a convincing demonstration.[21]

Lyle said, "Upon reaching the beach there was no evidence that the first wave had landed and the enemy beach positions were still intact. The Rangers were trained to rush across a beach and were over it before enemy mortars could short their fires. Two [Italian] machine-gunners attempted to fire, but as they opened up they found Rangers in the positions with them and were promptly destroyed."

Lyle's combined companies entered Gela and began cautiously traversing the silent streets they had memorized from the scale model. Whenever an incautious Italian soldier appeared from a doorway or from around a corner, he was swiftly shot down. Lyle's first sergeant encountered a roadblock but quickly cleared it with a grenade and a few bursts from his Thompson submachine gun. From the west edge of town, a gun battery was spotted in the dark and immediately mortar rounds were placed on it.

After finding a ditch that led to the battery, Lyle directed his men in the assault. As two machine guns kept the Italians' heads down, a squad of Rangers advanced with Bangalore torpedoes to blast a hole through the wire that encircled the position. At about this time, shells from the *Savannah* came crashing down on the battery that contained 3-inch coastal guns, obliterating it; Lyle requested the naval fire cease so that his men could finish mopping up. By 0630 hours, the position had been taken. Lyle's casualties had been light: one man killed and eight others slightly wounded—far from the 75 percent that Darby had warned might be incurred.[22]

Shortly thereafter, the growing, growling noise of aircraft engines was heard—German aircraft. Darby recalled, "Twenty of them dived on the beach, their machine guns chattering nervously. In an instant they were out to sea, still strafing. Then they were over the ships and gaining altitude in a wide circle to return to the landing area." Darby said that one of his men claimed to have shot down one of the attacking Me 110s with a long burst from his Browning automatic rifle.

By this time supplies, artillery pieces, and anti-tank guns were being delivered to the beach by the workhorse DUKWs; mountains of boxes and crates full of supplies were piling up on the sand. Engineers stayed busy trying to locate and defuse buried mines, although occasionally a DUKW would run over one and detonate it.[23]

The Americans had gotten a tenuous toehold on the southern Sicilian coast. Roaring in behind the Rangers was the 1st Infantry Division, ready to strengthen that hold and enlarge it. But the danger was just beginning. Very soon the Rangers, the 505th PIR, and elements of the 1st Infantry Division would find themselves in the middle of one of the most difficult fights of the entire Sicily campaign.

■ ■ ■

Aboard the *Monrovia*, Patton was listening to radio reports of the firefights as they were happening in real time. The battle had just begun; how soon would he be able to go ashore and orchestrate it? "We may feel anxious," he believed, "but I trust the Italians are scared to death." The exhilarated general added, "I would not change places with anyone I know right now."[24]

5

THE BIG RED ONE ARRIVES

Nothing in Hell must stop the Ist Division.

—Terry de la Mesa Allen

In the ports of Algiers and Tunis, the 1st Infantry Division loaded into the Navy's new attack transport ships known as LCIs, a type never before used in war. The LCI was more than half the length of a football field, could hold an entire infantry company (two hundred men), and had a top speed of sixteen knots (eighteen miles per hour). But its flat bottom and shallow draft (less than six feet) meant that the men in it were in for a stomach-churning ride in to the beach at Gela, code-named "Dime Beach."[1]

Hewitt's great fleet cast off its lines from ports across Algeria and Tunisia on 6 July and sailed into the night. Bringing the 1st Infantry Division to Gela was Rear Adm. John L. Hall's Task Force 81, made up of the light cruisers *Boise* and *Savannah*, eleven destroyers, two LSTs, six transports, thirty-three landing craft, eight minesweepers, and ten patrol torpedo boats.[2]

For a few hours at least, the invasion was out of Patton's hands. Everything had been set in motion; now it devolved to the landing-craft coxswains, the battalion commanders, the company commanders, the platoon leaders, the individual soldiers. Patton had done all he could do, had hopefully aroused in each man a lust for battle, a desire to kill, and the drive to make the other poor dumb sonofabitch die for his country. Now he could only pace and helplessly monitor the situation from the *Monrovia*, listening to reports coming in from the various units that had been let loose to storm the beaches of Sicily.

For better or worse, this mighty endeavor was his creation. As war correspondent Hal Boyle wrote, a "fire of pride" burned in Patton's eyes as he stood on the bridge of the *Monrovia* and watched ships carrying the men—his Seventh Army—plow through the blackened sea, their white contrails the only indication of their existence. Boyle discerned, "It was to him not a ship's deck he stood upon but a peak of glory."[3]

■ ■ ■

Coming in on the wet heels of the Rangers at Gela's Dime Beach—divided into four sectors code-named Beaches Yellow, Blue, Red 2, and Green 2—was the 1st Infantry Division, one of America's most experienced combat formations. Created in 1917 and known as the "Big Red One" because of its unit patch, a scarlet number one set in an elongated, olive-green pentagon, the division performed exemplary service in France during the Great War.

It also proved that it had lost none of its fighting spirit during the Torch invasion and subsequent campaign in North Africa. Indeed, so passionate was Patton about including the division in his plans for Husky that he told Eisenhower, "I want those sons of bitches. I won't go on without them." Patton got them—and inserted them into what many correctly thought would be the hottest of the Americans' three invasion beaches—Dime Beach at Gela.

Leading the 1st was Maj. Gen. Terry de la Mesa Allen, one of Patton's longtime friends and fellow polo players. Born on April Fools' Day, 1888, at the Fort Douglas Military Reservation in Salt Lake City, Utah, Allen was an unconventional commander. "Before they made him, they broke the mold," one of his men once quipped. Allen had a streak of the maverick in him and was just as likely to rub someone the wrong way as he was to earn their praise. In fact, Patton and Bradley would become so displeased with Allen that both he and his assistant division commander would lose their jobs within just a few weeks.

Wiry, with smile-lines crinkling the corners of his eyes but with the heart of a warrior, the hard-drinking Allen was casual in his dress and appearance and was not inclined to be overly strict with his men on such matters; their fighting qualities were vastly more important to him than spit and polish and a sharp crease in a pants leg. As a consequence, he was sometimes in hot water with his superiors who questioned what they assumed was a lax manner of commanding. Allen couldn't care less. His motto was, "Nothing in Hell must stop the 1st Division." Allen was known for getting the job done, and his leadership of the Big Red One was crucial in order for Husky to succeed in the very center of the invasion area. If Allen's men failed, then the entire operation was in jeopardy.

Allen came from a military tradition. His father, Sam Allen, was an Army colonel, and his maternal grandfather was Col. Carlos Alvarez de la Mesa, a Spanish national who fought on the Union side in the American Civil War. Allen wanted to carry on the tradition; he had won an appointment to West Point but was dismissed for poor grades. Undaunted, after graduating from the Catholic University of America in Washington, DC, in 1912, he enlisted in the Army as a private, earned a commission to second lieutenant, joined a cavalry regiment, and, much like Patton, served on the Mexican-American border against *banditos*. With America's entry into the Great War, Allen went overseas with the 90th Division, where he was awarded the Silver Star for bravery and a Purple Heart for wounds suffered.

After the war, Allen remained in the cavalry and was such an accomplished horseman and polo player that he was selected for the U.S. Army Olympic polo team, which took third place in the 1920 Antwerp Olympics.

During the interwar period, Allen continued to impress and advance, catching the eye of George C. Marshall, who promoted him from lieutenant colonel to brigadier general without the customary stop at full colonel. After briefly commanding the 2nd Cavalry Division in early 1941, he became the assistant division commander of the 36th Infantry Division, a Texas National Guard outfit. Five months after America's entry into World War II, Allen was given command of the 1st Infantry Division, which was then sent to Great Britain to prepare for combat.[4]

■ ■ ■

Having spent the last six months fighting its way across much of North Africa, the 1st Division was as battle-hardened (some would say battle-weary) as it could be. But the division had, as Omar Bradley believed, an overinflated opinion of itself. Not that the opinion wasn't deserved. In the Great War, the Big Red One had proved its toughness in several battles: Cantigny, St. Mihiel, and the Meuse-Argonne offensive. Proud of the fact that it was the first U.S. Army division ever created by the War Department, the men who served in its ranks thought of themselves as special, something above the ordinary. Their commanding general thought so, too. After all, their sleeve patch said they were Number One.

Terry Allen was more concerned with how a man fought than how he looked and often blurred the sacrosanct line between officers and enlisted men. An officer friend of his once commented, "He was a darn good officer, a little bit wild at times, but he was a soldier's officer, a great officer. All the enlisted men thought he was God as far as they were concerned. Whenever they would stop to bivouac, the officers might get together and have a little party. Terry would get a bottle of booze and go down with the enlisted men and have a few drinks with them. They just idolized him."[5]

His relaxed style, however, rubbed some people the wrong way; Omar Bradley was one. According to Bradley, during the downtime after the German surrender in North Africa, "While the Allies were parading decorously through Tunis, Allen's brawling 1st Infantry Division was celebrating the Tunisian victory in a manner all its own. In towns from Tunis all the way to Arzew the division had left a trail of looted wine shops and outraged mayors. But it was in Oran, the city whose troops had liberated it after the Torch invasion, that the division really ran amuck."[6]

Allen Towne, a medic with the 1st Division's 18th Regiment, recalled, "The 1st Infantry Division had a reputation for being different from other Army units, and when the division returned to the vicinity of Oran after the Tunisian battles were over, the soldiers let off steam. They caused trouble with some of the supply and other noncombat units. This was called the 'Second Battle of Oran.' The division commander winked at this lack of discipline. He thought the men were owed some fun and relaxation."[7]

Bill Faust, another 1st Division soldier, said the division desperately needed time off. "If you can imagine thousands of battle-hardened troops hitting this Mediterranean seaport on a beautiful May evening at one time, in [woolen] clothes that reeked with the sweat and sand of the Sahara, and just pure body odor stink from weeks without showers, those being baths taken from water held in one's helmet. It had been months since we had a real shower. Our first obstacle that we encountered was the spit-and-polished [military police] in their spotless suntan [cotton] uniforms. They met us at the [Oran] city gates and quickly informed us we were not permitted in the city as we were not in the proper uniform." Soon, fists began to fly.[8]

According to Bradley's list of grievances, "The trouble began when SOS [Services of Supply] troops, long stationed in Oran, closed their clubs and installations to our combat troops from the front. Irritated by this exclusion the 1st Division swarmed into town to 'liberate' it a second time.... When the rioting got out of hand, Theater sternly directed me to order Allen to get his troops promptly out of town.... The incident indicated a serious breakdown in discipline within the division. Allen's troops had now begun to strut their toughness while ignoring regulations that applied to all other units." An admonition by Bradley to Allen that all units needed to play by the same rules went unheeded.

Allen's assistant division commander was Theodore "Teddy" Roosevelt Jr., the son of the "Rough Rider" president and a cousin of President Franklin D. Roosevelt. Ted had also served as a battalion commander with the 1st Infantry Division in World War I, was one of the founders of the American Legion, had been a successful businessman, and served as Assistant Secretary of the Navy, governor-general of the Philippines, and governor of Puerto Rico. Arthritis and a war wound from the 1918 Batlle of Soissons caused him to go around with a cane.

Bradley felt that Roosevelt, too, was cast from the same mold as Allen, and said that the two leaders did not possess

> the instincts of a good disciplinarian. They looked upon discipline as an unwelcome crutch to be used by less able and personable commanders.... Had he been assigned a rock-jawed disciplinarian as assistant division commander, Terry could probably have gotten away forever on the personal leadership he showed his troops.

> But Roosevelt was too much like Allen. A brave, gamy, undersized man who trudged about the front with a walking stick, Roosevelt helped hold the division together by personal charm.

Three quarters of the way through the Sicilian campaign, at a town called Troina, both officers would discover that personal charm was insufficient to retain command.[9]

While still in North Africa, Bradley remarked, "Both men were exceptional leaders revered by their men but both had the same weakness: utter disregard for discipline, everywhere evident in their cocky division. It was clear that the division needed firm discipline and intensive training. I was not certain that Allen or Roosevelt had the inner toughness to impose the discipline and training or the willingness to take orders from and play on the same team with the higher command."[10]

Eisenhower, too, was unhappy with the state of discipline in the Big Red One. One day Ike drove into the 1st Division camp with his staff car emblazoned with a starred flag but failed to elicit any salutes. Maj. Gen. John P. Lucas, Ike's deputy commander, made an inspection trip to the 1st Division's training camp shortly before Husky kicked off and also came away with a negative opinion. In his diary, Lucas wrote, "[Ike] is not satisfied with the 1st but neither am I. The division has been babied too much. They have been told so often that they are the best in the world, but as far as real discipline is concerned they have become one of the poorest. They look dirty and they never salute an officer if they can help it."

Dirty and undisciplined or not, Patton knew it would be far better to have an experienced, battle-tested division landing on D-Day than one like the 36th that had never fired a shot in anger. Therefore, he requested that Ike select the 1st Division to be a major part of Operation Husky.

A member of Allen's staff recalled, "Allen was very much surprised. He had thought that we would probably have a longer rest period out of the line. . . . Patton had looked over the new divisions that were coming and he decided that he needed at least one division that had made an amphibious landing in the Mediterranean."

Originally, the 36th Division had been considered for Husky, but Ike agreed with Patton that a more experienced division was necessary. And so the 1st was assigned what many considered the most difficult landing spot—Gela—right in the very center of the American invasion area.[11] The division's long-term objectives were the cities of Enna and Nicosia—some fifty miles north of the landing beaches and over some of the most forbidding terrain on the island.[12]

Befitting the division's "number one" designation, the 16th and 26th Infantry Regimental Combat Teams (RCTs) would be the first "straight-leg" (non-airborne) division into Sicily; the 18th RCT was initially held in reserve. Division artillery and supporting tanks from Hugh Gaffey's 2nd Armored Division would not arrive until later on D-Day because of sand bars, buried land mines, the blown-up concrete pier that delayed the offloading of heavy equipment, and a miscommunication between Patton and Hewitt.[13]

■ ■ ■

Capt. John Finke said that shortly after dark on 9 July, "We changed course to the northwest, then due north to approach the coast of Sicily. During the night we were hit by a storm of gale-force intensity, which made life difficult for the first-wave troops who were loading their landing craft. As a valuable dividend, however, the storm made it extraordinarily hard, if not impossible, for enemy aircraft to keep track of us on the way to our landing areas."[14]

Medic Allen Towne never forgot the rough voyage: "The intensity of the storm increased as night set in, and it was difficult to sleep. . . . Some of the men started for the galley but got seasick and immediately went back to their bunks. . . . During the night I was awakened by a tremendous jolt. I first thought we had been hit by a shell or torpedo, but soon word was passed to us that we had collided with another ship. No serious damage occurred."[15]

Aboard the troop transport *Samuel F. Chase*, Sgt. Harley Reynolds, Company B, 16th RCT, recalled,

> We were only aboard one night and part of the next day when the beautiful Mediterranean seemed to turn upside down, very sudden like, within minutes. Waves from the front were breaking over our bows and washing assault boats from the decks of our ships after breaking them loose from the chains and cables lashing them to the deck.

Reynolds said the order came down to sink the washed-overboard landing craft so that they wouldn't damage the *Chase*.

> We had anti-aircraft guns on deck and the gun crews were called to "man your guns." It was very dangerous and they belted themselves into their seats as the seawater was splashing over the decks. They were shooting at the assault boats that had been washed overboard from our ship as well as boats from other ships that we passed getting tossed around. . . . The gunners were ordered to sink them so that no trail would be left in the sea for the Germans or others to spot.

Hundreds of men aboard the *Chase* were suffering from seasickness combined with the fear of the unknown and the very real threat of impending death. Reynolds recalled, "Fear was beginning to show in many that, I think, was brought on by the seasickness—especially after we were told we were going to invade Sicily and shown a sandbox model of the beach, along with the aerial pictures. At this time we were told also of our assignments and places in the line of the invasion. With the seas as rough as they were, it was hard getting a good look at the model. Hardly any of the men were reviewing the sand models. They could have cared less as this point—they were too sick."

Finally, at around midnight, an announcement was made for all men to report to their loading stations. "We shook hands with friends and wished them the best," Reynolds said. "Even though the weather was letting up, the waves were still five to six feet high as we went over the side of the ship and down the rope net ladders. You had to time your release from the ladder so as to let go while the wave was at its crest and go down with the LCVP. If a man let go while at the bottom of the wave, he met the boat coming up; a very solid and jarring landing. A man in the boat ahead of ours did just that and broke a leg in the fall. They did not make any effort to lift the man back aboard the *Chase*; I assume he went into shore and then came back when the boat returned for another load."

Once the men were in the landing craft, the pitching and rolling of the *Chase* was forgotten, merely a pleasant memory compared to what they were now experiencing. There were no seats in the LCVPs and the men were slammed from side to side and forward and back as the boats were bounced about like bathtub toys. Men who thought they had no more vomit left inside them discovered that they did. The ride into shore seemed to take forever.[16]

■ ■ ■

Going ashore with one of the 1st Division units was an unnamed *Life* magazine correspondent. He wrote, "Two miles from land the formation of landing boats were caught in the searchlights. Machine guns rattled on the shore. Said the ensign in charge of the boat to the coxswain, 'Get down or you'll be shot.' The coxswain replied, 'I don't care if I do get shot. I'm going to land these boys at the right place.'"[17]

Also coming along was *Life* reporter Jack Belden, who used almost every word in his vocabulary to capture what it was like for the average GI arriving at Sicily. Describing his rollercoaster ride in an LCVP, he wrote that it was "totally unlike anything we had experienced on the ship. It pitched, rolled, swayed, bucked, jerked from side to side, spanked up and down, undulated, careened, and insanely danced on the throbbing, pulsing, hissing sea. The sea itself flew at us, threw the bow in the air, then, as it came down, swashed over us in great roaring bucketfuls of water."[18] To many GIs, it was an unamusing amusement park ride that lasted more than an hour.

As the LCIs and LCVPs approached the shore, Italian gunners, suddenly alert, homed in on the large, lumbering, whale-like ships. Adrenalin levels went sky-high. Cpl. Sam Fuller, a member of the 16th RCT (and a future Hollywood writer, actor, and director who would create the 1980 film *The Big Red One*, starring Lee Marvin and Mark Hamill), wrote of the chaos of the landing at Gela:

> D-Day . . . The black sky is filled with death. Tracers streak from ship to shore. Big guns seek out the enemy's stationary coastal guns. Flashes on the horizon. Shells bursting on the beach. The sound is like one long rolling peal of thunder. The crash of guns blends insanely with the quiet, calm command piped over the ship's broadcaster: "First wave—to your station."
>
> Big guns duel. Crimson splotches on the horizon. A fire breaks out. . . . It is like 4th of July . . . the greatest fireworks in history. . . . The elements are against us. The sea is furious. 0057 hours, the first wave is lowered away. Rope nets smash against the sides of the boat. A man falls but is

> not seriously hurt. Two men below in the landing craft clutch at the ends of the rope ladder, hold it taut. Others descend. Will this be the finish before we begin? How can such a small craft remain alive in a whirlwind of fury?[19]

At around 0230 hours on the morning of 10 July the boats carrying the 16th and 26th RCTs hit the beach at Gela and the wretched, retching, seasick men piled out of their landing craft into the face of sporadic Italian fire, glad to be free from their seaborne misery but now thrown into the cauldron of combat.

Charles Hangsterfer, a member of the 16th RCT, said, "Just before we landed, a spotlight from shore focused on our invasion craft and somebody began to shoot at us. It was on us for only a short time; the Navy shot just one salvo and put the searchlight out."[20]

The earlier landing by the Rangers had not cleared all of the Italian positions. Despite that, the Yanks charged forward, overrunning enemy bunkers and foxholes, capturing surprised Italians who were in many cases only too happy to give up.

Sam Fuller and the rest of the men in his unit rode in with the bobbing, heaving LCI and headed toward the flaming, exploding shore. After what seemed like an eternity, the landing craft scraped the beach, knocking the men off their feet. The ramp dropped and the men tried to sprint through water. Fuller wrote, "Little, dark, death-dealing figures we are, soaked waist-high, guns held aloft, dashing through the surf, sprinting across the sand toward the enemy!"[21]

The beginning of morning nautical twilight was at 0400 hours, and as the landscape transformed from black to gray, pockets of Italian soldiers in hidden defensive positions in buildings and bunkers along the beach that had been bypassed during the Rangers' earlier landing fired a few desultory rounds at the Americans, then came out with hands held high.

■ ■ ■

The landing started out easily—too easily, some said—then the hell began. The Rangers' landing had been the trip wire and those Italian defenders who hadn't already been killed or captured opened up on Allen's men. Kesselring had also quickly mobilized his air force and now warplanes were roaring over the landing beaches from their bases across Sicily and from the southern Italian peninsula.

At 0424 hours a flight of ME 109s, Ju-88s, and Italian fighter-bombers streaked over Dime Beach and Gela, bombing and shooting up anything that looked American. Eleven enemy dive-bombers then targeted the cruiser *Philadelphia* and attack transport *Thomas Jefferson* (APA 30) but caused little damage.[22] Just then a Stuka dive-bomber flew through a curtain of anti-aircraft ordnance and set fire to LST 313 that had beached itself at Gela carrying men of the 1st's 33rd Field Artillery Battalion; she was abandoned and later scuttled.

At 0458 hours the destroyer USS *Maddox* (DD 622), under the helm of Cmdr. Eugene S. Sarsfield, was attacked by a Ju-88 and a squadron of Italian planes about sixteen miles off the Gela beachhead.[23]

Sailors often have it the worst in any war. While those on deck manning guns—even though wracked with fear at seeing an enemy ship or plane heading their way—have the comforting sense that they are fighting back, those high up on the bridge often feel like sitting ducks when enemy planes swoop in. And those sailors down below—whether in the noisy, sweltering engine room or the ammunition locker or in closed-off, windowless compartments—have no idea of what is taking place "up top." The sounds of the big guns booming in their turrets—or the staccato *pom-pom-pom* of the Oerlikon anti-aircraft guns blasting away—echo off the steel bulkheads and send great shudders through the ship.

Everyone working below decks knows that if his ship is hit, he is likely to be trapped with little or no chance of escape. To save the ship every man also knows that the compartment in which he is working might have to be flooded and sealed off. The air of terror is heightened by being unable to see anything or fight back; no man knows when his battle station will be torn apart by a shell or bomb and he and his fellow screaming sailors will be thrust into fiery black water from which there is no escape.

So it was on the *Maddox*. One bomb hit the ship's magazine, causing a tremendous explosion that sent men and ripped shards of steel flying into the sea. *Maddox* disappeared beneath the waves two minutes later, carrying

8 officers and 203 men to their deaths; a German plane came in and strafed the survivors in the water. Sarsfield, probably wounded, remained aboard the sinking wreckage to direct the evacuation of seventy-four other sailors but then perished with his ship. He was posthumously awarded the Navy Cross.

About fifteen minutes after *Maddox* exploded and went under, a few American aircraft showed up—but it was too late; the enemy had already done his damage. Then, after the American planes departed, German aircraft returned and this time focused on the minesweeper USS *Sentinel* (AM 113) off Licata, where the 3rd Infantry Division was landing, and repeatedly attacked her. Her crew fought back just as hard, downing two enemy planes and damaging at least two others with her 3-inch gun—even as she was sinking. She suffered nine men killed.[24]

■ ■ ■

While Patton was concerned that the Big Red One was struggling to gain a foothold at Gela, nineteen miles to the southeast the 45th Infantry Division was about to receive its first taste of combat—and a bitter taste it was.

6

HERE COME THE THUNDERBIRDS

I am most impressed with Middleton.

—George S. Patton Jr.

Heading for Cent Beach at the small fishing village of Scoglitti was the 45th Infantry Division—an amalgamation of two regiments of the Oklahoma National Guard (179th and 180th) and one from the Colorado National Guard (157th). This would be its first combat action. It had sailed directly from Virginia to North Africa and was now—ready or not—thrust into war.

A few miles off Cent Beach, the men of the 45th Division began climbing over their transports' gunwales in the predawn darkness and down into their bobbing landing craft. They had their orders: after reaching land, they were to move rapidly inland to take the towns of Vittoria, Biscari, and Comiso and the Biscari and Comiso airfields. Securing Highway 115 that ran parallel to the coast from Gela on the west to Ragusa on the east was also part of the mission.[1]

Unlike Patton, Truscott, and Gavin, the round-faced, balding, and bespectacled Troy Middleton, age fifty-three, looked more like a bank president than a combat commander. Yet he was highly respected as a true military leader by both the men under him and those above him. Born on 12 October 1889 on a Mississippi plantation (many of his relatives had fought for the Confederacy), he enlisted in the Army when he was twenty and became a standout football player for his unit.

In 1913 he received his officer's commission and, like Patton and Allen, served during the Mexican border campaign. The next four years saw him rise in rank as the crisis in Europe boiled over into a world war; at age twenty-nine Middleton became the youngest full colonel in the American Expeditionary Force. During the Battle of Meuse-Argonne (September–November 1918) he had led the 47th Regiment of the 4th Division in France.

Returning home, Middleton had a variety of assignments, including teaching at the Infantry School and the U.S. Army Command and General Staff School and as commandant of cadets in Louisiana State University's Reserve Officers Training Corps program. Retiring briefly from the Army in 1937, he became Louisiana State's dean of administration and, later, comptroller and acting vice president of the school. He was a longtime friend of both Eisenhower and Patton; during the interwar years, Ike persuaded him to leave the university and return to the Army, where he was sure that Troy would one day achieve the rank of general. He was right.

In June 1942 Middleton was appointed commanding general of the 45th Infantry Division. (By the time World War II ended, he would log 480 days in combat in charge of both the 45th Division and, later, VIII Corps—more than any other American general officer.[2]) With the possible exception of Terry Allen and Teddy Roosevelt Jr. of the 1st Division, Patton had no concerns about any of his field commanders. He noted in his diary, "I am most impressed with Middleton."[3]

■ ■ ■

The 45th Division was one of the more unique military formations in the U.S. Army—not because its table of authorization or table of organization and equipment was any different from the other sixty-seven U.S. Army infantry divisions formed before and during the war.

No, it was unique because, out of its 14,200 men, approximately 3,000 were Native Americans from Oklahoma—members of the Apache, Cherokee, Choctaw, Seminole, and Sioux tribes. Initially organized in the 1920s as a National Guard division made up of regiments from Oklahoma, Arizona,

New Mexico, and Colorado, it had as its insignia a mythical thunderbird—a creature of supernatural strength. Consequently, the division became known as the "Thunderbirds," exemplified by the red-and-yellow symbol on their shoulder patch.[4]

Despite the fact that the U.S. government had treated the North American continent's original inhabitants terribly over the centuries, when World War II broke out these three thousand young men made the decision that, regardless of the long history of ill treatment, the United States was still their country and they would defend it.

■ ■ ■

Brig. Gen. Raymond S. McLain, the 45th Division artillery commander, recalled the difficulties encountered while trying to get ashore that morning of 10 July:

> It seemed boats were circling everywhere. . . . Cox'ns were shouting orders from the deck to the boats, staff officers and radar experts were checking position by every known means. . . . We stood watching the boats form up and move off the line of departure. . . . Destroyers moved in with the assault waves. . . . As they reached the line of departure, the destroyers moved to the flank and soon opened a terrific bombardment. . . . It was some time later when fire was opened to the south in the direction of Camerina. The cruisers and the *Abercrombie*, a British monitor, also opened at the same time. The shells of all these guns were plain red traveling lazily through the air. The *Abercrombie*'s guns' trajectory was nearly as high as it was long. It was an awe-inspiring sight. It was delivering death and destruction to a country that had not seen war for decades.[5]

Machine-gunner Kenneth D. Williamson, Company D, 179th RCT, was nervous about his introduction to combat and was awed by the firepower demonstration the Navy was putting on: "An enormous naval bombardment commenced, the likes of which no one had ever witnessed before. This continued for hours."

The naval fire may have been impressive, but the advance to the shore was a jumbled, scrambled, confused nightmare for many of the landing craft and their occupants. Tossed by the waves, boats slammed into each other, ran aground on rocks, were knocked out by enemy fire or mechanical failure, ended up at the wrong beaches (two hundred of the 180th RCT Thunderbirds ended up intermixed with the 1st Division's 16th RCT between Gela and Scoglitti), and dropped off their troops into water that was too deep. Bodies of drowned soldiers and sailors lapped at the shore.

Williamson was in one of the later waves. He recalled waiting to load into the landing craft—a painful wait that seemed like hours: "We checked our gear and made ready for our own landing. Such gear! Whoever issued orders for what we would carry on our backs to shore must have been sitting behind a desk in Washington. We had full packs with two blankets, extra shoes, pup tent, two days' rations, canteen, gas mask, rifle, grenades, filled cartridge belt, and a bandoleer of ammunition. As I stood on deck, waiting to go over the side, my arches ached from what must have been a hundred-pound load.

"The coxswain had probably taken in a number of loads by then and knew the best points on the beach to land. He took us to a sandy spot for disembarking. We got our feet wet but that was a trivial price to pay for being safely ashore. We assembled on the beach, feeling some urgency to get inland, since we were very vulnerable to strafing or artillery barrages. Our officers organized us into a single-file column and we started off the beach into a dune area."[6]

Lt. Eddie Speairs, Company C, 157th, recalled, "The Navy guys were scared to death; they had never done anything like this. They were under fire for the first time in their lives. The Navy had not trained their landing crews well enough—we were scattered all over. The waves were eight, ten, twelve feet high—where do you get that kind of training?"[7]

■ ■ ■

One of the Native Americans heading to Cent Beach was a young Pawnee from a north-central Oklahoma town located at the top of a triangle formed by Pawnee, Tulsa, and Oklahoma City. Born in 1922, Brummett Echohawk was a sergeant in Company B, 179th RCT. Until recently, he had never seen the ocean. Soon he would also see something else new: mountains.

In the predawn hours of 10 July, Echohawk—the squad leader of his platoon's second squad—was riding the waves in a landing craft on its way to

Scoglitti, a small, wholly unremarkable fishing village of one-story buildings with red tile roofs on the southern shore of Sicily, between Gela, thirty miles to its left, and the 1st Canadian Infantry Division and 1st Canadian Army Tank Brigade landing at Pachino, about fifty miles to the east of Gela. There was hardly any beach; Scoglitti's buildings were built practically up to the waterline.

Echohawk recalled,

> Like old-time cavalry, the assault barges advance abreast and in a wavering line. Here and there a barge jumps ahead and then pulls back in formation again. The cavalry line advances at a walk and champs at the bit. The barges rev motors in short bursts as if snorting. As the line is dressed, the cavalry then moves into a canter.
>
> A destroyer looms at the right. It cuts the waves and glides up with a muffled roar. The destroyer escorts us inland through the early morning darkness. We can make out blue lights on her. Beautiful. A feeling of strength arises. The destroyer shepherds us in for several minutes. "Men!" booms a loudspeaker from the bridge: "Good luck and God bless you!" The destroyer falls back from the line of barges, then fades into the darkness. Motors cough and roar. Then the cavalry springs into a gallop.
>
> I think of things we've got to do. I picture in my mind the beach, barbed-wire entanglements, pillboxes, sand dunes, and the enemy. There is a violent tearing of the air. We flinch as red balls of fire comet over us and streak for the beach. Seconds later comes the sound of naval gunfire miles behind us. More red balls flash over. The dark coast of Sicily flickers and rumbles. Far behind us we hear salvo after salvo . . . Ahead are the beaches of Scoglitti, flashing and thundering like a summer electrical storm.

The boats carrying the 1st Battalion of the 179th were caught in a sweeping searchlight on shore, terrifying everyone, before the Navy's shells extinguished it. No one knew what lay ahead. Echohawk was sure that that he and everyone else were about to be blown away. Platoon sergeant Shield Chief gave a Pawnee war cry: "*A-a'e—ay, kiddi, didde, kiddi, didde!*" All along the shoreline came sounds and noises that had never before been heard on ancient Sicily.

Echohawk related, "There is a piercing Cheyenne war whoop followed with, 'It's a good day to die!' Rising, too, is a Creek Indian war cry—the gobble of a wild tom turkey. From an adjacent barge comes the shriek of a gander goose and the neighing of a stud horse."

The boats crunched against the sand, ramps dropped, and men piled out with bayonets fixed, falling into the surf, coming up soaked and cursing, yelling at the top of their lungs to fire up their courage. Shield Chief directed Echohawk to take his squad through a broken line in the barbed wire and dash into the dark toward the enemy positions. Ahead, the dune grass was on fire and smoking from the naval bombardment.

The men halted briefly and looked around for their platoon leader, Lieutenant Dobbins, but didn't see him. A quick decision was made to continue inland to their objective: an Italian garrison known as Point Zafaglione. The sky was beginning to lighten. Beyond the low dunes they saw the garrison.

Suddenly, more naval shells screamed in, obliterating the garrison buildings in smoke and dust. Italian soldiers streamed from the burning ruins, heading away from the advancing Americans. "We lower bayonets and charge," Echohawk said. "The enemy soldiers turn in surprise, fire wild shots, and run. We go after them. Some drop weapons, thrust up arms, and jabber. A gobble of wild tom turkey comes from a Creek Indian, Sam Bear, who says, '*Uks-kotit! Retsu-kih!*' (Kill them! Use knife!) Running hard, I go for a red-faced soldier wielding a pistol. He backpedals, whirls, and runs. Everywhere there is shooting, jabbering, and hollering. A voice rings out: 'Hold it!'"

Captain Glen Lee, the company commander, halted the attack; more Italians emerged from the shattered buildings, arms raised, fear in their faces. One of the Italians yelled, "*Americano Indiano!*" Another fell to his knees crying, "Mussolini sonovabitch!"[8]

■ ■ ■

Also coming ashore on 10 July was a young rifleman in Company K, 180th RCT. Among his combat load of ammunition and grenades, he was carrying several sketchbooks, pencils, pens, and bottles of India ink. His name was Bill Mauldin.

In addition to his combat duties, Mauldin was also a cartoonist for his unit's newspaper, the *45th Division News*. Because his trenchant, sardonic views of soldier life were deemed too precious to be cut short by his death in a combat unit, he would soon be "booted upstairs" to the GI's newspaper, *The Stars and Stripes*.

Mauldin created two weary, unkempt, mud-stained characters, "Willie" and "Joe," whose acerbic complaints and universal gripes about Army life with which almost every soldier could identify would earn him the ire of General Patton—and the 1945 Pulitzer Prize for editorial cartooning.

David Israel, a member of the 45th Division, noted, "Willie and Joe were two combat-hardened average American GIs who were bored by inaction, complained about Army food, complained about living in water-filled ditches, complained about trudging up mountains, complained about marching through valleys loaded down with rifle and backpack, complained about digging foxholes for non-caring officers, complained about being thousands of miles away from family and friends, but most of all complained about receiving senseless orders from Headquarters.

"Not everyone agreed with Mauldin's point of view. General Patton tried to get him court-martialed for making fun of officers, but Eisenhower overruled Patton's sensitivities." Patton would later threaten to ban *The Stars and Stripes*' distribution to his Third Army in Europe if it did not stop running Mauldin's cartoons that he claimed were "scurrilous attempts to undermine military discipline." His threats came to nothing.[9]

■ ■ ■

Another of the Thunderbirds was Sgt. Don Robinson, a journalist in civilian life and the editor of the *45th Division News*. In 1944 he published a book, illustrated by Mauldin, in which he described his impressions of life in North Africa—impressions that would not be appropriate for a chamber of commerce travel guide: "There wasn't a decently dressed Arab in the bunch. . . . The donkeys had more personality than the Arabs. . . . The native villages. . . . were the filthiest human habitations we were to see before reaching Barrafranca in Sicily. They were rock-walled, and the smells rose over the walls and drifted into the roads."

No one except the top brass knew the division's destination. As the ships carrying the 45th and other units prepared to depart from Oran, Robinson wrote, "Back on the ship we waited to up-anchor. It was hot in the harbor, there were flies, and the water didn't smell good, and we even tired of looking at the magnificent [naval] escort we were going to have. We were impatient, too, because we knew that when we put to sea we would find out where we were going to strike. We knew already that the 45th would land fighting, but where? There were the usual bets: France, Italy, Sicily, Sardinia, and that we'd continue on to the Solomons [in the Pacific]."

While engaged in the Army's usual "hurry up and wait" routine, Robinson recalled, "The ship next to us had ice cream and Coca Cola, of which we had had none since we left the States, and that seemed a long time ago. Our boys tossed money to the next ship, and the boys over there tossed back ice cream. Sometimes they missed, spattering the side and deck of our ship with the stuff while we mourned. I never got any."

After reaching Sicily, the transports came to a dead stop and the combat troops began climbing into the waiting LCVPs. Robinson said that early on the morning of 10 July an announcement came over the ship's loudspeakers: "'The first wave has landed, unopposed.' We cheered. A little later, enemy planes were in the air. *General quarters! Ack-ack!* It was the first time our ship had fired at the enemy. We could hear the thud of bombs, none near. There was nothing we could do but wait while all landing teams ahead of ours were called." It was now daylight.

> We were ready when the call came to report to our debarkation station. We stood there on the deck and watched boats shuttling troops to the shore. The cooks had coffee for us and, as we drank it and smoked, we talked quietly so we'd be sure to hear our orders. The landing craft came alongside under our net. Left leg over first, then down the tall net into the tossing boats. The sea was calmer now, but even so it was white-capped, and it made fully half the men seasick.
>
> We held the nets for those who followed. . . . The motors growled and we zigzagged toward the shore. Our craft flew an American flag, as much for our morale as for identification, and it looked better to me than it ever had before. A flag means most in battle.

On the bumpy ride toward shore, with water sloshing over the LCVP's sides and bow, Robinson heard the sound of rapid firing:

> Ack-ack opened up on something we couldn't see, but soon the object became apparent. A Messerschmitt was on the tail of one of our Navy planes, a much slower craft, apparently intended for observation. We sickened as the ME 109 stung the Navy craft and retired while our plane smoked and dived out of control to the beach. But another act was to come. A Spitfire was on the tail of the Messerschmitt, and the German pilot died in the sea.
>
> Since we had to crouch with our heavy packs, we were cramped. The boat was full. The sun was hot. The choppy motion of the small craft was hard for some to bear. Ack-ack puffed apart in the sky, leaving hanging black blobs of smoke. We couldn't see what was going on on the beach. The choppy motion of the boat was made worse by the sharp turns we made. There were other boats near us, some bearing men and vehicles to the shore, some returning empty, some bringing back the first wounded.
>
> As if it were moving rapidly toward us, the shore approached. We could see the landing craft unloading, backing away, returning to the ships. The beach was yellow, and green trees and cane lay beyond. There were little hills. There was a thud as the boat was grounded several yards off shore. The ramp dropped. Our guns drawn, although the fighting was now inland, we plunged into the surf up to our thighs. This was better than we thought. Some landings are made in water up to your neck. The fierce undertow knocked some of us to our knees. We tried to run to shore, but had to take it slowly. On the beach we scattered, found what cover we could between two little hills, and sat down.

Once ashore in sopping-wet wool uniforms, Robinson and his boat-mates rested and broke out their rations for lunch. "Gradually the thought struck each of us: 'Now I'm in Axis territory—Axis home territory!' We wondered what came next."

The small group was marched to an assembly area farther inland and told to dig in. Robinson stepped over a strand of barbed wire and began to dig. "It was good digging," he recalled, "but someone pointed out that I was digging in a mine field. I'd dug so far that I continued, nevertheless, while [Bill] Mauldin took cover in his foxhole. Nobody's fool, Mauldin."

> Naturally, once the holes were dug, orders came down to move.
>
> Enemy planes flew over our heads. Some fool blazed away at them with his rifle, unable to control his anger, but they were after bigger game than we. They were a beautiful sight in the sky. With the earth shaking, we still could recognize the beauty of it with the horror.
>
> A new sound filled our ears. The big guns on the ships were firing. We watched, not expecting to see anything, when a giant object appeared in the sky. It was a tracer shell. It arched over us, glowing green, and seemed to travel slowly off into the distance. We could follow it for miles. Another came, and another. Explosions followed after we saw the shells from the direction of the sea, and other explosions were like echoes from the enemy's positions. When we went to sleep, the sky was still filled with the tracers from the anti-aircraft and the big guns.

Robinson and his newspaper team continued for miles the next day. Their mission: Find a place to print the first American newspaper on Axis home soil. It would be some time before they discovered an intact print shop in Vittoria and accomplished that mission—printing a two-sided, single-sheet edition. They would continue to publish in each town the division captured for the rest of the war.[10]

■ ■ ■

The experiences of another of the Thunderbirds, 2nd Lt. Bill Whitman, a platoon leader with Company B, 180th RCT, were typical of what nearly every soldier who landed on Sicily went through on D-Day—mostly terror and confusion. He remembered,

> We sailed along the coast of North Africa, passing Algiers and Bizerte, in our attack transport, the USS *Calvert* [APA 32]. . . . The night of July 9th the convoy dropped anchor off the beaches of southern Sicily. We had arrived in the transport area. A terrific storm pounded the ships. The chaplains held their services and the men looked solemn. Colonel Forrest Cookson, our regimental commander, made a broadcast over the ship's loudspeakers to the troops throughout the ship. It went like this: "Men, tomorrow morning I

want 3,000 killers to hit that beach. Good luck to each and every one of you." Then came the order from the *Calvert*'s captain: "Land the landing force."

Debarkation time was set for 2:14 a.m. but was postponed forty-five minutes because of the rough seas and other factors. Later during the war, amphibious assaults were made during daylight hours. This was one of the lessons learned from our operation at Sicily. The night sky was filled with flaming shells and tracers as our cruisers and destroyers poured fire on the invasion beaches. A British monitor (the *Abercrombie*) was firing 16-inch shells at the shore. Our destroyers moved in, sweeping the beaches with their guns. The noise was unbelievable; every time one of the big guns fired, we'd cringe. Fire from the shore commenced with heavy enemy guns, and we all knew that 'they' were waiting for us.

Then it came time to crawl over the gunwales and down the "scramble nets" into the waiting landing craft. Whitman was in the boat behind the one carrying the 1st Battalion's commander, Lt. Col. William Schaeffer. "He was called 'King Kong' and was the ugliest man in the U.S. Army—maybe the Navy and Marines as well," Whitman said. "But he was a brilliant tactician; he knew von Clausewitz from cover to cover. He was an outstanding leader and should have been a regimental commander. His LCVP's engine refused to start and we could hear his curses of outrage as the unlucky coxswain attempted to get the engine going."

Whitman and another thirty men climbed down into their landing craft and set off for the flaming, exploding beach. With five-foot waves slamming the LCVP every which way, men soon lost their pre-invasion meals. "Men were lying on the bottom of the boat, rolling in the seasick filth, wishing that they were dead," said Whitman who, incredibly, did not get sick. "We reached the rendezvous area and joined the other craft in the circle. Planes attacked our transports and the bombs dropped. Flares lit the seas in an eerie light. Tracers from our ships probed the night sky, seeking the German and Italian bombers. The noise of thousands of guns spitting their tracers into the sky made conversation in the boat impossible."

After what seemed like a nerve-wracking eternity, the landing craft stopped circling and headed for shore. Whitman's boat was in the first wave, on the far left flank of the line of LCVPs. Suddenly a row of flares blossomed overhead. "We were illuminated—perfect targets," he said. "I thought that we were really going to get 'the works.' We did not. After what seemed like years, our boat hit the beach. It was about 4:30 a.m. The ramp went down and out we stumbled into the surf. We ran across the beach and to the sand hills beyond. There was some small-arms fire and I saw my first casualty; one man had been shot through the chest."[11]

■ ■ ■

A daring occurrence took place off Cent Beach on D-Day. To get an aerial view of the 45th's battlefield, the cruiser USS *Philadelphia*, commanded by Gordon J. Crosby, launched its two Curtiss Seagull SOCs (scout observation biplanes) over the battlefield. The slow (165 miles per hour) aircraft were armed with a fixed, forward-firing .30-caliber machine gun in the wing and a flexibly mounted machine gun in the rear; each also carried two one-hundred-pound bombs.

The pilot of SOC 8-CS-4, Lt. P. E. Coughlin, had with him a radioman, Richard Shafer. Their job was to radio back to the ship any enemy troop concentrations they saw in order to bring fire down upon them. They soon spotted a group of Italian soldiers working on defensive positions but, instead of radioing the coordinates to the cruiser, Coughlin decided to try and flush out the soldiers like a covey of quail. Flying low to the ground and circling the troops, he dropped one of his bombs but it was a dud. Nevertheless, the unnerved enemy scattered.

The Thunderbirds below Coughlin began pointing to a nearby hill where other Italians were lying in wait for the GIs to advance. The pilot flew around the hill, firing with his two machine guns and causing the enemy to again vacate their position. He dropped his second bomb but it, too, failed to explode.

Coughlin now wondered if he could use his plane to nudge the enemy toward the GIs where they could be taken prisoner. When the flexibly mounted machine gun jammed, Shafer used his .45-caliber pistol to show he meant business. Coughlin's maneuver worked; the Italians on the hill came out with their hands up, and Coughlin herded them toward the Thunderbirds, who took 150 of them prisoner. For their unusual actions, Coughlin and Shafer were both awarded the Navy's Distinguished Flying Cross.

Unfortunately, the *Philadelphia*'s other SOC, piloted by Lt. Cdr. R. O. Stevenson and accompanied by a radioman named Pierson, was shot down by an ME 109 and crashed into the sea; both men were lost.[12]

■ ■ ■

In the 180th's sector, things started badly—and got worse as the day wore on. The chaotic landing meant that some units weren't delivered to the correct beach; some three hundred men from the 180th RCT landed among the 1st Division's 16th RCT on beaches west of the Acate River—the boundary between the two divisions. One of those men was the regiment's commander, Col. Forrest E. Cookson. His LCVP landed at Gela rather than at Scoglitti, over twenty miles away; he and his staff were nowhere to be found.[13]

Omar Bradley, assuming that Cookson was either dead or captured, wanted Lieutenant Colonel Darby to give up command of the Rangers, be promoted to full colonel, and take over the 180th. But Darby turned Bradley down in order to stay with his Rangers. Patton was impressed: "This is the first time I ever saw a man turn down a promotion. Darby is really a great soldier."

Then Patton was approached on the *Monrovia* by Brig. Gen. Albert C. Wedemeyer, Marshall's chief of war plans, who had come from Washington to observe the invasion. He was so eager to lead men in battle that, when he learned of Cookson's disappearance, he begged Patton to demote him to colonel so that he could command the 180th. Patton was impressed again. He wrote, "General Wedemeyer asked to be reduced to a colonel so he could get the 180th. I sent him up to command it as a brigadier general. I have no real authority to do this, but like to help a fighting man."[14] But Cookson showed up thirty hours later and, deeply chagrined, resumed command of the 180th.[15]

■ ■ ■

Patton felt good, confident, in control. Except for a few glitches—normal for an operation of the size and complexity of Husky—Seventh Army's invasion was progressing well in its first few hours. The three infantry divisions had been slowed but not stopped at the water's edge and were now making good time moving inland. The airborne drop had been a scattered mishmash, but no large operation is ever perfect. Even Hewitt's warships were doing a fine job obliterating targets with their big guns.

But the general was growing antsy. He desperately wanted to go ashore, to be in the midst of his troops, to inspire them and give them courage, to lead from the front. He wanted the news photographers who had accompanied the invasion to photograph him giving orders, looking stalwart and general-like. But there was still too much to do aboard ship. He had to monitor the radio traffic, keep watch on Hewitt, and demand that his army receive better air cover. He planned to go ashore the following day.[16]

■ ■ ■

A curious episode is said to have taken place during the invasion. The Italians claimed that Patton had issued a radio message declaring that Allen's 1st Infantry Division, having difficulties at Gela, should be prepared to re-embark Navy ships and withdraw. General Emilio Faldella, chief of staff of Guzzoni's Sixth Italian Army at Enna, swore that he was handed an intercept of that message: "Bury the equipment on the beaches and be ready to re-embark—Patton." Other witnesses attested to also having seen the communiqué.

Only the Italians are thought to have seen such a message; neither Patton nor Allen nor Eisenhower ever made mention of such a directive.[17]

■ ■ ■

The 180th's official history lists a litany of problems that took place during the landings:

> The regimental team was landed on a twelve-mile front whereas under the plans as made it would have been landed on a front of only 3,000 yards. . . . All landings were delayed from two to six hours. . . . All Headquarters Company personnel should have been landed on Red Beach prior to 1000 on D-Day; all boat officers and boat crews had been given instructions to that effect but apparently made no effort to do so. . . . The unloading of vehicles was such that one platoon did not receive vehicles to which [they were] assigned . . . [Medical detachment] The 2nd and 3rd Battalion sections

> were handicapped by the late arrival of first-priority equipment . . . The 1st Battalion communications were landed in the vicinity of Scoglitti and no communications with any battalion, adjacent unit, or higher unit was instigated or installed . . . Elements of our 1st Battalion crossed their beach unopposed but terribly separated as the result of the erroneous landings made by naval coxswains.[18]

Yet somehow in his underground command center on Malta, Eisenhower received a report that expressed the exact opposite. "On the southern front," he noted, "we were almost amazed at the reports of progress in the American sector where we had thought it possible that Rear Admiral Alan Kirk, in command of the assault convoy [Task Force 85, into Cent Beach at Scoglitti] might even postpone the transfer to small boats for several hours, hoping for better weather conditions. It was so difficult for Admiral [Andrew B.] Cunningham to believe that landings in that area were feasible that he promptly took off in a destroyer to see what had happened. He came back and reported that the landings in the 45th Division sector constituted one of the finest exhibitions of seamanship it had been his pleasure to witness in forty-five years of sailoring." Why Cunningham's observation differed from that of the 180th RCT's is a mystery. Ike resolved that he and other members of his staff would sail for Sicily itself and personally view the invasion's progress.[19]

■ ■ ■

After reaching a place of relative safety inland of Scoglitti, Lt. Bill Whitman, Company B, 180th RCT, 45th Division, knew that he and his men were lost. The sun had set. He tried reading his map, but it was too dark. When the sky lightened the next morning of 11 July, he discovered that his unit had been landed at the wrong beach. As the only officer in his boat group, he was expected to take charge. "We were five miles too far to the left (west), towards Gela," he said, "so we started moving inland and bearing to the east. Soon I discovered some landmarks that were on the map and knew we were on the right track.

"We met some B Company boat teams and I added them to mine; I began to feel a little better. After a short while we encountered Captain Fleet, our company commander, and he took over command. We were still missing several boat teams." Fleet sent out some scouts and before long two Italian soldiers with their hands raised came toward the GIs. "They wore overseas cloth caps and mustard-colored uniforms," Whitman recalled. "The captain sent them back to the beach under the guard of about four of our men."

The Thunderbirds cautiously approached a small farmhouse, and Fleet had one of his men who could speak Italian ask the frightened couple in the farmhouse the direction to Biscari, where the regiment's objective—an airfield six miles to the north—was located. The GIs then began marching through a cultivated landscape covered with vineyards. After a while, the company took a break and downed some of their boxed rations. With the breakfast break over, the group continued up the road toward Biscari; the sounds of rifles, machine guns, artillery, mortars, and naval guns provided a soundtrack to the march. Approaching another farmhouse, Fleet's men suddenly came under sniper fire from the building's second floor. Fleet ordered Whitman to advance and recon the situation. It would be a fateful assignment.[20]

■ ■ ■

Meanwhile, earlier on 10 July, one more division had come ashore—Lucian Truscott's 3rd Infantry Division. What kind of opposition would they face at Licata?

7

MARNEMEN HIT THE BEACH

Polo games and wars aren't won by gentlemen.

—Lucian K. Truscott Jr.

Simultaneously with the landings of the Rangers, the Big Red One, and the Thunderbirds, the 3rd Infantry Division, made up of the 7th, 15th, and 30th RCTs, was assaulting Joss Beach at Licata—the far western flank of the invasion area.

Due to its heroics in France during the Great War, the 3rd Division had gained the moniker "the Rock of the Marne"—earned on 15 July 1918 when they held their ground at the Marne River near Paris while units around them retreated in the face of the last massive German offensive. The troops were thereafter called the "Marnemen."

Beefed up for Operation Husky to 27,650 men (rather than the standard 14,200), the 3rd Division sailed from Bizerte on 6 July. One of the attached units was a battalion of Sherman tanks from the 2nd Armored Division. Another was the 3rd Ranger Battalion, commanded by Maj. Herman Dammer; it would be the first American unit to reach Joss Beach.[1]

The 3rd Division's commander in this war, Maj. Gen. Lucian King Truscott Jr., looked like Hollywood's version of an American infantry division commander—steely eyes, forward-thrusting chin, a touch of gray in the hair, a leather bomber jacket, knee-high cavalry boots, flared riding breeches, a gravelly voice, and a swagger stick. But Truscott was no costumed actor striking a pose; he was the genuine article.

Born in Chatfield, Texas, on 9 January 1895, Truscott did not have the military as his first career choice. The son of a doctor, he taught school and became a schoolmaster in a one-room Oklahoma schoolhouse. An expert horseman, he decided to enlist in the Army's cavalry branch in 1917, just as the United States was preparing to enter the Great War, but he did not see action overseas.

A *Life* magazine feature noted that Truscott had been "a lieutenant colonel at the time of Pearl Harbor. Truscott served for four years as an instructor at Fort Riley [Kansas], two years as a student at the Command and General Staff School at Fort Leavenworth, and four years as an instructor there. On his first overseas assignment after the U.S. entered the war Truscott was attached to Lord Louis Mountbatten's Combined Operations Staff where he supplemented his book learning by visiting every Commando training unit in England and Scotland. He helped organize the first American Ranger unit." In 1942 he led "a special task force from the U.S. 9th Infantry Division on the difficult and bitterly contested mission of capturing Port Lyautey in French Morocco. Here Truscott received the Distinguished Service Medal for brilliant planning and leadership."

The general, the article went on, "has an abiding faith in the American soldier. 'At first,' Truscott has said, 'the doughboy is cocky and thinks he can knock the stuffing out of anyone in the world. But he's developed a lot. He had an amazing ability to adjust himself to the circumstances. When this is coupled with his knowledge of weapons and wonderful physical fitness, and when he is given good leadership, there's no doubt that he is the best material in the world.'"[2]

A skilled horseman, Truscott had been an outstanding, aggressive polo player who pushed the rules to the limit. In 1935 he had told his fourteen-year-old son, Lucian K. Truscott III, "Listen son, goddamit. Let me tell you something and don't ever forget it. You play games to *win*, not lose. And you fight *wars* to win! That's spelled W-I-N! And every good player in a game and every good commander in a war—and I mean really *good* player or *good* commander—every damn one of them has to have some sonofabitch in him.

If he doesn't, he isn't a good player or commander. And he never *will* be a good commander. Polo games and wars aren't won by gentlemen. They're won by men who can be first-class sonsofbitches when they have to be. It's as simple as that. No sonofabitch, no commander."

Upon Eisenhower's recommendation, the "sonofabitch" was appointed to command the 3rd U.S. Infantry Division in March 1943 as the Allies were planning Operation Husky.[3]

■ ■ ■

Lucian Truscott was Terry Allen's polar opposite. Stiff and formal compared to the relaxed Allen, Truscott was a hard-nosed disciplinarian who believed in training and physical fitness to the maximum. He developed what became known as the "Truscott Trot"—a marching pace of five miles per hour over the first mile, four miles per hour thereafter—much faster than the Army's usual standard of two-and-a-half miles per hour. The Truscott Trot would prove to be decisive when moving his men into position for attack.[4]

Patton considered the 3rd to be the best-trained, best-led division in what would become the Seventh Army and Truscott himself one of the best leaders. He once wrote in Truscott's officer efficiency report, "I know of no other major general who has more efficiently performed as a division commander." He rated Truscott fifth out of 155 general officers he knew.[5]

■ ■ ■

Before leaving Algeria for Sicily, Truscott remarked that only his force

> was provided with an adequate number of craft entirely suitable for a shore-to-shore operation. Thus, the Joss [beach landing] became the first real test of shore-to-shore operations under actual conditions of war with adequate equipment. . . . For this invasion, we were planning with equipment which had never been tried under operational conditions, some of which had never been seen by the Army and Navy staffs involved.
>
> For example, LSTs (Landing Ship, Tank) were designed to transport tanks and other vehicles to a beach where they could drive off under their

> own power. LCIs (Landing Craft, Infantry) were designed to transport and disembark an entire company [approximately two hundred men] upon a beach after the assault waves had landed from smaller craft.

But the lack of intelligence about enemy strength, disposition, and morale on Sicily worried Truscott; he felt that the maps that had been provided were out of date and inaccurate, and the aerial photographs were lacking considerable detailed information. "From our previous studies," he said, "we knew that Sicily was protected by coast-defense guns, pillboxes, wire, and other obstructions."[6]

■ ■ ■

At the far western end of this operation called Husky stood Licata, with its narrow streets and ancient buildings seemingly piled upon each other and a broad, crescent-shaped beach enclosed by steep cliffs. The Greeks and Phoenicians had built the first settlement here in ancient times, followed by the Byzantines, Arabs, Normans, and a host of others. But Truscott's men did not come as sightseeing tourists; they came here fully armed to add their names to Licata's long list of conquerors.

Joss Beach was divided into four sectors. From west to east, they were Red Beach (Rangers and 7th RCT), Yellow Beach (15th RCT and 443rd Antiaircraft Artillery [AA] Battalion), and Green Beach and Blue Beach (both 30th RCT). Elements of the self-propelled 443rd AA Battalion were spread across Yellow and Blue Beaches; Combat Command B of the 2nd Armored Division also came ashore at Red Beach. The southern shore of Sicily would soon erupt in a violent paroxysm, with planes darting everywhere, dropping bombs and firing their machine guns, falling in flames; ships crashing through waves and into each other; huge cannon on land and sea lashing at each other, blowing gigantic columns of metal and stone and fire into the sky. It was as if Mount Etna was releasing her fury at a new location.

■ ■ ■

As Rear Adm. Richard L. Conolly's Task Force 86 was bringing the 3rd Division through the inky blackness of morning, spears of light suddenly reached out from shore; Task Force 86's accurate gunners returned fire, quickly extinguishing the searchlights.[7]

Aboard *Biscayne* (APV 11), a converted seaplane tender and Conolly's flagship, Truscott looked off to his right and could see streaks of light and flashes of explosions miles away where Terry Allen's Dime force was landing. He said, "At the time we thought the battle was on and surprise had been lost." But it was Italian AA fire shooting at the planes carrying Gavin's paratroopers. "Then off to the westward, the thunder of naval guns broke the silence. It was the cruisers *Brooklyn* and *Birmingham* and their accompanying destroyers bombarding the coast off Agrigento in a diversion planned for deception."

Truscott added, "We knew that the Licata area was prepared for defense. Every beach was organized with pillboxes, beach obstacles, barbed-wire entanglements, rifle pits, machine-gun positions, anti-aircraft guns, and emplaced artillery. Would the garrison be standing by their guns awaiting our approaching craft? These were trying moments for commanders who could only wait!"[8]

■ ■ ■

As LCVPs were bringing Darby and the Rangers to Gela, Maj. Herman Dammer's 3rd Ranger Battalion, their faces blackened with burnt cork, would land first at Licata. Down the cargo nets draped over the sides of the transports crawled his men; the landing craft left the rendezvous area for shore at 0204 hours—a fifty-three-minute ride. Once reaching land they would be separated from Darby's Ranger command post at Gela by twenty miles.[9]

In the predawn darkness and confusion of H-hour, accidents were bound to happen. The destroyers *Swanson* (DD 443) and *Roe* (DD 418) rammed each other at 0255 hours and were so badly damaged that they were ordered to withdraw to Malta for repairs; the destroyer *Buck* (DD 420) took their places off Joss Beach.[10] LST 345 and submarine chaser PC 621 collided while trying to dodge aerial bombs.[11] Then, shortly before 0300 hours, an LCVP loaded with 7th RCT men broke loose from the davits holding it against the side of its transport and dumped the troops into the sea, drowning nine. The transport *William P. Biddle* (AP 15) accidentally ran into LST 382 off Cent Beach at 0530 hours, but neither suffered major damage.

Nearby, the damaged *Swanson* was pounced upon by an ME 110 at 0512 hours, but her gunners managed to shoot it down.

In the midst of the chaos, German and Italian planes swooped in and began strafing and bombing Conolly's vessels; the aerial attacks would continue until late into the night. Anti-aircraft bursts from the ships' gunners blossomed in the sky, but few Allied planes were seen doing battle with the enemy.

At Licata, on the 2,800-yard-wide sector named Red Beach, the invaders were confronted by the Italian 207th Coastal Division and its array of artillery and machine guns. But once the enemy batteries opened up, they were subjected to *Biscayne*'s smothering fire, thus allowing landing craft to approach Joss Beach; *Brooklyn* and *Boise* also joined in at 0700 hours.[12]

A feature known as the San Nicola Rock on the Rangers' right flank and the sixteenth-century Gaffi Tower on their left afforded the enemy excellent observation posts and flanking fields of fire. Behind the positions rose a sheer cliff sixty feet high. The battle here, which would also involve the 3rd Battalion of Col. Harry B. Sherman's 7th RCT, went on without pause for ninety minutes before this end of the beach was declared secure.[13]

Michael Chinigo, an American war correspondent with International News Service, was accompanying the Marnemen into Licata. When he heard a phone ringing in an abandoned Italian command post, he answered it in his best Italian. On the other end was an Italian general wanting to know if rumors of an Allied landing were true. Not true, Chinigo said, and hung up.[14]

As the struggle for Red Beach on the left unfolded, Col. Charles R. Johnson Jr.'s 15th RCT was attacking the center at Yellow Beach while the 30th RCT and 2nd Armored Division tanks were engaged at Joss Beach's eastern flank. The Italians fought back bravely during the initial encounter but were soon overwhelmed by superior firepower.[15]

Throughout the day enemy planes persisted in doing their share of damage, but they continued to be shot down by ships' gunners. Unfortunately, all of the cruisers' spotter planes were also knocked out.[16]

Landing craft headed for shore while under fire, but most made it to the beach. Men spilled out into the surf and onto the sand and rushed forward, dodging landmines and bullets. After delivering the first waves, the landing craft returned to their mother ships and began reloading; it went on for hours.

In the full light of morning, two destroyers pulled close to Joss Beach and covered the landings with a smoke screen. One wave of LCVPs was turned back by artillery fire, but Conolly's task force masked them with another discharge of smoke and the admiral ordered them back in.[17]

By 1100 hours most of the enemy resistance had ceased, and the 3rd Division claimed control of Licata. Truscott, observing from Conolly's flagship, was pleased with his division's progress. He radioed Hewitt and Patton, reporting that his men had nearly all of Licata and Joss Beach under control and that all operations were going "magnificently. . . . Shooting honors go to the Navy's cruiser which destroyed remaining enemy batteries." He also reported that Allied air cover "was tops" over Joss Beach—one of the few times that the aviation effort was sufficient. "Our assault battalions had landed before they were discovered and had quickly cleared the beaches of all resistance," he said. "In little more than an hour, ten infantry battalions including the Rangers with supporting tanks had landed and were about their business."

To Truscott, it was a textbook operation: "In seven hours the airfield, town, and port were in our hands, beaches and port were organized, and additional troops and supplies were flowing ashore in steady streams. All beach resistance has been smothered by the speed and violence of the assault and more than 2,000 prisoners were taken. Our own casualties were little more than a hundred."[18]

■ ■ ■

Not everyone was so pleased. A disgruntled, diminutive 3rd Division private from Kingston, Texas, named Audie Murphy splashed ashore at Joss Beach in one of the later waves. His dreams of glory in combat had faded. "Just trust the Army to get things fouled up," he said. "If the landing schedule had not gone snafu, we would have come ashore with the assault waves. That was what I wanted. I had primed myself for the big moment. Then the timing got snarled in the predawn confusion; and we came in late, chugging ashore like a bunch of clucks in a ferryboat.

> The assault troops had already taken the beach. The battle had moved inland. So for several hours we have tramped over fields and hills without

> direct contact with the enemy. It is true that the landing was not exactly an excursion. There was some big stuff smashing about, and from various points came the rattle of small arms. But we soon got used to that.
>
> A shell crashes on a nearby hill; the earth quivers; and the black smoke boils. . . . The second shell is different. Something terrible and immediate about its whistle makes my scalp start prickling. I grab my helmet and flip over on my stomach. The explosion is thunderous. Steel fragments whine, and the ground seems to jump up and hit me in the face. Silence again. I raise my head. The sour fumes of powder have caused an epidemic of coughing.

Murphy's platoon moved out. Once inland, the enemy-filled landscape rose upward and Murphy and his fellow dogfaces rose with it.

> As we plod over the hills in sweat-soaked clothes, the uneasiness passes from my stomach to my mind. So it happens as easily as that. You sit on a quiet slope with chin in hand. In the distance a gun slams; and the next minute you are dead.
>
> Maybe my notions about war were all cockeyed. How do you pit your skill against skill if you cannot even see the enemy? Where is the glamour in blistered feet and a growling stomach? And where is the expected adventure? Well, whatever comes, it was my own idea. I had asked for it. I had always wanted to be a soldier.[19]

■ ■ ■

After monitoring the activities at all three beaches all day, Admiral Hewitt sent a signal to his Western Naval Task Force: "Due to careful planning, excellent seamanship, gunnery, and engineering, and a high standard of proficiency and devotion to duty by all hands, the most difficult and complicated task of landing our troops on hostile shores has been successfully accomplished. Informed reports of especially meritorious acts and accomplishments have been many. I consider that all, from the Task Force commanders to the lowest ratings, have performed splendidly and are deserving of the highest praise. Well done. It is now our duty to support, maintain, and build up the forces which have been landed. Carry on."

But the admiral was highly critical of how the arrival of vital supplies was handled once they reached shore, as he noted in his after action report:

> Smooth, efficient operation of the assault beaches was not accomplished until after the departure of the assault transports from the Gulf of Gela. Beginning on D-Day, from H-hour onwards until D+3, beach conditions were chaotic. . . . Boats were arriving at all beaches in such numbers that unloading by the Shore Party was at no beach able to keep pace with the arrival of loaded boats.
>
> Many vehicles, upon being unloaded from craft, came to an end on enemy mine fields which had not been located and marked by the Shore Party prior to the arrival of the motor equipment. The destruction of these vehicles, and the lack of suitable exits and proper markers to show safe routes for traffic through enemy mine fields, soon created widespread confusion as trucks became blocked on the beaches.
>
> Eventually the beaches became crowded with miscellaneous personnel standing around idle. . . . Troops were observed loitering about on the sand dunes awaiting instructions as to movement. . . . Supplies were piled high on the beaches without any effort to accomplish segregation. Gasoline, ammunition, water, food, and assorted equipment were strewn about in a hopeless mass. No fire-fighting equipment was in evidence anywhere. As enemy planes made frequent strafing attacks along these beaches, fires were of infrequent occurrence.[20]

■ ■ ■

Ernie Pyle, a war correspondent for the Scripps-Howard newspaper chain, clacked out his impressions of the Husky landings on his portable typewriter in his usual conversational style:

> The fleet of 2,000 ships that carried the Allied invasion forces to Sicily was by all odds the most gigantic ever assembled in the world's history—many, many times the size of the Great Spanish Armada.
>
> In reading of this invasion you must remember that at least half of it was British. The planning was done together and our figures lumped together,

but in the actual invasion we sailed separate fleets, landed in separate areas. So when you read of 2,000 ships* in this fleet, you can figure half of it or more was British and also the 2,000 figure includes convoys that were at sea en route from England and America which arrived with reinforcements a few days later. But either section of the invasion, American or British, was a gigantic achievement.

After being with them throughout this operation, I must say my respect for the Navy is great. The personnel for this great task had to build as quickly as the fleet itself. We did not rob the Pacific of anything. We created from whole cloth. There were 1,000 officers staffing these new-type invasion ships and fewer than twenty of them were regular Navy men. The rest were all erstwhile civilians trained almost overnight into sea dogs.

The American invading force was taken from Africa to Sicily in three immense fleets sailing separately. Each of these three was in turn broken down into smaller fleets. It would have been utterly impossible to sail them all as one fleet. That would have been like trying to herd all the sheep in the world with one dog.

I traveled with the section that was assigned to the western third of the Americans' designated territory. We had to take about fourteen miles of beach front. . . . At two beaches the opposition was trivial and soon over. On a fourth beach it was stronger and the beach wasn't occupied until after daylight but even so it was minor-league defense in every sense of the word. Our sector covered the territory on each side of the city of Licata.

When I went ashore, I landed about two miles east of the city, waded ashore, and hitchhiked a ride into town with a bunch of engineers in a jeep. Licata is a city of about 35,000 with a small river running through it. It had a big wide main street and a very nice little harbor. The buildings are of local stone, dull gray and very old but very substantial. The city is so colorless it blends into the surrounding dry countryside and you can't see it [from] a few miles away. A hill rises up right behind the city and there is a sort of fort on the top.

---

* The actual size of the combined Allied fleet consisted of 3,200 vessels. D'Este, *Bitter Victory*, 153.

When daylight came we looked at the city from the boat dock and could see the American flag flying from the top of this fort although the city itself had not surrendered. Some Rangers had climbed up there before daylight and hoisted our flag. The city hadn't been bombed. The only damage came from a few shells we threw into it from the ships just after daylight. The corners were knocked off a few buildings and some good-sized holes were gouged in the streets but the city got off pretty nicely.

[The Italian] defenses throughout our special sector were almost childish. They didn't bother to mess up their harbor nor to blow out the two river bridges which would have cut our forces in half. They had only a few mines on the beaches and practically no barbed wire. We'd come prepared to fight our way through a solid wall of mines, machine guns, artillery, barbed wire and liquid fire and we even expected to hit some new fiendish devices. Yet there was almost nothing to it. It was like stepping into the ring to meet Joe Louis and finding Caspar Milquetoast waiting there.[21]

But as smoothly as the first few hours of the invasion had gone all along the coast, the enemy was mounting a major effort to strike back.

8

D-DAY AT GELA

Sniping by enemy civilians as well as soldiers continued . . . throughout day and night.

—James Lyle

While the 3rd Division's landing at Licata was going relatively smoothly, the same could not be said for Terry Allen's 1st Division landing at Gela. The Big Red One, following the Rangers ashore at Dime Beach, seemed to have hit a snag. The 1st was supposed to have been augmented by its own division artillery and Combat Command B of the 2nd Armored Division, but the destroyed pier, profuse minefields, miscommunication between Patton and Hewitt, and heavy enemy fire from a number of pillboxes and machine-gun nests at the eastern end of Dime Beach, along with mortars and artillery from the Italians' XVIII Coastal Brigade, played havoc with the timetable.[1]

Cpl. Sam Fuller, 16th RCT, recalled going ashore: "We move inland. . . . A pillbox. Then another. A few machine guns. They are knocked out. The flat beach, some fifty yards wide, has no other constructions. Across steep dunes plod the soldiers. Behind these barriers an Italian company holds a defensive position. This is quickly disposed of and the Italians drop their arms. Others vainly fire a few brave rounds. All of them soon scatter, bolt. Most of them are captured later."[2]

One of the 1st Division's missions on D-Day was the capture of the Ponte Olivo airfield, about four miles north of Gela. It was expected that the 1st's

26th RCT would need to assist the small Ranger contingent in seizing Gela; when that proved to be unnecessary, Col. John W. Bowen's 26th RCT headed north but became ensnared in a large minefield that took some time to clear. Once through, the regiment marched toward the high ground west of Ponte Olivo; Terry Allen and his command staff had also proceeded quickly northward and established the division command post in a building along Highway 117, the road to Niscemi.

But neither Allen nor Col. George Taylor's 16th RCT, which had come ashore intermingled with the 26th RCT on the eastern side of the beachhead, had yet to make contact with Gavin's scattered paratroopers, who were assumed to be in control of Piano Lupo but who obviously were not.[3]

Allen was also severely hampered by a lack of intelligence about the enemy. One estimate said that there were 3,800 soldiers from either the 206th or 207th Coastal Division in "four coastal infantry battalions, one coastal artillery battalion, and three light antiaircraft [batteries]" in the vicinity of the Ponte Olivo airfield and perhaps two companies with heavy weapons. It was also assumed that there was "a local response force in addition to those enemy troops manning static positions," but no one knew for certain. The exact whereabouts of the Italian 4th Livorno Division were also not known, but it was assumed that it and at least one German division could be expected to counterattack, supported by strong air attacks, within a day or two of the landings.[4]

To accomplish his mission, Allen had ordered the 16th and 26th RCTs to aggressively move off the beach, employ a two-pronged movement to skirt the eastern and western sides of Gela, and seize the high ground at Ponte Olivo and Piano Lupo that dominated the northern highway approaches to the city. Allen counted on the Rangers being in control of Gela and on being able to use the Navy's muscle until his artillery could come ashore. He also expected elements of the 2nd Armored Division to arrive shortly.

But now, in the dark, early hours of 10 July, the Big Red One was still struggling to get ashore; the extensive minefields on Red and Blue Beaches would not be cleared until almost noon, and then only by the heroic efforts of men with mine detectors working under constant shellfire. Yellow Beach took several more hours to be at least somewhat cleared of the buried explosives.[5]

Dismayed to see the wreckage of the two-thousand-foot concrete pier that would hamper the arrival and offloading of Gaffey's tanks and the division's artillery, Allen pushed his troops forward and hoped that they would not meet enemy armor before the heavy weapons could come ashore.

Through sheer courage, the 16th and 26th RCTs advanced through Gela (much of which still contained bypassed pockets of enemy troops) without much difficulty. The 26th then veered off to the northwest, crossed the Gela River, and headed up Highway 117 to the west of the Ponte Olivo airfield, taking prisoners along the way.[6]

Tom Lancer, a 1st Division soldier, recalled, "After we landed, we went straight into Gela and occupied the town hall. The mayor had departed, of course, but lying on his desk was an Italian translation of *Gone with the Wind*, which he had apparently been reading. I went to the balcony and watched the POWs, mostly Italian, some German, being herded by the military police to the beach for evacuation by ship. . . . They were shuffling along."[7]

At around 0500 hours enemy warplanes made their appearance and roared down on the still-disembarking troops, their naval escorts, and the vulnerable, slow-flying aerial reconnaissance planes launched by the cruisers; no Allied fighters had yet appeared to duel with the German and Italian pilots. Four Heinkel He 111 medium bombers and four Focke-Wulf FW 190 fighter-bombers attacked the transports but were driven off by a heavy screen of anti-aircraft fire. Except for minor damage to the *Murphy* (DD 603), none of the vulnerable ships were hit.[8]

■ ■ ■

For the Germans, time was evaporating. Alerted earlier that morning by Kesselring that airborne troops were dropping between Gela and Vittoria, Paul Conrath, commanding the Hermann Göring Panzer Division, had ordered his soldiers to prepare to meet the threat. His plan was to hit the invaders no later than 0900 hours and, although his division was on the road by 0400 hours from Caltagirone, some twenty miles northeast of Gela, delay after delay conspired against him. The roads were unsuitable for tanks, his columns were attacked by a rare appearance of Allied warplanes, and he kept running into scattered groups of Gavin's paratroopers, who panicked his inexperienced soldiers and slowed him down.

Conrath had hoped to coordinate his attack with the Italians to his west, but his communications went out as paratroopers cut telephone lines wherever they found them. As a result, the German general was unable to contact any Italian units in his vicinity. Unaware that Italians were already moving toward Gela, he decided to make an attack on his own.[9] Indeed, Gen. Giandomenico Chirieleison, commanding the Livorno Division, had already sent one of his units, Gruppo Mobile E, to confront the Americans.

Without Italian help, Conrath split his panzer division into two regiment-sized *Kampfgruppen*, or combat groups. One group passed Niscemi in two columns; then, one of the columns branched off to the west onto Highway 117, crossed the Gela River, and headed toward the Ponte Olivo airfield and Gela beyond. The other half of this group, after rolling south of Niscemi, was to pass Abbio Priolo, turn east at Piano Lupo, cross the two-hundred-yard-long concrete Ponte Dirillo bridge, climb Biazza Ridge, and head toward Vittoria to attack the 45th Division.

Conrath's other *Kampfgruppe*, which he personally commanded, traveled south from Caltagirone toward Biscari, where he hoped to secure the Biscari airfield and interdict any advance elements of the 45th coming up from Scoglitti.[10]

Altogether, the German force had at least one hundred Mark III and IV tanks along with a few sixty-ton Mark VI Tigers from Panzer Detail 504; the Americans, Conrath was certain, had virtually nothing at this early hour with which to stop the onslaught.

The official history of the campaign says:

> Several tanks of the Ponte Olivo force were to make a feint north of Gela to deceive the Americans into believing that the city of Gela was the main objective. Instead, the main effort was to be made by the other tank column south along the Niscemi–Piano Lupo road to occupy Hills 132 and 123 (the southern edge of Piano Lupo). Joined by the tank battalion coming across the Gela plain from the west, the tanks were to strike south for the sparsely wooded area between the Biviere Pond and the Gulf of Gela.

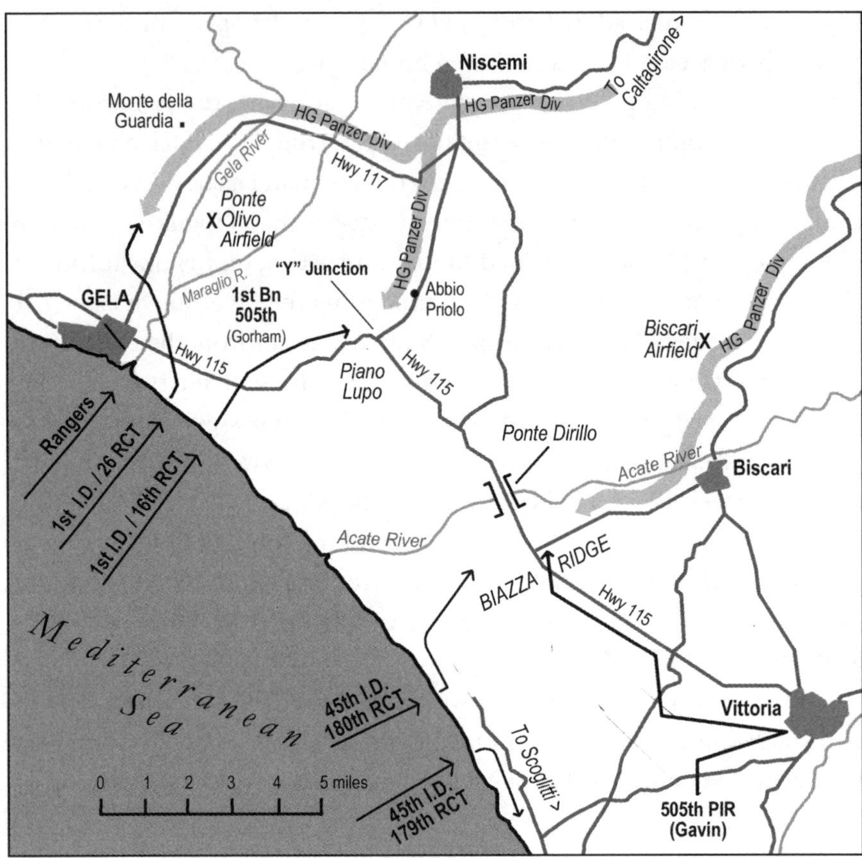

Map 8.1 ▪ The invasion area around Gela, scene of some of the fiercest fighting during the initial phase of Operation Husky

The infantry-heavy force, meanwhile, was to cross the Acate River at Ponte Dirillo and join the tank forces on Piano Lupo. From the sparsely wooded area near the shoreline the entire force was then to roll up the 1st Division's beachhead from east to west, while the Livorno Division, coming in from the west, was to overrun Gela and roll up the 1st Division's beachhead from the west.

Once the Americans had been stopped, Conrath's panzers were to head east, destroy the 45th Division's incursion around Scoglitti, and then continue on to strike the British-Canadian landing forces at Syracuse. The ambitious plan might have been tactically sound, but, as events proved, it had no chance of succeeding.[11]

Lying in the path of these Axis units were the Rangers in Gela, the 1st Division's 16th RCT heading toward Piano Lupo, the 26th RCT on its way to Highway 117, a smattering of Gavin's misdropped paratroopers, and elements of the 45th's 180th RCT approaching from the east.[12]

■ ■ ■

Terry Allen had reason to feel cautiously optimistic. By 0800 hours much of Gela was in American hands, and two hundred Italians had been taken prisoner. Word was also received from Taylor's 16th RCT forward elements that some of Gavin's paratroopers had been contacted near Ponte Olivo. But heavy enemy artillery barrages prevented the rest of the 1st Division from advancing out of Gela and toward Niscemi.

As D-Day morning wore on, the chaos and congestion at Dime Beach grew. With the rough surf, hidden sand bars, intermittent enemy air and artillery attacks, and nearly two hundred disabled LCVPs bobbing aimlessly about, the tanks and vehicle-towed artillery were not getting off the ships and to where they were needed—to the battlefront a few miles inland of Gela.[13]

The enemy's looming armor attacks on 10 and 11 July would be the largest and most powerful launched against an American unit in any theater, including North Africa, Anzio, and Europe.[14]

■ ■ ■

It is no exaggeration to say that at Gela on the first two days of Husky, the ships of Rear Adm. John L. Hall's Task Force 81/CruDiv 8 literally saved the beachhead.

At around 0830 the first enemy tanks were spotted rolling toward Gela by Lt. Cyril Lewis piloting a recon plane catapulted from the cruiser *Boise*, a ship and crew that had already seen considerable action in the Pacific. Lewis reported, "I dove down below 1,000 feet a couple of times and identified them as hostile." After giving target coordinates to the *Boise*, Lewis was chased off by two ME 109s.[15]

According to the U.S. Navy's official history of the Sicilian campaign, the group of Italian tanks and infantry was approaching Gela in an "almost formal, parade ground formation." Lewis had seen thirty-two ten-ton Renault tanks, sixteen three-tonners, and several World War I–vintage Fiat tanks of the Livorno Division's Gruppo Mobile E operating French-built Renault R-35 two-man light tanks in Italian livery, coming down Highway 117 from Niscemi—along with a company of motorized anti-tank guns, a motorized machine-gun company, and an artillery battery of eight 75-mm howitzers. The only Americans between this force and Gela were the Rangers and a few paratroopers; the 1st and 2nd Battalions of the 16th RCT were still a considerable distance behind them. Terry Allen also ordered Bowen's 26th RCT to bolster the line. To break up the Italian advance, the cruisers *Boise* and *Savannah*, plus the destroyers *Shubrick* and *Jeffers* (DD 621), standing six hundred yards offshore, began slamming Chirieleison's oncoming force with their guns (the ships would fire 572 rounds that day), completely halting the attack and sending the survivors fleeing. For the rest of the ships' time off Gela, their expert gunners responded to every request for fire.[16]

With the surviving Italian tanks having temporarily withdrawn, a Ranger company inside Gela discovered three abandoned 77-mm Italian artillery pieces and ammunition. Correctly assuming that the tanks would return, Capt. James Lyle, commanding the Rangers' Company A, formed three ad hoc gun crews from men who had previously had some artillery training and detailed them to operate the weapons. "Part of the basic training of all Rangers consisted of the utilization of captured enemy material," Lyle said. Before long, "the Ranger Artillery reported that it was ready to fire."

It was perfect timing. A group of Italian infantrymen tried pushing forward toward the western side of Gela, which Lyle's company was holding, but were halted by the Rangers firing their captured Italian artillery pieces. Lyle said the fire "took a heavy toll among the closely bunched enemy soldiers. Rifles, machine guns, and mortars joined in as the range closed. . . . Leaving behind numerous dead and wounded, the remnants of the Italian battalion fled."

A few of the tanks now returned to the battlefield. Lyle noted that "nine [Italian] tanks were observed approaching the town from the north. When the tanks were about 5,000 yards from the town, four stopped in a small group of trees and the remainder continued to move towards the town." Lyle ordered his 4.2-inch mortar platoon to lob shells onto the advancing tanks. Although none were hit, their commanders were so unnerved by the barrage that some pulled back while others rushed forward, reaching buildings at the northern edge of town; there they were systematically knocked out by the Rangers' bazooka teams. Then, after some range adjustments on the mortars, the four tanks concealed in the grove of trees were taken under fire; one was destroyed and the other three retreated out of range.

The three still-operable Italian tanks that had pulled back made one final thrust; the Ranger Artillery was ready for them and stopped them cold. Then, as Lyle recalled, the Rangers' guns laid a barrage on a large farmhouse about a mile to the north where enemy soldiers were observed. "About 200 enemy soldiers boiled out of this building, scattering in all directions, running into ditches and defiles, and disappearing out of sight."

What tanks could not achieve, perhaps warplanes could. In an effort to suppress the American naval fire, a formation of German bombers with fighter escort roared overhead to attack the American ships. Hall's gunners responded with their anti-aircraft weapons and "hundreds of bursting shells filled the air, shooting down several aircraft," according to Lyle. "After the bombers had passed, the fighter escort returned, strafing the ships and town and dropping a number of small bombs. When the smoke cleared . . . two large transports had received direct hits."

Although many of the civilian residents had initially welcomed the American invaders as liberators (before turning into refugees and fleeing Gela and other towns along the coast), Lyle reported, "Sniping by enemy civilians as well as soldiers continued to harass the units throughout day and night.[17]

■ ■ ■

The Italian shore batteries that hadn't been knocked out in the initial fighting opened up a fearsome assault on the LSTs in the harbor; the *Boise*'s fire was shifted from the tanks to the enemy gun emplacements lining the beach. At 0939 hours the cruiser's guns began saturating the concrete-enclosed 75-mm cannons and field guns closer to the beach; the destroyer *Jeffers* joined in. Not all the shore batteries were silenced, however, and they continued to target the LSTs and the troops and vehicles that were offloading at Red Beach 2, causing that beach to be closed temporarily at 1010 hours.[18]

■ ■ ■

After the Italian tanks were halted, and before the floating reserve known as Force Kool under Hugh Gaffey could arrive, tanks from Conrath's force joined the battle. He ordered one column of infantry-supported armor—twenty Mark III and IV Panzers—to attack Darby's Rangers and Taylor's 16th RCT north of Gela while he sent another column against the 45th Division's 180th RCT that had landed on the east side of the Acate River.

Historian Carlo D'Este noted, "Tanks and infantry were not accustomed to working together, and the leaders of the Hermann Göring demonstrated no understanding of such a need in terrain which, for the most part, was wholly unsuitable for armored warfare."[19]

Regardless, on came the steel wave accompanied by battalions of infantry. As the force reached small-arms range, Allen's men opened up on the infantry with machine guns, rifles, and mortars. Again, fire from ships offshore helped to break up the formations.

The 1st Division's intelligence officer wrote, "[The 16th RCT's] units moved through the wadis* and the [German] tanks had no way of depressing their guns enough to get at them. The eroded wadis were so deep that tankers without infantry, that first day, would have had to get out of their tanks and fight on foot. This a tanker won't do if he can help it. So, that was one reason why the German tank attack was a failure. The [1st Division] infantry just got in tank-proof terrain. . . . I, frankly, was very surprised to find that the tanks appeared in the middle of the afternoon of the first day. They almost overran our position."[20]

---

* The Arab word *wadi* refers to a dry creek bed; the 1st Division had fought in plenty of them in North Africa.

■ ■ ■

From his vantage point atop Biazza Ridge, Jim Gavin could see the broad, treeless Gela Plain covered with enemy armor moving toward him like a herd of buffalo stampeding in slow motion. Without a working radio, he sent a runner back to the beachhead, which he hoped was in American hands, to request reinforcements—and prayed they would arrive in time.[21]

One of Gavin's paratroopers, Sgt. Bill Bishop, Company G, never forgot the terror of being confronted by a sixty-ton Tiger: "Me and a fellow named Duke Boswell were laying within two or three feet from the tank treads in a small ditch. They would shoot at a single man with the 88s they had on those tanks. They killed a bunch of people with that 88. They ran over one man's legs. Of course he died from shock."[22]

■ ■ ■

Bill Darby noted, "The rest of D-Day morning was hectic. There were still snipers and enemy-held pillboxes in town. About noon, eighteen huge German Tiger tanks lumbered into Gela for the second counterattack. For a time it looked bad. I called for the 4.2-inch rifled chemical mortars and for cruiser fire. The chemical mortar troops plopped their twenty-five-pound shells against the tanks in the streets. Captain [Charles] Shunstrom turned a captured 77-mm against them, too. Twelve tanks were blasted out of action" and three more retreated.[23]

■ ■ ■

Sam Fuller of the 16th RCT said, "Two [tanks] appeared in front of the 1st Battalion; six more hit the 2nd. At 0900 the 2nd Battalion received a staggering blow from ten to sixteen tanks on the Niscemi Road. . . . sometime later 1st Battalion was confronted by thirty tanks. [But] enemy morale seemed to be sagging. If it were possible to get by the tanks, it appeared likely that Niscemi might be reached that day."[24]

The daring-but-doomed Italian tankers, probably the bravest on the island, refused to break and run, choosing instead to continue advancing into the face of certain death. Darby called upon his mortar crews, noting that the Italian infantrymen were approaching in mass formation: "Our mortars, holding fire until they were about two thousand yards away, laid down several hundred 4.2-inch shells in a minute's concentrated firing. The Italian thrust disintegrated."[25]

■ ■ ■

Morning melted into afternoon. Terry Allen pushed the 16th and 26th RCTs and the 1st Recon Troop further north toward Piano Lupo. He also radioed the division's situation to Patton aboard the *Monrovia* and pleaded for the arrival of the armor and anti-tank guns; in response, at 1340 hours Patton ordered the Navy to land Maj. Gen. Hugh Gaffey's 2nd Armored Division at Gela—pier or no pier.

Unfortunately, the Navy did not get the word. Force Kool under Hugh Gaffey, consisting of the desperately needed reserve of tanks, was held under Hewitt's immediate command. The admiral said,

> This group, composed of the transports *Orizaba* and *Chateau Thierry*, and sundry landing craft under Captain K. S. Reed, U.S.N., had been moved in close to the *Monrovia*, in a position of readiness to land as directed. We were awaiting word from General Patton.
>
> About 1530, I received a visual signal from Captain Reed to the effect that General Gaffey said he had orders to land, and that he, Reed, requested instructions. I immediately showed the signal to General Patton, alongside me on the bridge, and asked him what it meant. He said, "Oh! Yes! I gave orders an hour ago to land the reserve at Gela to support the 1st Division."

Unfortunately, according to Hewitt, Patton had given the orders "in usual Army fashion to his Chief of Staff, who had transmitted them via slow Army channels direct to General Gaffey, without informing anyone in the Navy, which, of course, had to do the landing."

Hewitt, in his most diplomatic manner, said to Patton, "Well, General, it is too bad that neither I nor any member of my staff were informed of your wishes. If we had been, General Gaffey's force would have been on the way ashore long ago." The problem was soon worked out and the armor began landing at Dime Beach—but not until 1700 hours. Had there been further delay, the consequences could have been catastrophic. With both men on the same ship it is unknown why they didn't communicate more efficiently about a matter so vital.[26]

■ ■ ■

Despite the pounding they had just taken, Conrath's men still refused to give up. At about 1600 hours a group of surviving Tiger tanks made another push toward Gavin's 505th paratroopers atop Biazza Ridge. Just as they rolled to within fifty yards, a barrage of shells from the *Boise* and *Savannah* screamed overhead and slammed into them, blowing them apart. Prudently, Conrath withdrew the remaining Tigers out of range to prepare for another thrust, but the beating his shaken soldiers had just endured caused him to call off another immediate attack.[27]

About two hours later word reached Gavin that reinforcements from the U.S. 2nd Armored Division, along with more infantry, had landed and were on their way to bolster the paratroopers' position.[28]

The German ground attacks on 10 July had accomplished nothing. By 1845 hours Conrath realized that he held the losing hand and pulled his forces back out of naval gunfire range. With night approaching, the 16th RCT seized the Piano Lupo high ground, but the Ponte Olivo airfield had not been taken. By now, three of the 1st Division's four field artillery battalions—the 5th, 7th, and 33rd—had finally reached Dime Beach, and their motor transport was hauling the guns into firing positions to be ready in the event of another German attack—which was coming.[29]

■ ■ ■

As night pulled a shroud over the battlefield, Lieutenant Colonel Dante Leonardi received orders: The next day, his 3rd Battalion of the 34th Infantry Regiment, 4th Livorno Division, was told, "You will attack the Americans in the early hours of 11 July." There were no other essential details. As Leonardi was moving south by truck that evening, Allied aircraft strafed his column, resulting in two dead, twenty wounded, and five vehicles damaged. It was not an auspicious beginning to the unit's introduction to combat.

At 2300 hours Leonardi's unit reached the Ponte Olivo airfield, a place that seemed deserted. After dismounting and continuing south on foot in the dark for several more miles, they contacted other units that had no more information than they had. At Monte Casteluccio Leonardi found the 155th Bersaglieri Motorcycle Company, part of Gruppo Mobile E, led by Lieutenant Franco Girasoli, who had been wounded during the day's attack on the beachhead. His company, the only Italian infantry unit in the area prior to Leonardi's arrival, had been torn apart; what was left of it was scattered around Biazza Ridge.[30]

■ ■ ■

Terry Allen liked night operations—he had conducted several in North Africa—and thus ordered the 16th and 26th RCTs to make and maintain contact with the enemy once the sun had set. Late on 10 July he also ordered the two regiments to head for the division's two major objectives, the Ponte Olivo airfield and Niscemi.

Colonel Bowen's 26th RCT was advancing up the left side of the Niscemi-Piano Lupo road with the 16th on its right, while Lt. Col. John T. Corley's 3rd Battalion, 26th RCT, marched up Highway 117 toward Monte della Guardia. Corley's men were heading toward the high terrain west of the highway that overlooked the airfield, but they ran into heavy enemy fire that halted the battalion's progress.

Meanwhile, Lt. Col. Charles Denholm's 1st Battalion, 16th RCT, was headed northward toward the hamlet of Casa del Priolo while Company G of Lt. Col. Joe Crawford's 2nd Battalion marched parallel to the 1st Battalion along the west side of the road. Although the 1st Battalion reached Casa del Priolo without encountering the enemy and began digging in, Company G of the 2nd Battalion panicked at the sight of German tanks to its left front and without authorization withdrew back toward Gela.

Surprised and angered by this move, and fearing that the German tanks would attack his unprotected left flank, Crawford ordered Companies E and F to fill in the gap left by Company G's departure and to dig in on a ridge at Abbio Priolo, about a thousand yards northwest of Casa del Priolo. After hooking up with some of Gorham's paratroopers, these companies would reach the ridge early the next morning.[31]

■ ■ ■

In a remarkable display of courage, at around 2230 hours on 10 July Company G of the 505th's 3rd Parachute Battalion held against German forces on Biazza Ridge during a battle in the dark. One historian described the clash: "The American parachutists, a hodgepodge collection of engineers, cooks, orderlies, riggers, clerks, and riflemen, had no field guns, antitank guns or tanks, and would be vastly outnumbered in the looming confrontation." This hodgepodge somehow stopped the enemy—but only for the night.[32]

Taken by surprise, the Germans temporarily withdrew, but they would not be gone for long. A counterattack pushed the Company G paratroopers off Biazza Ridge, but Company H quickly took up the fight, fixing bayonets and surging back into the melée. Hand-to-hand fighting broke out and the Germans once again pulled back, only to return minutes later for one last effort; it failed to break the defenders. After numerous skirmishes in the dark, the 1st Division and paratroopers established new defensive positions and waited for dawn.[33]

■ ■ ■

Meanwhile, unloading operations back at the beach had been going on all day and into the night, and the 18th RCT, Allen's floating reserve, along with the 41st Armored Infantry Battalion, finally arrived, moved past Gela, and took up positions in the gap between the 16th and 26th RCTs. The majority of the Sherman tanks of the 2nd Armored Division would not arrive until 0200 hours on 11 July, as they were delayed in offloading due to the demolished pier and uncleared minefields; the LSTs would now have the opportunity to try out the pontoon causeways, which worked successfully.

The follow-up landings would be none too soon, for that night the enemy armor was preparing to launch another counterattack, even bigger than the previous one.[34]

German and Italian bombers also attacked again that night. "The planes dropped magnesium flares to light the transports," a sailor remembered, "and bombs fell on the ships in cascades, clumps, and clusters." Fortunately, serious damage was averted.[35]

■ ■ ■

With the surprisingly strong response by Italian and German aircraft over the Seventh Army invasion area, a passive air defense system was launched: barrage balloons. The Royal Navy had had three years of combat experience in the Mediterranean and had successfully employed the tethered balloons against constant low-level aerial attacks; the United States also saw the value of the apparatus and deployed three Army barrage balloon battalions to North African ports to support the American landings. During the second day of Husky, a total of one hundred balloons—whose steel cables were designed to discourage enemy pilots—were floated two hundred feet above the ships offshore and the beachheads, but not on the first day, when the ships and unloading parties were subjected to attacks by the Luftwaffe and Regia Aeronautica.[36]

■ ■ ■

On the night of 10 July, hours after the paratroopers had dropped and the infantry and tanks had gone ashore, Eisenhower and his staff left Malta on a British destroyer to visit Patton and Hewitt. When he arrived the following morning, Ike said, "The German was pulling back, presumably to strengthen his defenses in the critical Catania area. . . . Up to that moment, no amphibious attack in history had approached this one in size. Along miles of coast line there were hundreds of vessels and small boats afloat and antlike files of advancing troops ashore."[37]

■ ■ ■

With the fighting finished for the night, a temporary cemetery was created for the fallen paratroopers. Gavin, who had been slightly wounded during the battle, watched with tears in his eyes as his men were laid to rest.[38] Several days later he found a few minutes to write a cheery letter to his daughter Barbara: "Dear Babe, Well, it was a good fight but the censor will not let me tell you about it. I didn't miss a minute of it. Believe I got a Purple Heart [for a minor wound to the leg]. Never felt better in my life. Tell you more about it some other time. Love, Pappy."[39]

■ ■ ■

To Patton, floating helplessly offshore on the *Monrovia*, the reports that had flowed into his command center during D-Day painted a picture of partial success and worrying confusion. Perhaps his presence on shore the next day would straighten things out. It would not be a moment too soon, for 11 July—D-Day plus one—would arguably be the most critical day of the entire Sicily campaign—the day when the enemy made his last, best attempt to shove the Americans back into the sea.

9

D-DAY PLUS ONE

THE CRISIS

A Tiger tank is an awesome thing to encounter in combat.

—James Gavin

The best time to defeat an amphibious operation is in its first few hours, before the invaders can get organized and have all their assets on shore and ready for deployment. Having missed that opportunity early on 10 July, the Germans' and Italians' last best chance was shortly after dawn on 11 July—D-Day plus one.

Congestion and confusion on the beaches at Gela were still a major problem. Not all of the American troops, tanks, artillery, and essential equipment had come ashore; supplies had piled up on the sand; the front line had not pushed more than ten miles from the coastline; certain territorial gains had not been consolidated; the airborne troops were still scattered; and American airpower had yet to take control of the skies.

The Germans and Italians still held a slim numerical advantage over the Yanks, but they had a very small window of opportunity to use that advantage before the odds swung in Seventh Army's favor.

■ ■ ■

The sun rose and began heating the southern Sicilian coast like a blowtorch. At about 0830 hours Gavin's paratroopers, moving northwest, reached the point where a railroad line crossed Highway 115. A half-mile away was a slight rise, perhaps one hundred feet high, covered with a large grove of olive trees planted in rows; it was called Biazza Ridge. Fighting for it had gone on during the night. Gavin had been taught to "seize the high ground," so he ordered Lt. Col. Ed Krause's 3rd Battalion and the engineers to do just that. He didn't know that Italian soldiers from the Livorno Division, and some Germans, were still on top of it.

Gavin soon discovered that fact when he directed Lt. Ben Wechsler's engineer platoon to seize the ridge and they were met by bullets sizzling through the air. "I was with Wechsler, and in a few hundred yards the fire became intense," Gavin said. "As we neared the top of the ridge there was a rain of leaves and branches as bullets tore through the trees, and there was a buzzing like the sound of swarms of bees. A few moments later Wechsler was hit and fell. Some troopers were hit; others continued to crawl forward. Soon we were pinned down by heavy small-arms fire."

While his men traded fire with the enemy, Gavin scrambled down to bring up Krause's men but Krause was not there; with no working radios, he had gone back to contact the 45th Division to see if he could enlist the Thunderbirds' help. However, Krause's executive officer soon arrived with more paratroopers and also a 45th Division platoon, and the battle of Biazza Ridge resumed. Suddenly, in addition to machine-gun bullets, mortar and artillery rounds began to hit Gavin's men.

As wounded paratroopers fell back, they brought word that a few German tanks had joined in the counterattack. Fortunately, some mortars and a couple of 75-mm pack howitzers of the 456th Parachute Field Artillery had been air-dropped and were now being brought up to give the lightly armed paratroopers a fighting chance. More paratroopers eager to get in on the action also arrived.

An advance patrol from Conrath's panzer division was up ahead and added their 88-mm voices to the fray; more paratroopers went down dead and wounded. "The [enemy] fire increased in intensity," Gavin said, "and our wounded were coming back in greater numbers."

Normally, howitzers are fired using a high-arc trajectory, but near the top of Biazza Ridge they were called upon to provide direct-fire support. German panzers began rolling up the northwest slope of the ridge, which gave Gavin an idea. He quickly gathered the 75-mm gun crews together and told them, "We're staying on this goddamned ridge no matter what happens," and he said that they should "stay concealed and engage the less heavily armored underbellies of the tanks when they first appeared at the top of the rise. It was a dangerous tactic, but the only the thing we could do; tanks are vulnerable in that position."

Gavin spotted a tank slowly moving about four hundred yards ahead among a small group of buildings. "A Tiger tank is an awesome thing to encounter in combat," he said. "Weighing more than sixty tons, armed with an 88-mm gun and machine guns, it was far more formidable that anything we had ever seen, and we had nothing in our own armored forces to compare with it."

One of Gavin's 75-mm gun crews bravely chose to take it on. Lying prone beside their weapon, they waited until the tank more fully exposed its belly. But the tank got off the first shot; its round exploded in front of the crew, "knocking the troopers like tenpins in all directions," Gavin reported. "I was standing just to the left rear, watching the action, and I was knocked down, too." The gunners, who were miraculously unhurt, regained their composure and quickly returned to their piece and fired at the tank but only blew off a chunk of a nearby building. "In the smoke and dust the tank backed out of sight. That was the last we saw of it," Gavin said.[1]

■ ■ ■

That morning a dozen Italian bombers flew over the Gela area; one naval transport was hit and two others suffered damage from near misses, adding to the confusion in the harbor and delaying further offloading. The aerial attacks would continue all day, with almost no response from Allied air.[2]

■ ■ ■

The 1st Division's 16th and 26th RCTs continued to advance without much difficulty after their previous night's encounter with the enemy. Word was also received from forward 16th RCT elements that some of Gavin's paratroopers had been contacted near Ponte Olivo. Allen had reason to feel cautiously optimistic. By midmorning much of Gela was in American hands and more

Italians had been taken prisoner. But the main objective—the Ponte Olivo airfield—was still under enemy control, and would be until 13 July.[3]

■ ■ ■

Hewitt's warships, meanwhile, continued to prowl along the coast, responding to desperate calls from shore parties for gunfire against concentrations of German and Italian forces while fending off sporadic attacks by enemy warplanes and dodging occasional shells from still-active Italian coastal batteries. Transports were also busy hauling vital supplies, ammunition, and vehicles to the beaches and, in turn, taking wounded G.I.s to the ships for medical care. Allen's men continued to bear the brunt of the enemy's attempts to wipe out the beachhead.

The situation quickly turned grim for the Yanks. At Abbio Priolo on the 1st Division's right flank, Conrath's panzers smashed into Taylor's 16th RCT with the force of a gigantic armored fist. "Fighting with the equipment at hand—little more than the individual soldiers' arms—the regiment met the head-on attack of the Hermann Göring Panzer Division, the elite armored division of the German Army," said Cpl. Sam Fuller.

"When the German counterattack hit in full force," said Fuller, "chances were good that the [16th] regiment would be pushed back into the sea. There could be no retreat. It had to be a question of victory or annihilation. On July 11th the 16th Infantry fought one of the most desperate battles in history. It was purely a defensive battle—a struggle for existence."

The 2nd Battalion knocked out two heavy panzers, and the 3rd Battalion knocked out another. Fuller continued, "However, five more remained, out of range, to 3rd Battalion's front and an undetermined number were spread out across the regimental front. An additional thirty were concentrated at a crossroads less than a mile to the north. Other smaller groups were scattered in the same general area. Part of the group of thirty took the few 37-mm anti-tank guns under fire. . . . Cannon Company,* the one salvation

* From July 1943 through the war's end, each U.S. Army infantry regiment was authorized to have one 118-man "Cannon Company" that was equipped with six towed M3 105-mm howitzers to provide its main organic direct-fire anti-tank fire support. War Department Field Manual 7-37, *Cannon Company, Infantry Regiment* (Washington, DC: War Department, 28 March 1944).

in this emergency, had not yet arrived. Two 57-mm's were knocked out and most of their crews lost."

Seeing his regiment begin to falter under the weight of the armored assault, Colonel Taylor issued strict orders to his battalion and company commanders: "Under no circumstances will anyone pull back. Take cover from the tanks but don't let anything else get through. Cannon Company is on its way. Give orders for everyone to hold positions."

Taylor then messaged the division: "Situation critical. We are being overrun by tanks. In Colonel Crawford's area [2nd Battalion] the enemy has placed ten tanks in front of him and has ringed him with an additional thirty. We have no idea what is going on to the east of us."[4]

From his command post in a building along the Gela–Ponte Olivo Road, assistant division commander Teddy Roosevelt phoned Allen: "The situation is not very comfortable out here. The 3rd Battalion has been attacked by tanks and has been penetrated. The 2nd Battalion is in support but that is not enough. If we could get a company of medium tanks it sure would help. If we are to take the Ponte Olivo airport, we must have those tanks."[5]

■ ■ ■

Admiral Hewitt wrote in his Action Report that at 0919 hours reports coming in from Dime Beach said, "Situation at Yellow and Blue beaches very bad due to enemy land mines. Casualties being evacuated to transports by ship's boats. Traffic in this area to be sent to Red Beach 2 until others are cleared."

Minutes later the Italian beach gunners laid a heavy barrage onto Red Beach 2, where troops and vehicles were coming ashore and wounded men were lying on the sand waiting to be evacuated; Yellow beach also came under renewed fire. Hewitt ordered the *Boise* and *Savannah* to temporarily redirect their fires from the approaching Italian tanks in order to suppress the enemy's artillery that was targeting the beach.[6]

■ ■ ■

Lt. Bill Whitman, Company B, 180th RCT, 45th Division, remembered his encounter with a German panzer. "The enemy fire had slacked off," he said, "which made things a lot easier for me." But then he came to a small clearing and had a face-to-face encounter with a German tank. "Seconds after I saw it, it fired its 88-mm gun in my general direction. I was so close—a matter of yards—that it blew my glasses and helmet off."

Whitman scrambled back to his company commander and told him about the tank; his company commander, Captain Fleet, decided to attack the panzer with a 60-mm mortar, bazookas, and rifle grenades, but by the time the attacking force reached the farmhouse, several more tanks had appeared.

"The small mortar shells pounded the fronts and turrets of the tanks," Whitman said. "Our rocket launchers fired but the rockets and rifle grenades just bounced off. Our fire seemed futile at the time. We learned later that the tank commanders were so confused as to what weapons we had that they failed to take advantage of the situation by coming into the vineyard and overrunning us. In fact, all they did was remain stationary and fire their machine guns at us. Why they didn't pound us with their 88-mm guns I will never know, unless they were out of shells for them."

More elements of Company B, 180th RCT, arrived and quickly came under fire; the panzers were soon joined by German infantry. "Lieutenant Brown's 1st Platoon on the left side of the road was overrun by tanks and had to pull back," said Whitman. "This permitted the Germans to move in and place flanking fire on us from the right. First Lieutenant George Proctor, a very good friend of mine, was shot down and run over by a Tiger tank."

Suddenly enemy aircraft appeared overhead. According to Whitman, "We lost most of Company B in this hellish vineyard. What the German and Italian machine guns and tanks didn't get, the German planes did. At one point I was hugging the ground when there was a shout from the rear. I turned my head just in time to see two German planes come swooping low towards us, their guns blazing. The ground opened into hundreds of little furrows as the bullets stitched it—and the backs of some of the men."

The GIs were in a fix. They had no supporting weapons and their radios did not work, probably because of the salt-water bath they had received during the wade-in. Scores of men were missing. Then Captain Fleet ordered Whitman and several men to find the enemy's flank.

They reached another stone farmhouse that was crawling with Italian soldiers and took them under fire. Whitman dropped flat behind a stand of cactus but, whenever an Italian bullet tore through the cactus, the juice would squirt into his eyes. Another bullet hit the ammunition clip he was loading into his M-1 Garand rifle, numbing his hand. Sicilian dust and dirt jammed his rifle. With the situation rapidly deteriorating, Fleet decided to pull back to a vineyard, then circle around a hill and come up into the rear of the vineyard where he hoped his men still were. Whitman said,

> The only trouble now was that the Germans and Italians had moved men and weapons that cut off our return route to the vineyard. We fought a withdrawal down a valley to our left rear, moving further away from our men in the vineyard.
>
> We reached a road and, as we were resting a moment, one of the men suddenly screamed, "Look, look—a tank!" There on the top of the hill that we were going to climb was a German tank. It opened fire with its machine gun and our captain was shot through the lower leg. He crawled behind some rocks where he was safe from the fire, and the rest of us scattered on that bare hillside.

Alone, Whitman decided to head over the top of the hill. "As I neared the crest, two Italian soldiers appeared on the top; they had rifles. I raised my useless jammed rifle and aimed it at them. They threw theirs down and took off running. When I reached the top of the hill I could not see any of our men; when they had seen the tank they had scattered in all directions, not having anything with which to fight it. I sat down behind some bushes. The sun was very hot; July in the Mediterranean is no time to be running up hills in woolen uniforms."

After resting for a while, Whitman moved along a trail and reached another farmhouse where, by using hand gestures, he convinced the frightened old farmer to give him some water. Whitman also tried asking if there were any Germans (*Tedeschi*) around; the farmer gestured that they were all around. Whitman departed the farm and, with an inoperative rifle, made his way down another trail; he eventually ran into more men from his battalion who gave him a vague idea of where he might find the rest of his company. From then on it was a matter of dodging the enemy, who seemed to be everywhere.

Whitman came to a small valley where he heard German being spoken. "I got under some bushes and covered myself with leaves as over a hundred

Germans in black uniforms came over a rise and into the valley. They set up camp. And on top of one of the hills some Italian soldiers pulled an artillery gun into position and started firing it in the general direction of the sea."

Soon the sound of airplane engines—German ones—mixed with the booming of the gun. "I was able to look up through the bushes and could see formation after formation of [enemy] bombers heading toward the sea. Soon there was the sound of explosions and anti-aircraft fire. After a while I saw the planes returning. It looked to me like there were just as many as went overhead before—they were on their way back from attacking Allied shipping off the coast."

Off in the distance Whitman could see black clouds of smoke billowing into the sky, and he wondered how many American ships had been sunk. "My morale at this time was very low as I was beginning to think that the invasion had failed, and we had been driven back into the sea. This feeling was made stronger when I saw Germans walking some American soldiers along a path. There were about five Americans with their hands tied behind them."

Whitman decided to strip himself of almost everything he carried—watch, wallet, ring, insignias, maps, and ID card. "I remembered my training on items of intelligence," he said. "I knew that the enemy gave captured officers much more intense interrogation than enlisted men; that is why I got rid of my insignia of rank and ID card. There was no other way that one could tell that I was an officer. This movement was to be almost my last for that day, night, the next day, and almost the next night. . . . I thought of surrender but rejected it, as we had been trained never to surrender as long as we were armed or there was an alternative. I was still armed; I had two grenades and a trench knife." He crawled deeper into the bushes and hoped no one would spot him.[7]

■ ■ ■

At 1100 hours the 1st Division's 26th RCT reported that enemy tanks had broken through their lines and rolled into Gela, and were destroying the mountains of supplies that had been delivered to the 531st Engineer Shore Regiment on the beach.[8]

A 1st Division officer observing from the high ground wrote, "The Big Red One called for naval support. We could see the destroyers in pairs run in, turn just short of the breakers, and bring broadsides to bear on the hostile tanks."

But the hostile tanks that survived the shelling were still rolling uncomfortably close to Allen's command post. Bill Behlmer, an anti-tank gunner, recalled, "The Hermann Göring Panzer Division encircled us. Tanks everywhere. We thought we could outlast them. The 57-mm's which had replaced our 37-mm cannons performed beautifully. Finally, their big guns had us zeroed in and the German armored infantry were advancing. We knew we had to change our position but we couldn't get the trucks up the hill to move our guns. We could see we were surrounded and got going. The Germans captured our guns and spiked them. The cruiser *Savannah* and our own artillery saved the day. The *Savannah* steamed back and forth on the beach knocking out the tanks."[9]

Then, like the cavalry appearing in the nick of time in a Hollywood western, Cannon Company arrived and began blasting the panzers; over a dozen were destroyed in a matter of minutes. Not long thereafter, the first Shermans of Combat Command B arrived and added their firepower to the battle.[10]

■ ■ ■

The skies were strangely devoid of Allied aircraft, which could have done much to stop the Axis attacks. Historian Gerald Astor wrote, "During the first desperate days on the Sicilian shore, the air command, under the British, pursued its own agenda—interdiction of roads and supply depots. No tactical air support arrived to rip into the German armor that threatened the 1st Division."[11]

British historian Hugh Pond echoed that sentiment: "Here was a first-class opportunity for fighter-bombers: dozens of tanks in full view on an open plain. Yet not one Allied plane appeared, despite urgent signals from the ground troops. The Air Force had laid down strict instructions that all requests for air support had to be made at least twelve hours before it was required; here the need was pressing and had to be met within minutes, not hours."[12]

Admiral Hewitt was sharply critical of the U.S. Army Air Forces. He said, "The weakest link in the joint planning of the U.S. forces was the almost complete lack of participation of the Air Force. . . . Contacts with the Air Force were maintained with difficulty and information of the development of the Air Plan was unknown to either the army ground forces or the Navy. Eventually an Air Plan was promulgated but it was found to be completely unrelated to the Military Attack Plan and the Navy Attack Plan. . . . It contained detailed data on Air Force equipment and supplies to be landed over the beaches, but gave no specific information to the Naval and Military commanders of what support might be expected during the assault or what, when, or where fighter cover would be provided." Only on rare occasions did Army Air Forces planes arrive when and where they were most needed; the enemy's tank attacks at Gela was not one of those occasions.[13]

■ ■ ■

The bravest of the brave were the unarmed doctors and medics, including the 505th's regimental surgeon, Maj. Dan McIlvoy, who had high praise for Capt. Alexander "Pete" Suer, a Jewish dentist from Philadelphia who could speak some German. "He would plaster a jeep with Red Cross flags and carry German wounded to the front lines and swap them for our American boys who were also wounded."

During the battle for Biazza Ridge, Captain Suer also commandeered a captured Italian ambulance to take the wounded back to the beachhead so they could be transported to one of the hospital ships. He himself was wounded and evacuated.[14]

Pfc. Murray Goldman, one of McIlvoy's medics, remembered that on 11 July,

> I was told to move up to the vicinity of Biazza Ridge with part of the battalion aid personnel to where part of our battalion was engaged. Major McIlvoy and several others had gone ahead to establish the aid station. When I arrived at the place, I found the entire area under intense mortar, small-arms, and high-velocity artillery fire. However, the aid station was functioning and about twenty to thirty wounded were collected and being treated in a defiladed area in an olive orchard.
>
> Major McIlvoy was present and had procured an Italian truck, which was marked with the Geneva red cross. About this time, a runner appeared

> and excitedly reported that there were many wounded up ahead, exposed to enemy fire. The Major never hesitated; he jumped into the driver's seat of the vehicle and asked for two volunteers to accompany him, as he knew that the mission was extremely hazardous. Crosby and myself were the first aboard and we were off.

Goldman said that they drove into the area being raked by bullets, searching the fields for wounded. "Making a turn in the road, we came face to face with a German Mark VI tank. The Major drove the truck off the road and into a ditch and attempted to turn it around. We were immediately machine-gunned by the tank and several other positions on our flank. The concrete road marker that I was lying behind received a direct hit and the concussion stunned me. I cried out that I had been hit. The Major started toward me and was himself hit in the back by a mortar fragment. Nevertheless, he helped me to my feet and we both started back. We had proceeded about twenty yards when the truck we had used was blown to bits by a direct hit from cannon fire from the tank."

Although wounded, McIlvoy helped Goldman back to the aid station and spent the rest of the day and night supervising the collection, treatment, and evacuation of every injured soldier he could find. "When this job was done, he also supervised and started an evacuation in the city of Vittoria," Goldman said. "We had no transportation. Our medical supplies were only what we brought in by air and carried for the most part on our person; yet no wounded man failed to be evacuated to the rear within a short time after being wounded. Major McIlvoy's sincerity, courage, and devotion to this task was the inspiration with which we accomplished a task that even now seems almost impossible."

After the war Goldman recalled, "In our regiment, when the combat soldiers were awarded Combat Infantry Badges or jump pay, the medics did not receive these badges or extra pay since they were not gun-carrying combatants. The enlisted men of the regiment volunteered to give money out of their own pockets for a so-called combat medic pay, which the medics turned down."[15]

■ ■ ■

From what George Patton could piece together from the various reports coming in to his command center, the invasion seemed to be going as well as could be expected. The Rangers seemed to have quickly gotten control of Gela. Truscott's 3rd Division and elements of Gaffey's 2nd Armored Division were moving inland from their beachhead at Licata. Middleton's inexperienced 45th Division Thunderbirds had landed without too much trouble at Scoglitti—despite some units being deposited at the wrong beach—and had taken the airfield at Comiso. Even the scattered paratroopers were beginning to bring order to the chaos.

But it was the 1st Infantry Division's progress, or lack thereof, that concerned him. Coming ashore after the Rangers, Allen's men seemed to have hit a snag. They were supposed to have driven all the way to the Ponte Olivo airfield by now, but the unexpected counterattack by German and Italian armor had stopped them. They also should have been augmented by their own division artillery and Combat Command B of the 2nd Armored Division, but factors beyond their control were delaying their arrival.

Patton believed deep down that a leader must direct his troops from the front, not from some safe rear area. So, after floating offshore on the *Monrovia* for a day and listening to the invasion's progress through radio reports, Patton decided it was time to go ashore and make a personal reconnaissance of the situation.

Patton was also upset with Hewitt over the previous day's tank fiasco, although his lack of communication with the admiral was just as much to blame as the other way around. "Hewitt is a perfect fool," he wrote in his diary, "but Admiral [Spencer S.] Lewis, his chief of staff, is good. [Am also] having trouble making Hewitt take over prisoners so as to relieve [Army] guards, or move his LSTs, now empty, back for the next load."[16]

Patton, resplendent in his crisply tailored khaki uniform and shiny cavalry boots, with a long cigar clamped between his teeth, swung his legs over the ship's railing and climbed down the rope ladder into Hewitt's barge and set off for Gela, paying no attention to the shells that were still exploding and bullets that were kicking up spouts of water. He was off to do what he could to influence the battle's outcome—or die trying.[17]

Along with his chief of staff, Lt. Gen. Hobart "Hap" Gay, Patton planned to head for the 1st Division's command post a few miles up the Niscemi road and raise holy hell with Allen, but upon learning that Darby's command post was atop one of the tallest buildings in Gela, he decided to make that his first stop.

Darby and Captain Lyle were on the building's roof observing one of the attacks by Italian tanks and German panzers against the Rangers and paratroopers about eight hundred yards to the north. The captured 77-mm Italian guns as well as the 4.2-inch mortars went into action, slowing but not stopping the advance. The situation was becoming critical.

As the two officers pressed their binoculars to their eyes with bullets snapping through the air and shells exploding everywhere, a voice behind them said, "Captain, your chinstrap is unbuckled." As it was the practice to not buckle the strap when incoming artillery fire was expected or being received,* Darby said over his shoulder, "Hell, yes—we always unbuckle the chinstrap when receiving incoming fire."

Then the two men turned around. Standing there was General Patton. Lyle recalled, "With a quick 'Yes, sir,' the chinstrap was secured." Patton then questioned Darby about the situation and was informed that it was rather tenuous. After watching the enemy formation continuing to advance, the general seemed unconcerned. He remarked, "Kill every one of the goddamn bastards," then turned to a nearby naval liaison officer and growled, "Hey, you with the radio, if you can contact your goddamn Navy, tell them for God's sake to drop some shellfire on that road." The officer did as ordered, and soon a blizzard of shells blanketed the line of advancing tanks and troops who were as vulnerable as George Pickett's men at Gettysburg.

Lyle recalled, "When this curtain lifted enemy troops could be seen staggering around as if thoroughly dazed."

Shortly thereafter the 1st Battalion of the 41st Armored Infantry Regiment, 2nd Armored Division, arrived to fill the gaps in the forward lines. Patton told the battalion commander, "Colonel, your outfit will make an attack in the very near future. After the attack I want to see blood and guts hanging from every man's bayonet! Do you understand?" Patton then turned and withdrew to his vehicle in an attempt to find Allen.

Once Patton had departed, the lieutenant colonel turned to Darby and asked, "Do you think the general expects my outfit to carry out his instructions?"

---

* The belief was that a buckled chinstrap could decapitate or seriously injure the wearer if a shell went off nearby and the force of concussion yanked it backward.

According to Lyle, "Darby cast a cold eye at him. 'General Patton expects every order he issues to be carried out to the last word.'" Darby then ordered Lyle and his company to enter the impact area and kill or capture any of the enemy still alive. Lyle noted, "In the area where the enemy had been stopped by the Navy, there were human bodies hanging from trees and some blown to bits." Lyle's men also rounded up some four hundred dazed Italian soldiers.[18]

■ ■ ■

As soon as he left Gela, Patton was met by a 3rd Division officer who had made the journey from Licata via the coast road with ten of Gaffey's Sherman tanks. Patton told the officer to tell Gaffey "to close the gap between Gela and the 1st Division and to send a company of tanks to help Darby. This was done. Darby counter-attacked at once to his left and took 500 prisoners. We also destroyed seven [enemy] tanks east of Gela. After I got the situation of the 3rd Division from the officer who had made the trip, General Roosevelt arrived and I talked to him about the failure of the 1st Division to carry its objective last night. The chief reason, as far as I can see, is that the division attacked without anti-tank guns and without moving up their artillery."

Patton was off again to find Allen. "While we were driving down the road we met Allen coming in and halted on a hill. This was about 1530. While we were there fourteen German bombers came over and were attacked by the anti-aircraft." A piece of anti-aircraft shrapnel hit a few yards from Patton and Gay. "During this attack we saw two bombers and one other plane shot down," Patton said. Germans also shelled the road while Patton and Gay were heading west to Gaffey's command post, but they escaped injury.[19]

After Patton returned to the beach, at least twenty-four Ju-88s targeted the Liberty ship SS *Robert Rowan*. At 1710 hours Patton observed as its cargo of fuel and ammunition turned into a spectacular orange ball that sent a huge cloud of ugly gray smoke and pieces of ship high into the sky.[20]

■ ■ ■

Lt. William Campbell, 18th RCT, 1st Division, also witnessed the attack by the Ju-88 bombers as he was approaching Dime Beach at Gela in a landing craft, mechanized (LCM) at about 1545 hours. "They came on a level approach," he recalled, "and they appeared to be flying slowly. An incendiary bomb dropped into the number-one hatch on the [supply ship] *Robert Rowan*—with all that high-octane gasoline and all that ammunition inside. Soon the ship was smoking and the troops abandoned it. They came down the side of the ship and we picked them up in the LCM; we dropped our ramp to help them aboard. Destroyers also came alongside and dropped nets. We picked up all the men. Then the ship blew up and went to the bottom."[21]

Patton recalled, "Before our eyes a tremendous explosion threw white and black clouds several thousand feet into the air. The ship was literally blown in two, but at present writing, some six hours later, the rear half is still afloat. Most, if not all, of the army personnel on board, who numbered only one hundred and fifteen, were saved"—a number that was not correct.[22]

While on the beach Patton also noticed what he said was "the most stupid thing I have ever seen soldiers do. There were about 300 500-pound bombs and seven tons of 20-mm high-explosive shells piled on the sand, and, in between the bombs and boxes of ammunition, these soldiers were digging foxholes. I told them that if they want to save the Graves Registration burials that was a fine thing to do, but otherwise, they'd better dig somewhere else.

"About the time we got through explaining this to them, two bombers came over and strafed the beach, and all the soldiers jumped right back into the same holes they had dug. I continued to walk up and down and soon shamed them into getting up."

Once back aboard the *Monrovia* that evening, Patton recorded in his diary, "This is the first day of the campaign that I think I earned my pay. . . . God certainly watched over me." But he also confided to his diary that he still was not pleased with Terry Allen and the 1st Infantry Division. Something would have to be done.[23]

■ ■ ■

Still, there was grudging appreciation for what Allen and his men had done. Once the beachhead was secure, Omar Bradley commented, "I question whether any other U.S. division could have repelled that charge in time to save the beach from tank penetration. Only the perverse Big Red One with its no less perverse commander was both hard and experienced enough to take that assault in stride. A greener division might easily have panicked and seriously embarrassed the landing."[24]

Allen was fulsome in his praise of the naval support provided by Rear Adm. John L. Hall's Task Force 81: "Hall will always be remembered by the 1st Division for his courageous support of the division in their landing at Gela. He not only landed the division there with maximum efficiency and seamanship but he kept his ships close-in off-shore and gave the division highly effective naval gunfire support. This effective support has not been accomplished without heavy losses in the naval spotter aircraft in Admiral Hall's fleet."[25]

■ ■ ■

On that same day, Truscott's division captured Licata and was heading north toward Campobello, twelve miles away. The enemy had erected barriers and obstacles along the way, only to have them quickly overcome.

Eight miles north of Licata, the 3rd Division's 15th RCT had managed to push up to Favoratta where an act of extraordinary courage took place. When Scottish-born 2nd Lt. Robert Craig was four, his parents immigrated to Toledo, Ohio; a week before Pearl Harbor, he enlisted in the Army, eventually being commissioned a second lieutenant through the officer candidate school. He was then assigned to be a platoon leader in Truscott's division.

On 11 July he and members of his platoon came under fire from a hidden machine-gun emplacement. After three other officers failed to knock out the position, Craig advanced against the gun and killed its three crewmen. A few minutes later, with his unit pinned down again, he ordered his men to withdraw to safety while he tried to find the other enemy machine gun that was delaying his platoon's advance. After spotting it, Craig crawled to within thirty-five yards of the position before being discovered. He became the division's first Medal of Honor recipient. His posthumous citation reads,

> Charging headlong into the furious automatic fire, he reached the gun, stood over it, and killed the three crew members with his carbine. With this obstacle removed, his company continued its advance.

Shortly thereafter, while advancing down the forward slope of a ridge, 2nd Lieutenant Craig and his platoon, in a position devoid of cover and concealment, encountered the fire of approximately 100 enemy soldiers. Electing to sacrifice himself so that his platoon might carry on the battle, he ordered his men to withdraw to the cover of the crest while he drew the enemy fire to himself. With no hope of survival, he charged toward the enemy until he was within 25 yards of them.

Assuming a kneeling position, he killed five and wounded three enemy soldiers. While the hostile force concentrated fire on him, his platoon reached the cover of the crest. 2nd Lieutenant Craig was killed by enemy fire, but his intrepid action so inspired his men that they drove the enemy from the area, inflicting heavy casualties on the hostile force.[26]

■ ■ ■

During the drive, a firefight broke out between Lucian Truscott's 3rd Division and a mixed force of Italians and Germans. Disregarding his safety during the firefight, Truscott said, "I stood in the middle of the road, absorbed in watching the brief action."

Once the skirmish was over, Truscott revisited the battlefield. The torn-up ground was littered with the shattered bodies of men, twisted into silent, grotesque poses. Nearby, smoke and flame drifted into the air from the burning hulks of vehicles. Ancient stone buildings had gaping holes in them. The general observed, "A dozen or more Germans lay dead, a number of wounded were being cared for by American aid men, and several prisoners were being marched off. It was the first time I had seen Germans killed by infantry fire in front-line action."[27]

■ ■ ■

During his second night alone on the battlefield, Lt. Bill Whitman was still hiding beneath a bush, separated from his men and close to a group of Germans. He was terrified when a German soldier lay down to sleep under the same bush where he was hiding. The lieutenant could think of only one solution; when he was certain that the German was sound asleep, he quietly unsheathed his trench knife, clapped his hand over the German's mouth, and plunged the blade into him twice.

> All he did was give a little sigh. I felt his wrist—there was no pulse. I lay back and waited for dawn.
>
> With dawn came a pleasant surprise—the Germans were moving out! I heard the Germans call a name many times and I assumed that it was the dead man's who lay next to me in the bushes. I waited about two hours and then gradually moved slowly out of the bushes. I took my rifle even though it was jammed, and slowly climbed one of the hills.

From his vantage point he looked down and saw American jeeps and troops moving north along a road. The invasion had not failed!

Famished and dehydrated, Whitman was finally able to sneak out of the field where he had been surrounded by enemy forces for more than a day and reunite with his unit. But his adventures—and those of the 45th Division—were not yet over.[28]

■ ■ ■

Lieutenant Colonel Dante Leonardi's 3rd Battalion, 34th Infantry Regiment, 4th Livorno Division, had weathered the steel storm of D-Day plus one, but just barely. The battalion's three companies had all suffered heavy losses without being able to hold onto their meager gains. Despite desperate pleas for reinforcements, no additional troops were available, and by nightfall what was left of the battalion was ordered to fall back to Monte Castelluccio and hold it at all costs.

Outflanked, outnumbered, and nearly out of ammunition, the remnants of Leonardi's battalion tried their best to hold the hill. But hundreds of American shells saturated the position, followed by an infantry attack. Those who survived the firefight were taken prisoner.[29]

■ ■ ■

The German attack around Gela also disintegrated. The combined effects of infantry weapons, 57-mm anti-tank fire, 75-mm Sherman tank fire, and the naval bombardment were too much for Conrath's men and machines to bear; the survivors began pulling back, leaving the detritus of war scattered across the Gela Plain. But it was only a temporary withdrawal; that evening the Germans would try once more, this time with the infantry that had not accompanied the earlier armor attack. Once again, the attack was beaten back.[30]

With the danger to Gela over, Bill Darby set up his command post in a restaurant, where "we found a supply of cognac and champagne. But a visiting staff officer from a higher headquarters commandeered our site. Although the Rangers were ordered out, they figured their cache of spirits hadn't been requisitioned, so they took it with them."[31]

■ ■ ■

Omar Bradley once said that amateurs study tactics; professionals study logistics. That is a truism, for no army (or air force or navy, for that matter) can long sustain operations without an unbroken pipeline of bullets, bombs, boots, bandages, bayonets, food, fuel, flashlights, vehicles, radios, uniforms, tools, spare parts, and all the myriad accoutrements of war. The logistics effort required to support the invasion—all of it either from storage facilities in North Africa or brought by sea from the United States and Britain—was truly staggering. In 1943 alone 9,295,760 tons of all categories of supplies were shipped to Mediterranean ports; as much as half of that amount was allocated for Husky (both for American and British use).[32]

The three American assault beaches received a total of 17,766 dead-weight tons of essential supplies in just the first three days. Over the next few weeks, by ferrying ships back and forth to and from Tunis and Bizerte, hundreds of thousands more tons were delivered to Sicily.[33]

■ ■ ■

As the battle for Gela and Biazza Ridge passed into history, a disaster of major proportions was about to take place in the skies above Sicily.

10

DISASTER IN THE SKY

If they want a goat, I am it.

—George S. Patton Jr.

There is nothing "friendly" about "friendly fire" incidents, as Patton well knew. He had had his own brush with death at the hands of nervous American anti-aircraft gunners on 9 December 1942 while flying into Algiers to meet with Eisenhower, and he sensed that the same thing could happen with Husky II.[1]

As early as 3 July, Patton began worrying that, while the 505th PIR's airborne drop in the early morning hours of 10 July might surprise enemy forces, a subsequent drop by the 504th twenty-four hours later—Husky II—could receive a blistering reception.

Commanding the 504th PIR was thirty-one-year-old Col. Reuben H. Tucker III, described by Jim Gavin as "a tough, superb combat leader . . . probably the best regimental commander of the war."[2] Husky II would involve the 1st and 2nd Battalions of the 504th PIR, minus the 3rd that had been attached to the 505th. They were scheduled to drop onto the DZ previously secured by Gavin's men and then be ready to halt expected enemy incursions toward the Gela beachhead.

The 82nd Airborne Division's commander, Maj. Gen. Matthew Ridgway, was also concerned. He had come ashore with the seaborne troops on D-Day and was waiting for Gavin's men to arrive at their objective, the Farello airfield, near Gela. They were not to be seen. He had been previously concerned about the possibility of his troops being scattered in the dark, and now it seemed that his worst fears were coming true. He had tried to ensure that the Navy's ships, bristling with anti-aircraft weapons, would provide the transports carrying the two battalions of the 504th a clear corridor through which to pass.

Historian Martin Blumenson noted, "Naval commanders were reluctant to guarantee this access, for anti-aircraft gunners had to respond quickly to planes appearing suddenly, particularly at low altitudes." Ridgway finally got that assurance, but only if the planes flew precisely along a predesignated route, "with the last leg of that route over land." The course was worked out and the information provided to Patton and Hewitt.

But on the morning of 11 July, there was still much uncertainty as to whether the Navy had gotten the information and disseminated it to all ships. Patton had sent messages to all his division commanders as well as to Bradley, in command of II Corps: "You will warn your command to expect flights of friendly troops. Flights will pass between 2230 and 2400 hours approximately, length of flight [over Sicily] approximately forty minutes. Flights will drop parachutists or release gliders. Advise respective naval commanders." To ensure all division commanders received it, the message was even brought ashore by hand.[3]

But just before Husky II was about to lift off that evening, Patton, sensing disaster, tried to contact the air command at Kairouan/Enfidville, Tunisia, to postpone or perhaps even cancel the drop, but he was unable to get through. He wrote in his diary, "Went to office [his quarters on the *Monrovia*] at 2000 to see if we could stop the 82nd Airborne lift, as enemy ground attacks were heavy [during the day] and inaccurate Army and Navy anti-air [gunners] were jumpy. Found we could not get contact by radio. Am terribly worried."[4]

American anti-aircraft gunners on both land and sea were worried, too—but not about American troop transports overflying the Bay of Gela. All day long on 11 July—beginning early in the morning and continuing throughout the afternoon and evening—the Luftwaffe and Regia Aeronautica flew sorties—five hundred of them—against targets in the Seventh Army area alone. The naval gunners were in no mood to regard any planes overflying their areas to be friendly—even if they had received the messages about the impending arrival of American planes. Screw the orders—better to shoot first and ask questions later, many of them no doubt thought. To make matters worse, there seemed to be no effort by the U.S. Army Air Forces to drive enemy planes away.

Late on 11 July another enemy aerial attack had just swept across Hewitt's American fleet sitting like ducks offshore. Samuel Morison wrote, "Within a few minutes the German air attack swirled like a cyclone into the Cent area. Four flares dropped near Admiral Kirk's flagship. Pandemonium broke loose. Everybody let go, several men in *Ancon* [ACG 4] were injured by other ships' flak, and [the destroyer] *Anthony* [DD 515] shot down a bomber flying low across her bow, heading for [the cruiser] *Philadelphia*."[5]

As if planned with precision timing, as soon as the last German plane departed, the C-47 and C-53 transport planes carrying Tucker's paratroopers approached. At 2315 hours Admiral Kirk alerted all his ships in Task Force 85 that the paratrooper-carrying planes were about to arrive and to refrain from firing at anything in the sky. His message read, "Do not—repeat—do not shoot toward the beach unless you have a definite target, as friendly paratroopers are landing from friendly planes." But the gunners, still sweating from the German air attack minutes earlier, could not be persuaded to hold their fire—even if ordered to do so by an admiral.[6]

■ ■ ■

After making their left turn at the southeast corner of Sicily, the C-47s headed west and crossed the coast at Sampieri, southeast of Gela and Scoglitti. The first wave's mission, dropping paratroopers at the German-constructed Farello airfield, happened without incident at 2240 hours. But as the second wave approached the shoreline, guns below opened up on the unarmed transports that could be heard but not seen in the all-enveloping darkness.[7]

Aboard one of the ships was gunner Gordon Manley. He recalled, "Ships had been warned that American transport planes carrying parachutists would be flying over . . . but twenty minutes before they arrived German bombers made an attack. It was while this attack was being fought off, with great difficulty because of the dense smoke, that the transport aircraft arrived. They were right in the middle of the action before the naval gunners realized they were there. Most of the transports flew round the smoke thinking it was a cloud, but others coming in below it were confused with German aircraft, and these were the ones that were mistakenly shot down."[8]

Friendly fire wasn't just coming from ships; gunners on the ground were also guilty. "The anti-aircraft fire we jumped into was from the 180th Infantry of the 45th Division," said 504th jumpmaster 1st Lt. C. A. Drew. "They had not been told we were coming; later we learned that the Divisional Headquarters had been warned, but word never had got to the 180th infantry. . . . We jumped into a steady stream of anti-aircraft fire. . . . There were four men killed and four wounded from my platoon. Three of them were hit coming down and one was killed on the ground because he had the wrong password." Other paratroopers also suffered a similar fate when they gave the wrong password.[9]

The Thunderbirds were heartsick when they later discovered what they had accidentally done. George Fisher, the 180th's official historian, noted, "It was a dreadful night, and one felt it all the more when he realized that Americans had killed Americans. Gradually it sank in. Those planes going down were not German planes—they were American planes shot down by Americans. The feeling it gave one was so utterly sickening as to defy description. . . . As if to provide light for the tragedy in the olive groves, a huge comet-like blazing object roared in out of the southern sky and crashed into the Anti-Tank bivouac area." It was a C-47 full of paratroopers. In addition to those on board who died a fiery death, two men of the anti-tank unit on the ground were killed.[10]

Near Gela, 1st Infantry Division Sgt. Harley Reynolds watched in horror as the tragedy unfolded above him: "Many planes were hit and began to fall from the sky, either in flames or just exploding and falling in pieces. We could see bodies falling alongside the planes. One plane in particular we saw falling in flames as men fell with their planes."[11]

Omar Bradley, commanding II Corps, was already on the ground in Sicily, having come ashore earlier in the day. He recalled, "Suddenly somewhere in that vast darkness a lone gun fired into the sky. And while I looked on helplessly from Scoglitti, the sky exploded in A-A fire. Soon spent fragments of A-A shells clattered on our tile roof. Like a covey of quail the formation split as pilots twisted their ships to escape . . . parachutists tumbled out of the twisting aircraft. Some landed on the division fronts where they were mistaken for German raiders and shot while hanging in harness."[12]

Within the transports, paratroopers were screaming unheard above the roaring of the planes' engines and the explosions outside. Some planes filled with white silk as jagged splinters of shrapnel sliced apart the parachute-deployment bags. The flying munitions also punctured non-sealing fuel tanks, turning some planes and the men inside them into torches.

Planes fell like autumn leaves, plunging into the sea or onto the rocky island. In some crippled planes, the pilots flipped the red standby lights to green, and the paratroopers who were able to stood up, hooked their parachutes to the static line, and shuffled to the door and began piling out regardless of whether they were anywhere near their assigned drop zones.[13]

Lt. Robert A. Uhrig, piloting one of the C-47s in the 316th Troop Carrier Group, 36th Troop Carrier Squadron, was carrying a twenty-man stick of paratroopers when bullets began piercing the aircraft's thin aluminum skin, ripping through the men inside. He wrote later in his diary,

> When we flew over the drop point, some of the paratroopers had been wounded, but most of them jumped anyway. One was hit so hard in the leg that he had to crawl to the door, but still jumped.
>
> Another one was also hit in the leg and his boot was so full of blood it was running over when he jumped. The only ones that did not jump were the ones wounded so badly they could not get to the door.[14]

Of the 144 planes flying the mission, 23 were shot out of the sky, killing 318 American paratroopers and air crewmen. Colonel Tucker's plane, which missed the drop zone the first time and had to double back, had more than two thousand holes in it by the time the men in it were able to bail out near Gela.[15]

When the surviving C-47s returned to their Tunisian airfields, four dead and six wounded paratroopers were aboard them. Also arriving back at Kairouan were eight planes full of disappointed paratroopers who, for various reasons, had not had the opportunity to jump.[16]

One of Gavin's officers who witnessed the tragedy was Maj. Mark Alexander, commander of the 505th PIR's 2nd Battalion. He and his troops had been mistakenly dropped southeast of Gela on 10 July. Now he recalled,

> After dark when we hit the coast road again, we could see the invasion armada in the water off Gela. From our strung-out position along the coast road, we saw two German bombers fly in, bomb the fleet, and fly off. I'd say about two minutes behind them came forty-eight C-47s carrying the rest of the 504th paratroopers. They came in at roughly the same altitude and from the same direction as the German bombers.
>
> The Navy opened fire. From where I was, I could see the planes were our own, but the Navy got excited and just kept shooting. Finally they stopped, but they had knocked down twenty-three planes. Some of them were able to make a hard landing on Sicily, but a whole bunch of men were killed. Even the 45th Division got in on the shooting. They thought the Germans were attacking.[17]

One of those 45th Division men was Kenneth D. Williamson, a machine-gunner in Company D, 179th Regiment, standing guard duty inland near Scoglitti. He vividly recalled the night of 11 July: "Things got hot and heavy—more planes, more ack-ack. The sky was filled with tracers. Crossfire was so magnificent that some of the tracers were impinging onto each other in the air. And the fire was effective—planes were getting hit, coming down in flames and exploding on the ground. One after another they came down."

Williamson later learned that the planes were American, not German. "Sure enough, there were paratroopers falling in our area—but they were our own paratroopers! Those magnificent guns had been shooting down our own force. No one had realized when the Germans stopped coming and the Americans started coming!"[18]

■ ■ ■

The 52nd Troop Carrier Wing of the Army Air Forces also suffered. They lost seven men killed, thirty wounded, and fifty-three missing.[19] The 82nd Airborne's assistant division commander, Brig. Gen. Charles L. Keerans Jr., was on board a plane that ditched at sea four hundred yards off the Gela beachhead. He survived the crash relatively unhurt and apparently made it to shore on the evening of 11 July, where he spoke with a sergeant from another unit. The two men separated and Keerans was never seen again. For years, Keerans was assumed to have died in the ditching, but the sergeant's story provided a different interpretation; however, his body was never found.[20]

Coast Guard Seaman Maurice Poulin, manning a 20-mm gun on the troop transport USS *Leonard Wood* (APA 12), recalled, "We had been under attack by German dive bombers. We did not know our paratroop planes were coming. We had orders to elevate guns seventy-five degrees and fire when attacked. We shot down many planes but had no knowledge whose they were."[21]

Paratrooper Spencer Wurst of the 505th PIR recalled, "Although I was unaware of it then, a major event in the Sicily operation concerning our sister regiment, the 504th PIR, had thrown the entire future of airborne warfare into question. To come over the beaches, the Air Corps had to fly over the naval convoy. The Navy had received strict orders that there be no firing. Maybe the word did not get all the way down, or the anti-aircraft gunners on the ships got nervous. Either way, they opened fire on the low-flying troop transport planes."[22]

Lt. George Merz, the pilot whose C-47 had ditched into the sea near Scoglitti a day earlier, had been evacuated to an offshore LCI. He recalled that on 11 July, while aboard the LCI that had rescued him, "At about 11 p.m., it was pretty dark and the Germans were attacking. They dropped magnesium flares and a string of bombs and sank about three vessels . . . and then the beachmaster [on the LCI] told everybody that enemy paratroopers were dropping behind our lines. . . . Then about fifteen minutes later, here came these planes at low altitude. Someone started shooting first, and then everybody started shooting. No one seemed to recognize them as C-47s."

Merz had recognized the earlier raiders as German Ju-88s, a twin-engine bomber with a silhouette vaguely similar to the C-47. "So almost everybody started shooting at our airplanes. A couple went over, white stars [painted on the wings and fuselage] in plain sight. One ditched behind us. . . . I went up on the bridge and told the LCI captain, 'Hey, you're shooting down our airplanes,' and he ordered me off the bridge."

The next morning the sea between the LCI and the beach was a forest of C-47 tails sticking out of the water. A Navy ensign on the LCI apologized to Merz, but the captain, perhaps embarrassed, never spoke to him again.[23]

■ ■ ■

Lt. Avis Dagit Schorer, a U.S. Army nurse working in the 56th Evacuation Hospital in Bizerte, Tunisia, remembered the stream of patients flowing in after the disaster of Husky II:

> Hospital ships arrived in the Bizerte harbor daily with wounded from the fighting in Sicily. We had American, British, Italian, and German patients. . . . The officer on my ward called the nurses and wardmen together shortly after the fighting started there.
>
> "I want to remind you that we give our finest care to everyone," he said. "It does not matter if they are American, other allies, civilians, or prisoners."
>
> One group of Americans was especially angry about their needless wounds. They were paratroopers flown in to support the ground forces.
>
> "Our own Navy shot us down," said a captain bitterly. He had both legs in casts and many shell fragments still in his body.
>
> "Maybe they couldn't tell the planes were American," I said, trying to ease his bitterness.
>
> "We were flying low in C-47s. Any idiot should be able to tell them from enemy planes."[24]

■ ■ ■

Adm. H. Kent Hewitt claimed afterward that he did not know about the 82nd's second scheduled airborne drop until he was at sea, by which time the mandated radio silence prevented him from voicing any concerns or objections. Brig. Gen. Paul L. Williams, commander of the Northwest African Air Force Troop Carrier Command (Provisional), scoffed at that excuse, saying that the Navy was informed of the second drop six days in advance of takeoff.[25]

■ ■ ■

Ike's aide, Harry Butcher, wrote, "When we reached our Advance Command Post headquarters in Pinto Tunnel [on Malta], Ike learned to his great chagrin and consternation of a report that twenty-three of our air troop carriers . . . had been shot down over American lines in Sicily. Immediately he dispatched a hot message to General Patton, demanding a quick report. This tragedy cast a pall of gloom over an otherwise interesting and fruitful day."[26]

Patton wrote in his diary that he had been blistered in a wire from Eisenhower that demanded

> a full investigation and statement of punishments for those guilty of firing on [the American transports]. It is my opinion that every possible precaution was taken by this headquarters to obviate firing on our own airborne troops and that the failure to do so was an unavoidable incident of combat. . . . As far as I can see, if anyone is blameable, it must be myself, but personally I feel immune from censure.
>
> Perhaps Ike is looking for an excuse to relieve me. I am having a full report made but will not try anyone [by court-martial]. If they want a goat, I am it. Fortunately, [John] Lucas, [Albert] Wedemeyer, and [Joseph] Swing [the commander of the 11th Airborne Division who was in theater to personally view the 82nd's drop] are here and know the facts. . . . Men who have been bombed all day get itchy fingers. Ike has never been subjected to air attack or any other form of death. However, he is such a straw man that his future is secure. The British will never let him go.

No one was ever court-martialed for the incident.[27]

Interestingly, Eisenhower mentioned the British "Ladbroke" glider tragedy in his memoirs, *Crusade in Europe*, but wrote not a word about the American friendly fire airborne incident against the 504th PIR, nor his unhappiness with Patton over it.[28] Patton's aide, Charles Codman, who had been an aviator in World War I, said nothing about it, either.

■ ■ ■

The Axis side was rapidly reacting to the Allied incursion. *Panzertruppe* Gen. Fridolin von Senger und Etterlin, the German liaison officer with Guzzoni's Sixth Army, roared down the dusty roads from his headquarters in Enna to get a glimpse of the invasion for himself. When he arrived at a hill being bombarded about five miles north of Gela and saw the massive America armada off the coast, he realized that Sicily would soon fall to the Allies.[29]

As tragic as the 504th PIR's drop had been, there was no time to stop and mourn. The next phase of Operation Husky needed to move into high gear.

British Eighth Army commander Bernard Montgomery and George Patton ride together in a command car. Their relationship was often contentious. NARA

U.S. Eighth Fleet commander Vice Adm. H. Kent Hewitt (*left*) and Rear Adm. Alan Kirk, commander of Task Force 85 NARA

USS *Monrovia*, Hewitt's flagship for the Sicily invasion *NARA*

American soldiers jump off an amphibious DUKW truck as an LST burns after being attacked by enemy bombers at Gela, 10 July 1943. *NARA*

American vehicles and supplies come ashore at Gela, 12 July 1943. The vehicles exiting the LST are utilizing a new American invention—the pontoon causeway. *NARA*

A German tank lies destroyed on the Gela Plain after a failed attempt to drive American forces back into the sea on 11 July 1943. Naval gunfire proved to be decisive in saving the beachhead. *NARA*

Waving white flags, residents of Palermo greet American troops and 2nd Armored Division tanks as they enter the city on 22 August 1943. *NARA*

Because the retreating Germans had destroyed existing bridges along the north coast highway, Army engineers rapidly built temporary wooden structures so the pursuit could continue. *NARA*

General Patton talks with Lt. Col. Lyle W. Bernard, 3rd Infantry Division, a few days after Bernard's amphibious landing and battle at Brolo on Sicily's north shore, 11 August 1943. *NARA*

A burial party, with civilian and POW help, lays to rest an American soldier killed in the fighting around Fratello, August 1943. *NARA*

Driving between shattered buildings and a dead horse, Patton and his entourage tour Messina, 17 August 1943. *NARA*

A view of the temporary American military cemetery at Gela. After the war, the remains of the fallen soldiers were reinterred at the new Sicily-Rome American Cemetery at Anzio-Nettuno, Italy. *NARA*

11

MASSACRE AT BISCARI

Nothing can be done about it.

—George S. Patton Jr.

On 12 July—D-Day plus two—a major change of command was made to the American side. Rear Adm. H. Kent Hewitt was relieved of his duties as commander of American naval forces at Sicily. He headed to Malta to receive a new assignment: command of a reconstituted Western Naval Task Force that would conduct the amphibious landings and fire-support missions for Operation Avalanche, the invasion of Italy at Salerno scheduled for 8–9 September 1943.

It seems extraordinary that the commander of a heavily Navy-dependent operation such as Husky would be removed just two days into it for reasons other than health or dereliction of duty, yet the historical records show nothing that would indicate that the change was anything but administrative. It also seems—at least publicly—to have had nothing to do with the Navy's accidental shooting down of American planes on 11 July. Furthermore, Patton had said nothing about wanting Hewitt to be replaced because of the personality clashes the two men had had, and the admiral did not indicate that he requested the transfer to get away from the general whom he always seemed to irritate.[1]

Rear Adm. Richard Lansing Conolly, commander of Task Force 86, was installed as Hewitt's successor—a move that pleased Patton. Conolly, U.S.

Naval Academy class of 1914, was born in 1892 in Waukegan, Illinois, and had distinguished himself well before Husky. In August 1918 as a lieutenant aboard the destroyer USS *Smith*, he and eight others were sent as a salvage party to the transport USS *Westbridge*, which had been disabled by a German torpedo. The group remained on board and risked their lives for five days "steering by hand and handling the lines from the tugs while the ship was towed 400 miles to port." For this action, he received the Navy Cross—the U.S. Navy's highest award.

Conolly had also commanded destroyers during the bombardment of Wake Island immediately after Pearl Harbor in December 1941. In April 1942 he was in command of Destroyer Squadron 6 that escorted the USS *Hornet* on its voyage to carry Jimmy Doolittle's B-25 bombers to their historic raid on Japan. In March 1943 he was transferred from the Pacific to the Mediterranean to take part in Operation Husky.

During his time in the Pacific, he earned the nickname "Close-In Conolly" for his insistence that fire-support ships should be extremely close to the beach during amphibious assaults, believing that enemy fortifications could be neutralized only by direct hits from the shortest possible range. He followed his own dictum during his support of the 3rd Infantry Division at Joss Beach.

A better replacement for Hewitt would be hard to imagine.[2]

■ ■ ■

As the Yanks were mopping up the last vestiges of enemy resistance north of Gela, an incident occurred during the battle for the Biscari–Santo Pietro airfield, located atop a plateau ten miles north of Scoglitti. In July 1943 the airfield had the misfortunate to lie in the path of the 45th Infantry Division.

The airfield was home to the Regia Aeronautica's 504 Gruppo and was ringed by stout walls and pillboxes built low to the ground. The attacking Americans—Lt. Col. William "King Kong" Schaefer's 1st Battalion, 180th Regiment—correctly assumed that the airfield was heavily defended, but they did not know if the Italians would fight or surrender. Nor did they know that a company of German Tiger tanks and two infantry battalions from the Hermann Göring Panzer Division were also stationed there.

The attack had been launched on 10 July, and Schaefer's outnumbered men quickly discovered themselves in an untenable position, hammered by machine guns, tank rounds, mortars, and artillery that forced the battalion to withdraw south of Highway 115. Schaefer, who had been injured during a practice amphibious landing at Oran, found himself and two other officers surrounded in a culvert with no chance of escape; the three men were taken prisoner. (Schaefer would sit out the war as a German prisoner of war [POW] in the infamous Colditz castle near Leipzig.)

The Germans dropped their full arsenal on the Americans, including raids by strafing aircraft. After suffering heavy casualties—and the loss of Schaefer—Maj. Roger S. Denman took over command of the battalion. Then Denman was wounded, and his place was taken by another officer who also became a casualty.[3]

There were hundreds of extraordinary acts of individual heroism performed by the Thunderbirds before the airfield objective was finally taken on 14 July—four days after the battle for it started. But two terrible war crimes were about to take place.

■ ■ ■

On the morning of 14 July Sgt. Horace T. West, a cook with Company A, 180th, was directed to escort a group of two German POWs and forty-five Italian men from the 153th Machine-Gun Battalion to the rear for interrogation.

One report of the incident said, "After marching the POWs a mile, West halted the group and selected eight or nine to report to the regimental intelligence officer [for interrogation]. He then borrowed a Thompson sub-machine gun from his company's first sergeant and told him he was going to kill the 'sons of bitches.' He instructed his comrades to 'turn around if you don't want to see it.' West then murdered the disarmed POWs at close range, reloaded, and began firing single shots into the hearts of the POWs still moving." Supposedly West's motive was revenge—he had earlier witnessed three German soldiers take two captured American soldiers into a bunker and murder them.[4]

The next day, 15 July, the bodies decomposing in the sun caught the attention of a 45th Division chaplain, Lt. Col. William E. King, who reported what he saw to Lt. Col. William O. Perry, the division's inspector general.[5]

■ ■ ■

Later that same day at a different part of the airfield, thirty-six Italians surrendered after an intense firefight. Capt. John T. Compton of Tulsa, Oklahoma, the commanding officer of Company C, 1st Battalion, 180th RCT, was furious and frustrated that he had been unable to overcome the opposition; a dozen Company C men were wounded in the attempt. Compton was also angry because enemy snipers had earlier shot at his medics who went to help the wounded—a violation of the Geneva Convention.

A speech that Patton had given in Oran on 27 June also stuck in Compton's mind. The general had told the assembled Thunderbird officers to watch out for dirty tricks; it was not uncommon, he said, for the enemy to pretend to surrender. A favorite tactic was for a small group to drop their weapons and emerge into the open with their arms raised. When the Americans came forward to take prisoners, the "surrendering" soldiers would hit the dirt and the rest of their comrades, still in hiding behind them, would mow down the exposed GIs. Patton warned the officers to always be on their guard for this sort of treachery and to show no mercy if the enemy attempted this trick.[6]

At the airfield, as the thirty-six Italians, some in civilian attire, stepped into the open, Compton had an interpreter ask if they were snipers; no one answered. At that Compton assembled a twenty-four-man firing squad, lined up the POWs, and ordered the firing squad to kill them all from six feet away.[7]

Neither Compton nor West was a grizzled war veteran who had spent months on the front lines watching his buddies being blown to bits; they had been in combat for exactly four days. They were new to war and to killing, unlike the battle-hardened SS troops who murdered their way through towns and villages on the Eastern Front during Germany's Operation Barbarossa in 1941. An American lieutenant testified at Compton's court-martial that the Germans were not above committing atrocities, and that such conduct was far from unusual. He told of an incident when his driver was tied to a tree and shot by members of the Hermann Göring Division. "Then we encountered another German trick," he said. "They would rise without weapons, waving their hands in the air and shouting '*Kamerad!*' Then, when we went to round them up, they would fall flat and other Germans, concealed behind them, would open up on us. We lost many men due to this. Casualties were severe, and the procedure of taking prisoners was abandoned by both sides."

The two massacres went unreported for three more days and the battle for Sicily went on, but Patton's reputation soon would be stained by the Biscari incidents.

■ ■ ■

On 15 July reports of the massacres reached Omar Bradley, who immediately went to see Patton, who had just written a letter to Beatrice: "As you will have seen by the papers, we did it again and are attacking right now," he told her, "and having quite a war. . . . The enemy has been booby trapping his dead, which has made our men very mad, with the result that there are more enemy dead than usual. Yesterday I drove over one of our local battlefields and smelled dead men for some ten miles. It is a very strong disgusting odor. Our losses have been relatively small, but we have lost some good men."[8]

Patton seemed unconcerned with the accounts of what had happened at the Biscari airfield, dismissing them as "probably an exaggeration, but in any case to tell the officer [Compton] to certify that the dead men were snipers or had attempted to escape or something, as it would make a stink in the press and also would make the civilians mad. Anyhow, they are dead and nothing can be done about it."[9] He did, however, order that West and Compton be court-martialed.[10] Then the incidents were forgotten by Patton, as he returned his attention to the ongoing battle for Sicily.

During the investigation into the execution, Compton said in his defense, "George S. Patton, in a speech to assembled officers, stated that in the case where the enemy was shooting to kill our troops and then when we came close enough on him to get him, decided to quit fighting, he must die. Those men had been shooting at us to kill and had not marched up to us to surrender. They had been surprised and routed, putting them, in my belief, in the category of the General's statement."

At his general court-martial, Compton testified that he remembered Patton's exact words to a group of officers prior to Husky:

> When we land against the enemy, don't forget to hit him and hit him hard. We will bring the fight home to him. We will show him no mercy. He

> has killed thousands of your comrades, and he must die. If you company officers in leading your men against the enemy find him shooting at you and, when you get within 200 yards of him and he wishes to surrender, oh no! That bastard will die! You will kill him. Stick him between the third and fourth ribs. You will tell your men that. They must have the killer instinct. Tell them to stick him. He can do no good then. Stick them in the liver. . . .
>
> When word reaches [the enemy] that he is being faced by a killer battalion, a killer outfit, he will fight less. Particularly, we must build up that name as killers and you will get that down to your troops in time for the invasion.

Other witnesses testifying at the trial recalled Patton saying essentially the same thing.[11]

■ ■ ■

Several lesser-known atrocities were also committed by the invading Americans. On 10 July, according to Sicilian historian Giovanni Bartolone, a group of civilians were evacuating Biscari by car, heading toward nearby Vittoria. Among the refugees in the vehicle were Biscari's mayor, Giuseppe Mangano, his wife Carmela, teenaged son Salvatore, and four others. A group of soldiers from an unknown unit (possibly the 505th PIR) stopped the car and ordered everyone out. The soldiers, supposedly drunk, began to hit the civilians, and when the civilians started to fight back, they were shot and killed.

Another mass killing took place on 13 July in the farm community of Piano Stella di Caltagirone, a few miles from the Biscari airfield. A civilian known as Fiore was said to have shot and killed a paratrooper who dropped in front of his home. Seven men who had not committed any hostile acts toward the Americans were rounded up and machine-gunned to death; Fiore was not among them. An American attempt to hide the bodies and a complaint to the Carabinieri followed, but no one was held accountable.

A third massacre of civilians took place at Canicatti, near Agrigento, on 14 July. It began when reports of looting by civilians of a food depot and a soap factory were made to the city hall. An American lieutenant and fourteen military police (MPs) were sent to investigate; they managed to arrest about thirty or forty looters, many of them desperately hungry women and children.

Lt. Col. George Herbert McCaffrey, a civil affairs officer, appeared on the scene and directed the MPs to shoot the looters; the MPs refused. So McCaffrey pulled out his pistol and began firing into the group at point-blank range, killing at least eight. McCaffrey was later appointed military governor of Palermo and was never brought to account for his actions at Canicatti.[12]

It is unknown whether Patton was informed about these three additional atrocities. At any rate, his attention was diverted by a new development that had just occurred—one that would alter the course of the campaign.

12

RECONNAISSANCE IN FORCE

I really feel like a great general today.

—George S. Patton Jr.

Much had been accomplished in the few days following D-Day. Patton's Seventh Army had established three beachheads; defeated German and Italian armored attempts to drive them back into the sea; fought off repeated aerial attacks; captured the Comiso, Ponte Olivo, and Biscari airfields; and were now starting to drive into the interior of Sicily, pushing the enemy before them. Casualties, while heavy in places, had not been as bad as feared. Thousands of prisoners—mostly Italian—had been taken.

The U.S. Navy, save for the friendly fire disaster on 11 July, had also performed well. Fire support from cruisers and destroyers had stopped Axis attempts to crush the invasion at the water's edge, and the delivery of crucial supplies was unprecedented; by D-Day plus three, more than 66,000 American troops had been moved ashore, along with 17,766 tons of cargo and 7,396 vehicles. Two-thirds of an airborne division had been dropped.[1]

Not everything was sunshine and roses in the American camp, however. Despite their supposed friendship, Patton continued to rub Omar Bradley the wrong way. Bradley also sensed that many of the Seventh Army soldiers were growing tired of Patton's grandstanding and displays of pomposity. He wrote,

> To his troops, an Army commander is little more than a distant figure who occasionally shows himself on the front. As a consequence the impressions of those men are formed directly from what they see.
>
> George irritated them by flaunting the pageantry of his command. He traveled in an entourage of command cars followed by a string of nattily uniformed staff officers. His own vehicle was gaily decked with oversize stars and the insignia of his command. These exhibitions did not awe the troops as perhaps Patton believed. Instead, they offended the men as they trudged through the clouds of dust left in the wake of that procession. In Sicily Patton the man bore little resemblance to Patton the legend.[2]

■ ■ ■

Suddenly a gigantic monkey wrench was shoved into the works by none other than Patton's British nemesis, Bernard Law Montgomery. Seeing his Eighth Army's drive spearheaded by Miles C. Dempsey's XIII Corps running into stiffer-than-expected resistance on the way to Catania, Monty decided that he would rather have Oliver Leese's experienced XXX Corps protecting his left flank than the green American 45th Division.

Studying a map, Monty saw that a series of highways ran northward from Caltagirone and around the west side of Mount Etna, then angled to the northeast through Nicosia, Troina, and Bronte, ultimately ending up at the Allies' goal—Messina. He ordered Leese to take that route; he would tell Alexander—who usually did what Monty wanted—to tell Patton that the 45th Division, which was at that moment traveling up Highway 124 from Caltagirone toward Caltanisetta, must turn over that highway to XXX Corps.

On 13 July Patton got the bad news when he met with Alexander and members of his staff. "They gave us the future plan of operations, which cuts us off from any possibility of taking Messina," Patton steamed in his diary. "It is noteworthy that Alexander, the Allied commander of a British and American Army, had no Americans with him [at the meeting]. What fools we are."[3]

So the switch was made. Patton, who probably could have appealed to Eisenhower but didn't, was furious. But he quickly came up with something to salvage American pride: "I asked General Alexander's permission to advance and take Agrigento [twenty-five miles northwest of Licata], which is beyond the line specified for the front of the Seventh Army. He stated that if this could be done through the use of limited forces, in the nature of a reconnaissance in force, he had no objection."

Just what constituted a "reconnaissance in force" is open to conjecture—a company, a battalion, a regiment, a division, several divisions? Since Alexander didn't specify the size, Patton would use his discretion. Studying his own maps, he saw that he could probably also capture Porto Empedocle, a short distance from Agrigento; Palermo, the island's capital and a prize worth taking, was just sixty miles straight north from there. In addition, he could resupply Seventh Army through Porto Empedocle and other ports along the west coast rather than having to rely on the port at Syracuse in the British zone.

Patton boldly embarked upon his new plan. He told Bradley to pull the 45th back and around the 1st Division's left flank, then have both divisions head north. If Montgomery and Alexander were going to give him the freedom to take his mobile columns through wide-open country, that's exactly what he would do.[4]

Patton then concocted another idea—to form a Provisional III Corps under Geoffrey Keyes made up of the 3rd Infantry Division, 82nd Airborne, the Ranger Force, and a regiment of the 9th Infantry Division that was due to arrive shortly, sweep the western half of the island, then go like hell for Palermo. After taking the capital, Seventh Army could turn east and make a run for Messina along the north coast. If all went well, he might even be able to beat the Eighth Army to Husky's most important objective.[5] He would have Conolly's naval forces support the Provisional Corps' drive by landing troops and equipment on the western coast and shelling the enemy whenever necessary.

■ ■ ■

On 17 July, with Axis fortunes faltering, Germany chose to reinforce its presence on Sicily. *Panzertruppe* Gen. Hans-Valentin Hube—an experienced, highly decorated commander whose units had taken part in the invasions of Poland, France, the Netherlands, and the Soviet Union—arrived with his XIV Panzer Corps headquarters staff to take command of all German forces on the island and, shortly thereafter, all Italian forces as well.

Bolstering the German lines was the arrival of the 1st Parachute Regiment, 1st *Fallschirmjäger* (Airborne) Division, flown in from Italy; their timely drop helped to quash British attempts to take the Primosole Bridge north of Syracuse. Another division was also brought in—the 29th Panzer Grenadier. Hitler doubted that two more divisions would be enough to turn the tide of battle, but perhaps they could slow the Allies' drive long enough to give heart to the Italians and make possible the evacuation of Axis forces from the island. Hube quickly set about establishing a series of defensive lines designed to stall the Allies' twin advances toward Messina and buy time for the escape. According to Albert Kesselring, "Hube was the right man at the right place."[6]

■ ■ ■

Also on 17 July Churchill messaged Eisenhower: "Further congratulations on the unfolding success of the Sicilian Campaign. I should be grateful if you would give my compliments to Admiral Hewitt. The weather gave occasion, according to reports made by the Admiralty, for a magnificent display of American seamanship." Of course, Churchill was not yet aware that Hewitt had departed Sicily four days earlier and was in North Africa, helping to plan Operation Avalanche.[7]

■ ■ ■

Patton wasted no time—on 17 July Keyes' new Provisional III Corps on Seventh Army's left flank captured Porto Empedocle and Agrigento (which were out of the range of the *Philadelphia*'s and *Birmingham*'s guns) while Bradley's II Corps on III Corps' right flank took Caltanissetta on 18 July, just short of Highway 121, the main east/west lateral road through the center of Sicily. The march on Palermo had begun.[8] The Seventh Army's successes caused Alexander to make an about-face when it came to his assessment of the combat capabilities of the American soldier. He told a *Life* magazine reporter, "After the fighting they have done, the Americans are fine fighting troops, indeed. There is no comparison between the Americans in Sicily today and the Americans six months ago. They are at least 100% better."[9]

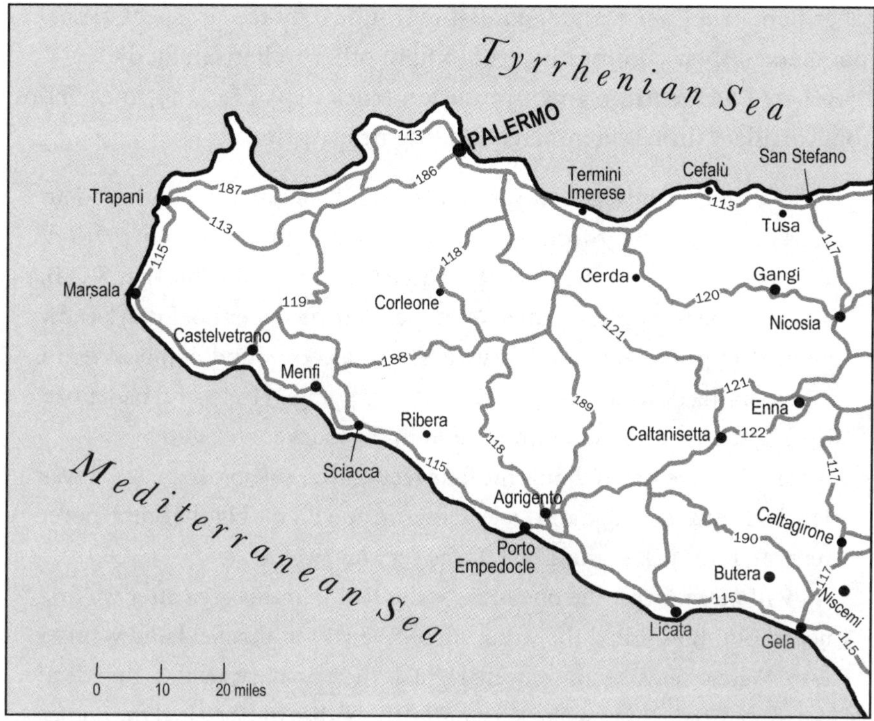

Map 12.1 ▪ Western Sicily, where Patton's "reconnaissance in force" took place during the march on Palermo

One unique advantage the U.S. Army had over the British was the large number of soldiers with Italian heritage who filled the ranks. Many were fluent in the language and could communicate with the Italian soldiers, talk them into surrendering, speak to them like brothers, gain their empathy, and extract valuable information during interrogations.

It is understandable if more than a few of the Italian American soldiers also had second thoughts about firing on their ancestral homeland. As noted by historian Stefano Luconi, "Italian-Americans in the United States reacted to the first major Allied operation on Italian soil in a variety of ways. On one hand, they wanted to show complete allegiance to the United States and were emphatically committed to the cause of war against fascism. On the other hand, they were understandably troubled by the prospect of seeing members of their community sent to fight other Italians in Sicily."[10]

Robert P. Argentino, an ammunition truck driver for a 155-mm "Long Tom" artillery unit, remembered landing near Agrigento:

> It was a tough landing. We were under fire. I was very lucky—I had an angel on my shoulder from surviving the German dive bombers [that] came down and strafing. I used my machine gun and I hit that S.O.B. and I saw the plexi-glass shatter. Whether I downed it or not I don't know but he dropped a bomb and I saw it. It was a 500-pound bomb. When I saw it coming down I thought my mother is going to feel awful bad. I had three-and-a-half tons of ammunition [in the truck].
>
> Here it came down, but it hit four feet on the side of the truck. I was right by the water's edge and water came up and hit me but the bomb never went off. I was just soaking wet. I was very lucky.
>
> I will never forget the one night we pulled into this area after we first moved out. Boy, it had the worst smell. We laid in this field and went to sleep. When we woke up we were right at the cemetery, next to the [dead Italian soldiers]. They had been bringing the bodies in. They had the bodies stacked one on top of another about eight feet high.

Argentino said that his father was from Palermo and his maternal grandparents had lived near Calabria, giving him some qualms about going to war against people who could have been his relatives. "I felt bad about it because you don't know if you're killing one of your relations."[11]

Samuel Buretta of Philadelphia, a corporal in the 45th Division, was temporarily put in charge of captured Italian soldiers and commented, "It hurt me to see those men behind barbed wire because I knew in my heart that they didn't want to fight us in the first place, and now only wanted to go home. So, while I had them, I put them to work in humane ways. I put my heart and soul into that job. When I saw them being cheated on rations, with bread and other staples being diverted for personal gain by others, I fought for them and put a stop to the practice real fast."

Despite being a third-generation Italian American from Hazelton, Pennsylvania, Daniel Petruzzi, who considered himself "one-hundred percent

American," could not avoid feeling the prospect of fighting other Italians—perhaps his own relatives—as "crazy" and "unpleasant." In particular he felt that fighting other Italians was the "killing people of our ancient blood."

Anthony Costanzo, from Jamestown, New York, a corporal in the 1st Division's 16th RCT, simply commented, "Sicily! Jesus Christ! My grandma lives in Sicily!"[12]

■ ■ ■

The Big Red One and the Thunderbirds continued to advance up the highway leading north from Gela—sometimes on foot, sometimes by truck. Ahead were Caltanissetta, Pietraperzia, Sperlinga, Cerami, Troina—towns no one had ever heard of in geography class. And at each, one more GIs would fall.

On 18 July the 45th Division reached war-damaged Caltanissetta, and the next day the 1st Infantry Division pulled in behind them. Medic Allen Towne recalled, "Whenever we set up our aid station near a large village or city, we would have older Sicilian men stop in and talk to us. They would speak English well; most of them claimed that they used to work in the States when they were younger. When they had saved enough money, they came back to Sicily, got married, and lived the life of a rich man."[13]

Patton couldn't understand why anyone would want to live in Sicily, let alone move *back* there. He soon came to hate the island and the conditions in which the battle for it had to be fought: "This is a truly horrid country in climate, fleas, mosquitoes, sand bugs, mountains, and inhabitants."[14] He wrote, "The people are just on the verge of starving and look utterly hopeless. . . . Of all the countries I ever been in, this is the most utterly damned. Dust, filth, bugs, and natives. . . . The people of this country are the most destitute and God-forgotten people I have ever seen."[15] Patton also noted in his diary, "At Caltanissetta we killed at least 4,000 civilians by air alone and the place smelled to heaven as the bodies are still in the ruins. I had to feel sorry for the poor devils."[16]

Jim Gavin was more sympathetic to the plight of the Sicilians. The airborne commander told his daughter, "We all read of conditions of these Axis-controlled countries but none of us really appreciated how deplorable things were until we encountered conditions here. The state and the local fascists took everything. Most of every crop and just about all the meat goes to the individuals in the inside of the local political circle. There appeared to be no way for the people to beat the system."[17]

There was no greater contrast between the lives of the peasants and the patricians than Patton's headquarters. He noted,

> We had lunch in the Fascist Palace which, strangely enough, was not much hurt. It was truly magnificent, all velvet and brocade and gold chairs, and we had lunch of C rations in the state dining room on a silk tablecloth, lovely china and silver, with toilet paper [for] napkins.
>
> My policy of continuous attack is correct. The farther we press, the more stuff we find abandoned that should not be abandoned. The Italians are fighting very well in the face of certain defeat. They must crack soon.[18]

■ ■ ■

Col. Bill Darby, the Rangers' commander, noted that Keyes' Provisional Corps "was sent out in striking columns towards Castelvetrano, Marsala, Trapani, and finally Palermo. I was to command one of these columns: 'X Force.' On paper, X Force comprised the 39th Regimental Combat Team [of the 9th Infantry Division], a battalion of 155-mm 'Long Tom' artillery guns, and my three Ranger battalions. However, events had moved so swiftly in the first week of invasion that units were split up and out of communication with their major headquarters. Though I had command, no one could tell me where all my troops were bivouacked. Answers to my questions invariably suggested that the troops were somewhere 'up ahead' along the coastal road."[19]

■ ■ ■

Since landing at Licata on 10 July, Truscott's 3rd Infantry Division had been the Seventh Army's spearhead, stabbing northward, jabbing away at attempts to slow it down, cracking the island in half like a pistachio and overcoming all opposition in its path. Now, on 19 July, the division was within striking distance of the capital.

Truscott said, "General Patton disliked the idea of playing second fiddle to Montgomery with the secondary mission of protecting Montgomery's flank and rear while Montgomery was adding fresh laurels to those of his recent victories [in North Africa]. And Palermo drew General Patton like a lode star. It was General Patton's view that he could split the enemy's forces and protect Montgomery's flank and rear by capturing Palermo."

Truscott said that Patton's plan, with one eye on future headlines in the newspapers back home, was "to break through the mountainous region immediately to the north of us, whereupon he would commit the 2nd Armored Division in a spectacular sweep to capture Palermo, which would be touted as the first great exploit by American armor. We knew by this time that most of the German forces in Sicily were now opposing the Eighth Army, and that most of the enemy forces remaining in the western end of the island would be found on the main route between Agrigento and Palermo in the 3rd Infantry Division zone."

He also knew that Patton, a longtime advocate of armored warfare, would like to see much of the credit for the capture go to Hugh Gaffey's tankers, but "I had some reservations, for I was commanding an infantry division of which I was justifiably proud."

Truscott saw that his line of advance would take him through rough country and mountains some four thousand feet high, narrow roads with hairpin turns, and bridges that the retreating enemy could easily defend or demolish. "Since demolitions would constitute our greatest obstacle," Truscott said, "it seemed to me that the faster we could traverse the distance, the less time the enemy would have for demolitions and destruction," so, at 0500 hours on 19 July the 3rd Division's drive to Palermo kicked off.[20]

Standing by the side of a road Truscott watched two battalions march past at their usual brisk "Truscott Trot." He marveled,

> In blistering heat and stifling dust, these soldiers plowed their way forward like waves beating on an ocean beach and at a rate which Roman legions never excelled. At the tail of each battalion I stopped the battalion surgeon and chaplain and asked how many men had fallen out so far. In both cases the answer was none.
>
> Both battalions had moved by motor all night, had attacked cross-country soon after daylight, and both had already covered twenty-five miles on foot since morning. For both there was another ten miles before halting.

That afternoon at about 1700 hours General Keyes caught up to Truscott and informed him that Patton now wanted the 2nd Armored Division to become the spearpoint of the drive toward Palermo. An unhappy Truscott remarked, "The . . . stage was now set for the big armored push. The Rangers had fallen behind and complained of exhaustion. Keyes relieved them from my command and placed them under his [Provisional] Corps control. His only other instruction was that no elements would cross the Blue Line except on order."[21]

The next week would be spent slogging over more of the hot, dusty, cactus-studded hills of Sicily, through one wrecked village and across one stone-dry riverbed after another, destroying roadblocks, avoiding minefields, and overcoming opposition, always in pursuit of an elusive enemy who would seem to make a determined stand, only to melt away like a rabbit disappearing from a predator. Yet both prey and predator suffered heavy losses during the chase, with artillery and aircraft seemingly coming out of nowhere.

■ ■ ■

Big moves beyond Sicily were afoot. With the Sicily campaign less than half finished, Eisenhower won support from the combined chiefs of staff for Winston Churchill's idea for the next phase of the war in the Mediterranean: multiple landings on the mainland of Italy in early September. A three-pronged assault would see a combined American-British force land at Salerno (Operation Avalanche) while two all-British assaults would take place at Calabria on the toe of the Italian "boot" (Operation Baytown) and at Taranto, in the arch of the boot (Operation Slapstick).[22]

During this time, while riding in a convoy near Villarosa, about eight miles west of Enna, 1st Division medic Allen Towne was amazed at how steep and narrow the roads were. He recalled, "We were going up a mountain road and a Sicilian was coming down in his two-wheeled wagon pulled by a donkey. The donkey got scared by all the vehicles and started running down the steep road. The donkey lost his footing, slipped and fell, and started sliding down the hill on his side, pulling the wagon and driver. The last I saw of them was a frightened man jumping off his wagon and this donkey and wagon still sliding down the steep hill."[23]

■ ■ ■

The Allies decided that, as a further inducement for Italy to quit the war, Rome should feel some of the pain that had been visited upon German cities by American and British bombers. "All agreed," said Ike, "that the Eternal City should not be uselessly damaged—indeed, this was the policy we pursued with respect to all the relics of the ancient civilization of Italy—but it was common knowledge that the Germans were taking advantage of our restraint to use Rome as a principal link in the communication system. . . . Later we were authorized to bomb the [rail] yards, taking particular care to avoid damage to Rome and the Vatican City."[24]

All Italians had hoped that the fighting would be confined to Sicily and that Rome and all other historic Italian cities would be spared. Such was not to be. The first blow came on the scorching afternoon of 19 July 1943 when some 270 American B-17, B-24, B-25, and B-26 bombers struck Rome during Operation Crosspoint, dropping 350 tons of ordnance on the San Lorenzo freight yard and steel factory, as well as nearby residential blocks east of the main train station and the La Sapienza University and medical school, killing almost 1,500 civilians. The Littorio and Ciampino airports in the city were also hit.[25] Only five American planes were lost to the German fighters that rose to intercept them.[26]

The carefully selected air crews had been instructed "to avoid historical and religious points by means of large aerial photographs on which such places as Vatican City, St. John Lateran and others were outlined in red with the legend nearby: 'Must on no account be damaged.'" But bombs do not always fall where they are intended.

After the strike Pope Pius XII sent a letter to one of his cardinals condemning the bombing, saying that the Basilica of San Lorenzo Fuori le Mura, located on the edge of the rail yards and "venerated by all Catholics for its antique memories, is now in great part destroyed. . . . In our quality as bishop of this sublime city we did everything possible . . . that our well-beloved Rome might be spared the horrors and wreckage of bombings. Rome is sacred not only to the Holy See but to the whole Catholic world."[27]

Just like at Hiroshima and Nagasaki almost exactly two years later, the bombing of Rome was a punch designed to convince one of the three main Axis partners that it was time to drop out of the war.

■ ■ ■

If the bombing of Rome and the impending fall of Sicily did nothing else, it sealed Mussolini's fate. On the same day of the aerial attack on Rome, Hitler summoned the disheartened Duce to a meeting at the secluded mountain town of Feltre in the southern Dolomites north of Venice. The German dictator was furious that two German divisions were fighting fiercely in Sicily while 300,000 Italians were surrendering just as fervently. As journalist William Shirer wrote, "Without much success the fanatical German leader tried to rekindle the sunken spirits of his ailing friend and ally. . . . Despite Hitler's promises [of more military aid], the atmosphere . . . was most depressing. Mussolini was so overwrought that he could no longer follow his friend's tirades. . . . The *Duce*'s despair worsened when during the meeting reports came in of the first heavy daylight Allied air attack on Rome." And when Mussolini returned to the Eternal City, he discovered, in addition to bomb damage, that his former friends in the Fascist Party—and a large portion of the Italian public—had turned against him. Riots and demonstrations foreshadowed his fate.[28]

■ ■ ■

Dismayed by his depressing meeting with Mussolini at Feltre, and realizing that he could no longer count on Italy's steadfast dedication to the war, Hitler, who had always forbidden his field marshals and generals from giving up an inch of ground, began thinking that a German withdrawal from Sicily, with an evacuation across the Strait of Messina to the toe of the Italian peninsula, would soon become necessary. Preparations began to be made.[29]

■ ■ ■

On 20 July Enna, an ancient walled city perched atop a daunting mountain that had been home to the Axis headquarters in Sicily, fell. The Canadians of Leese's XXX Corps had been assigned to take it but found the defense too tough; Bradley's II Corps stepped in. His intelligence officer noted, "It took the Saracens twenty years in their siege of Enna [to capture it]. Our boys did it in five hours."[30]

After the 1st and 45th Divisions marched into Enna, beating out a Canadian unit by eight minutes, Patton was feeling magnanimous. "I sent a dispatch to General Alexander saying that we [both the Canadians and II Corps] arrived at the same time. I will bet they claim to have got there first," he told his diary.[31]

That same day Patton had Keyes send the 82nd Airborne Division westward from Agrigento to Marsala and Trapani, and the 2nd Armored and 3rd Infantry Divisions northward toward Palermo, almost as though they were two "flying columns." Bradley's II Corps, with the 1st and 45th Infantry Divisions rolling like an unstoppable juggernaut, covered the right flank of this dramatic drive.[32]

Then Patton wrote to Beatrice, "Our men are really grim fighters, and I would hate to be the enemy. . . . The whole country is literally strewn with smashed trucks, guns, and tanks. . . . In my opinion, their so-called Tiger tanks with the 88mm's [main guns] are a flop. They are too slow. . . . My theory of keeping on attacking has certainly worked."[33]

The next day Patton took a moment to gloat in his diary, "I really feel like a great general today. All my plans have so far worked. I hope God stays with me." One reason for Patton's ebullient mood was that he had just learned that "the British have a pretty bloody nose south of Catania. . . . They have asked for the 78th Division [to come from North Africa to Sicily], which last week they said they did not need."[34]

Now Palermo was within his grasp. Once he captured it, he could make a hard right turn and dash along the northern coast to Messina and likely beat Montgomery there. "Alex has no idea of either the power or speed of American armies," he boasted in his diary. "We can go twice as fast as the British and hit harder."[35]

■ ■ ■

On 20 July Darby's Rangers, dubbed X Force, were ordered to advance from Ribera westward to the coast and make contact with the 9th Infantry Division's 39th RCT who were "somewhere up ahead." At the head of his column in jeeps, Darby tore up the road in search of the 39th. Through Sciacca the jeeps went and then on to Menfi, where elements of the 39th were finally found; they told Darby that enemy troops were in Castelvetrano. With night coming on, Darby decided his men needed some rest before going into battle.

The Rangers pulled into a grove of trees, and one of Darby's men, an expert scrounger, went out on a mission. He came back with several bottles of what Darby said "looked like whiskey or wine, attractively wrapped in lead foil. My staff and I prepared for a party. Pouring healthy drinks, we rose to toast the president, the king of England, and others.

"The first drink went off with a few wry faces; after the second, even the avid Ranger thirsts were stopped while they checked the bottles. They couldn't translate the small Italian printing on the label but the words in large print across the foil were *Vermi Fuggio*—Worm Medicine."

After catching some sleep, Darby and his stomach-cramped Rangers attacked a bridge before the town at dawn. "The action was sharp," he recalled, "but a well-executed envelopment caught the Italians on the flank; they threw down their arms."[36]

■ ■ ■

On 21 July Keyes messaged Patton, "Peanuts for breakfast"—a code that indicated Gaffey's 2nd Armored would be on the highway leading into Palermo by 0600 hours. Patton noted, "If the attack works out, it will be a classic example of the proper use of armor. I told Gaffey and [Col.] Maurice Rose [who headed 2nd Armored's Combat Command A] to take chances—to smoke the enemy and then charge him with tanks. I am sure that this will work as the enemy is jumpy and justly so, in the face of the power we can put against him."[37]

The next day Patton journaled, "Left for the front. . . . The road discipline was superior. Whenever I passed any of the 2nd Armored Division, all the men first saluted me and then waved. It was quite cheering."[38]

But 2nd Armored's advance was no Sunday drive in the country, as the division's after action report noted, "The entire movement from Agrigento to assembly areas west of the Belice River was made along one road in the face of most difficult conditions. All important bridges had been blown out, necessitating bypasses through precipitous gorges or in some cases through railroad tunnels. Engineers worked unceasingly on these bypasses improving them, widening the trails, clearing mines, both on the roads and on adjoined shoulders and fields."

In addition, 2nd Armored was continually harassed by Italian and German forces employing anti-tank weapons. It often took hard fighting by the accompanying elements of the 82nd Airborne, 3rd Infantry, and 39th RCT to overcome these obstacles. The distance from the Belice River to Palermo was sixty miles—a distance the attacking force covered in just ten hours.[39]

As he observed Gaffey's Sherman tanks on 22 July suddenly being forced to halt, Patton went forward to check out the source of the bottleneck—a narrow bridge north of Castelvetrano. There on the bridge he found an immovable mule-drawn cart. Patton "had the mule killed" and thrown off the bridge along with the cart. He then whipped the frightened Sicilian cart driver with his swagger stick, breaking it. He later huffed in a letter to Beatrice, "Human rights are being exalted over victory."[40]

■ ■ ■

Jim Gavin's ground-bound paratroopers arrived at the town of Santa Margherita, a suburb of Trapani, late on 22 July after an all-night march and entered Trapani in trucks the following morning. He wrote,

"The only hazards en route were the fruit and caramelos [a hard candy] thrown by the Sicilians. Actually, the caramelos could sting if they hit you while you were in a fast-moving vehicle. As we reached the outskirts of Trapani, we encountered a roadblock and heavy artillery fire," said Gavin. The enemy batteries defending the port were quickly silenced by the firepower of the 155-mm "Long Toms" of the 34th Field Artillery Battalion, allowing the 505th paratroopers to occupy the city. "The regiment deployed, swept into the town with no casualties, and accepted the surrender of the admiral in command. Thus ended the Sicilian campaign for the 82nd Airborne Division."[41]

Gavin wrote to his daughter Barbara, "The civilians have been extremely hospitable. Some towns have actually turned out to welcome us with flags, flowers, and cheers. This is normally preceded by a rather tough fight in which some lives are inevitably lost. As warriors the Italians have been entirely unpredictable. Sometimes they fight intensely and are capable of inflicting heavy casualties, again for unexplainable reasons . . . they knuckle under with little struggle. It keeps us wary and mean anyway. Don't worry about me, as I am doing fine even if I can't write every day."[42]

The battle for Sicily went on, but the paratroopers' role in major combat was finished after Trapani. Jim Gavin noted that the airborne had learned much from its two less-than-perfect combat drops in July. One of the lessons was that the lightly armed paratroopers simply did not have the weaponry to defeat enemy armor and hardened positions such as reinforced concrete bunkers and pillboxes. The few anti-tank mines the paratroopers carried with them were ineffective, and "the American carbine in heavy combat was worthless." What were needed were anti-tank rocket projectors—bazookas—and plenty of them. The later issuance of the .45-caliber M1 Thompson submachine gun also proved popular and effective for close-quarter fighting.

To overcome the problems, practice jumps were conducted at the Comiso airfield. A sub-branch of Pathfinders, who would drop twenty or thirty minutes before the main body to mark the drop zones, was created. Despite Patton's and Bradley's high praise for the paratroopers, Gavin knew that the higher-ups in the War Department were pessimistic about the airborne concept. Britain's disastrous experience with glider-borne troops also weighed on the future employment of sky soldiers. Gavin even quoted a letter from Eisenhower to Marshall: "I do not believe in the airborne division." Despite that, Operation Overlord, the Normandy invasion, would again use a mass drop of airborne soldiers—with parachutes and gliders—in highly effective but still imperfect ways. But Gavin said, "It had been a near thing for the airborne effort."[43]

While the 1st Infantry and the 82nd Airborne Divisions prepared to depart the Mediterranean for Britain to train for their upcoming roles in Overlord, Truscott's 3rd and Middleton's 45th Divisions remained on the island and spent the next few weeks getting ready for their participation with Clark's Fifth Army in the Salerno invasion set for 9 September. They would in August 1944 also be utilized in Operation Dragoon, the invasion of southern France.

■ ■ ■

During the long march northward, Bill Mauldin, the cartoonist for the *45th Division News*, took time to write down some of his impressions: "Nobody's scared of us. If you try to look tough as you walk down the streets of a freshly-taken town, you feel a little silly, and don't impress anybody. Because no matter how bloody and tattered and sweat-stained you may be, these people can't get it out of their heads that you're an American tourist here to spend money.

"If you like to have your ego flattered, Sicilians can do it. Two [jeeps] going down a main street have the same effect as an Armistice Day parade at home. They even throw flowers at you. It's best to wear a helmet when driving through town, because some over-enthusiastic flower-throwers forget to take the pot off in their haste."[44]

■ ■ ■

Events were rapidly moving in the Allies' favor, but the Sicilian drama was not yet over. The final act—seventeen days long—was about to play itself out.

· 13 ·

PALERMO AND BEYOND

This is a decisive moment in the war.

—Winston S. Churchill

For the citizens of Palermo, 22 July 1943 was a joyous day. As Lucian Truscott was deploying his regiments in a semicircle around the capital to seal it off, his units encountered scattered opposition, but "Italians were surrendering in such numbers as to be embarrassing. Explosions could be seen in the city and it was evident that the Germans were about their work of destruction," he noted.

Desperate civilians kept sending requests to be allowed to surrender the city, but all were denied until about 1800 hours that day when Keyes allowed 3rd Division patrols to enter and protect the port. When Patton and Keyes arrived at Palermo late that evening, they found Truscott's men already inside.[1]

Despite Patton's desire to have Gaffey's tankers enter first, it was Truscott's men who achieved that distinction. Patton and his entourage approached "with banners flying and cameras grinding," a *Life* reporter wrote. "But inside the city they found the 3rd Division's Lieutenant Colonel John Heintges and his entire battalion quietly patrolling the streets."[2] When Patton greeted Truscott, his first words were, "Well, the Truscott Trot sure got us here in a damn hurry."[3]

Hordes of civilians clogged the streets, clapping, cheering, embracing the dust-covered troops, and jumping onto the hoods of vehicles to ride for a few blocks in an impromptu victory parade. Patton recorded his thoughts on his triumphal march toward the capital: "Those who arrived before dark . . . had flowers thrown on the road in front of them, and lemons and watermelons given to them in such profusion that they almost became lethal weapons."

Patton said that the governor had left, "but we captured two [Italian] generals, both of whom said that they were glad to be captured because the Sicilians were not human beings but animals. The bag in prisoners for the day must have been close to 10,000."[4]

■ ■ ■

Also on 22 July U.S. Navy warships were closing in on Palermo's harbor, led by Capt. Charles Wellborn's Destroyer Squadron 8 and Cdr. William Messmer's Minesweeper Division 17. The first American craft to actually enter the debris-clogged harbor, however, were the four PT boats of Motor Torpedo Boat Squadron 15, commanded by Lt. Cdr. Stanley M. Barnes.

Barnes recalled, "At dawn . . . we were off Ustica [a tiny volcanic island forty miles north of Palermo]. First thing we saw a fishing boat putt-putting toward Italy. Going over, we found a handful of very scared individuals crawling out from under the floor plates, hopefully waving white handkerchiefs. This was the staff of the Italian admiral at Trapani. The only reason we didn't get the admiral was that he was late getting down to the dock and his staff said to hell with him. . . . One of the other boats spotted a raft with seven Germans on it feebly paddling out to sea. We picked those up, too."

When his motor torpedo boats entered Palermo harbor, Barnes was astonished at the amount of destruction he saw ringing the waterfront—buildings blasted by Allied air raids and German demolitions, cranes toppled into the water, and more than fifty boats sunk or bobbing forlornly on the oil-slicked water. The infrastructure was completely destroyed—no water, sewerage, or electricity. One of the conquerors' first jobs was to try and restore the city's services and provide aid for the tens of thousands of hungry inhabitants.[5]

On that same day Lt. (j.g.) Edward Stafford, skipper of the sub-chaser SCE 692, entered the harbor that "hadn't even been swept for mines when we came in. There were wrecks all across the middle of the harbor. A ship—it must have weighed 2,000 tons—was sitting not *at* the dock, but *on* the dock. It had been blown out of the water, presumably by an American air raid, and the explosion lifted it onto the pier."[6]

■ ■ ■

Patton saw his drive to Palermo as something for the ages: "I feel that future students of the Command and General Staff School will study the campaign of Palermo as a classic example of the use of tanks. I held them back far enough so that the enemy could not tell where they were to be used; when the infantry had found the hole [in Palermo's defenses], the tanks went through and in large numbers and fast. Such methods assure victory and reduce losses, but it takes fine leadership to insure the execution. General Keyes provided perfect leadership and great drive. The praise should be his." He also noted, "I also believe that historical research will reveal that General Keyes' Corps moved faster against heavier resistance and over worse roads than did the Germans during their famous Blitz."[7]

■ ■ ■

Some postwar historians have taken Patton to task for having wasted valuable men, resources, and time heading for the alluring prize of the island's capital instead of going hell-bent for leather to cut off the Axis escape route at Messina. Most of the U.S. newspapers and magazines had no such reservations.

Life magazine played up the surrender of Palermo and featured several Robert Capa photos of Keyes taking the surrender of a scar-faced Italian general, Giuseppe Molinero. Patton uncharacteristically allowed a subordinate to receive the laurels for the triumph. In the 23 August 1943 issue of *Life*, only Keyes' picture appears in the four-page spread; Patton is mentioned but once. "Geoff [Keyes] really deserves most of the credit and I have handed it out to him via the press," Patton said magnanimously.

The article continued,

> Palermo knew it would never forget July 22—the day the Americans came. Together Keyes and Molinaro drove to the Royal Palace, where the Italian formally surrendered the city to the Americans. . . . Next day the U.S. flag rose over Palermo and the American troops rumbled through its streets

> to the accompaniment of a tremendous welcome by its citizens . . . and the people of the city once more got bread and macaroni.
>
> One reason the people of Palermo were glad to see the Americans was because they thought it would mean the end of the bombings. Beginning on June 23, 1940, when the first [British] air raid was made, Allied planes had bombed the city fifty-two times. By the time of the Sicily landings, Palermo's docks, shipyard, naval base, and waterfront buildings were demolished, and nearby Bocca di Falco airport heavily damaged.

The citizens' hopes for a cessation of bombing were dashed, however, because Axis planes continued to target the city for many days to come.[8]

■ ■ ■

Shortly after arriving in Sicily twelve days earlier, Audie Murphy became a casualty—of a malaria-carrying mosquito. Weak, sick, and vomiting, he refused to go on sick call, not wanting to let his buddies down. But he ended up in a field hospital for a few weeks anyway.

Murphy rejoined his company for the final push, passing through Palermo on the way to catch up with his outfit, observing the streets crowded with 3rd Division men looking for intimate interludes to take their minds briefly off thoughts of death. He commented, "Lines of soldiers, with their weapons slung on their shoulders, stand before brothels, patiently waiting their turn. Individual dignity has been transformed to fit the nature of war."[9]

■ ■ ■

While the newspapers and commentators back home were ecstatic with the news, Omar Bradley was not impressed, and his resentment toward Patton continued to grow. There was nothing militarily significant or glorious about "the capture of hills, docile peasants, and spiritless soldiers," he grumbled.[10]

Patton, of course, had a different view. He said, "On the morning of the 23rd, when I was inspecting the harbor, I passed a group of [Italian] prisoners, all of whom stood up, saluted, and then cheered."[11]

More importantly, Patton was pleased to show the British that Americans could operate with dash and verve while Monty was having a hard time crawling up the eastern coast against tough opposition. Certainly one of Patton's main goals was to prove to America's main ally that the American soldier took a back seat to no one.

Alexander messaged Patton, "This is a great triumph. Well done. Heartiest congratulations to you and all your splendid soldiers." Patton said, "I [had] told him once that Americans needed praise and here it is."[12]

■ ■ ■

American eyes now turned eastward. Wasting no time, Patton journaled on 23 July, "We started this morning capturing the north road [Highway 113 along the coast] and also moving artillery to support the final effort of the II Corps which will begin in a few days."[13]

Patton then wrote to Ike to tell him, if he didn't already know, what a superb job his Seventh Army was doing: "The performance of all the troops, infantry and armored, was outstanding, and the drive and leadership shown by General Keyes were of a superior order. . . . I have nothing but praise for all the General Officers concerned and nothing but outstanding admiration for the endurance, hardihood, and combat efficiency of the troops. . . . The supply arrangements, both from the SOS [Services of Supply, the forerunner of today's Quartermaster Corps], Navy, and our own Supply here have been very successful, and I have nothing but praise for all of those concerned."[14]

Eisenhower was also pleased with his subordinate's conduct of the campaign thus far:

> [Patton's] rapidity of movement quickly reduced the enemy ports to the single one of Messina; it broke the morale of the huge Italian garrison [at Palermo] and placed Patton's forces in position to begin the attack from the westward to break the deadlock on the eastern [Eighth Army] flank.
>
> Patton was a shrewd student of warfare who always clearly appreciated the value of speed in the conduct of operations. Speed of movement often enables troops to minimize any advantages the enemy may temporarily gain but, more important, speed makes possible the full exploitation of every favorable opportunity, and prevents the enemy from readjusting his forces to meet successive attacks.[15]

To the southwest of Palermo, other towns were also falling to American troops. On 23 July Darby's X Force captured Marsala, and Gavin's 505th PIR entered Trapani, greeted by cheers instead of bullets.[16]

■ ■ ■

Middleton's 45th Division was far from the cheers as it battled its way toward Termini Imerese. Instead of friendly villagers, lying in wait for the Thunderbirds were the 26th "Assietta" Infantry Division and two regiments of the 29th Panzer Grenadier Division.[17]

On 23 July the 2nd Battalion of the 157th RCT was ambushed while trying to establish roadblocks at a rail junction. "We took what cover we could in shallow places in the ground and sweated out fifty minutes of hell," said Vernon Edney, Company F. "Then the Germans blew up a bridge, throwing chunks of cement onto the prostrate men. The 158th Field Artillery Battalion dropped a barrage and pinned [the Germans] down and allowed our battalion to withdraw and try to outflank the Germans, but they had made their famous withdrawal toward Messina."[18]

■ ■ ■

Lt. Bill Whitman, Company B, 180th RCT, remembered the drive northward as an unrelenting slog fraught with danger: "All we did was hike, hike, hike. We had some minor skirmishes but nothing serious." On 24 July the 180th Regiment reached Termini Imerese but there was no time to rest; Whitman's company was then sent to Cerda, southeast of Termini Imerese. "Just before we reached Cerda, a mountain village, I was sent into a small town with a patrol. I had the mayor collect all the firearms in the village."

While there Whitman recalled seeing a large compound filled with thousands of Italian and German prisoners of war who seemed more like enemies than allies. "The Germans were on one side of the street and the Italians on the other," he observed. "All that they had was contempt for each other. They refused to eat together or associate with each other."[19]

A *Time* magazine reporter had a similar observation: "On occasion the Italians fought fiercely, gave up only when further combat was hopeless. But when they surrendered, they surrendered in crowds. As in North Africa,

Italian soldiers and officers hated the Germans. Soldiers complained that the Germans took all the food; Italian airmen, that the Germans took the good planes and hangars.

"The Germans showed the same contempt for the Italians that they had displayed in Africa. . . . The German soldiers fought well, and their divisions as a whole put up a performance which Allied commanders will remember when they assess the German Army's ability to defend the continent. But in captivity the Germans had the sound of men who knew that they were condemned to sacrificial defense, in an area which their superiors had expected to lose."[20]

■ ■ ■

The 45th's 179th Regiment was also clawing its way toward the coast. Sgt. Brummett Echohawk, with the 179th's Company B, recalled, "We fight not only German pockets of resistance but also the terrain and Mediterranean heat. Men fall out with heat exhaustion as we move throughout the day. Evening comes and we again build stone foxholes. For dinner I eat a dehydrated fruit bar and drink water. I have powdered soup but it takes fire to heat water, and that's dangerous. As the sun sets I notice that these mountains have no darting nighthawks, ring-singing insects, or whip-poor-wills; it is a lifeless place. Tired, we drop off to sleep."[21]

Bill Whitman recalled that his unit was

> loaded into trucks and moved up the coast road. I was riding in a jeep behind one of our trucks. . . . We could hear artillery fire as we rode along and soon we passed elements of our artillery firing from positions alongside the road. On we went. Several miles beyond the artillery we began to hear the sound of infantry battle: rifles, tanks, machine guns, mortars firing, faintly at first, and then louder and more distinct.
>
> A stream of vehicles was passing us, all coming back from the front. Then there were ambulances and jeeps carrying stretchers. We could see the feet sticking up through the rear windows of the ambulances. The jeeps had bodies on the hoods and on the litters in the rear. It was apparent that they were carrying dead men, as the faces were covered with blankets and there were no movements. . . . I guess each one of us

could visualize himself on one of those litters, especially with the sounds of combat ahead in our ears.

Eight miles later, Whitman's platoon dismounted and was ordered to prepare for a night bayonet attack against an impossibly strong German position at the coastal village of Castel di Tusa, five miles west of Cefalù. Poring over a map, Whitman said, "We made detailed plans for the attack but not one of us looked forward to it. Dread with a capital 'D' is what it was. Fortunately the attack was called off and we all began to breathe again."

The cancellation, however, didn't mean it was time to relax. "The next morning our Company B led the advance of the regiment and division," Whitman said. "The Germans had pulled back during the night. Up the coast road we walked, the sea on our left and high mountains on our right. This morning I was the lead man in the whole U.S. Seventh Army on this flank—I was leading the 'Point' up the road! We walked a quarter mile, a half mile, nothing! It was a beautiful morning. Each beautiful day was appreciated because we all knew that it might be our last."

The column that Whitman was leading came to a sharp bend in the road. He and the men behind him became extra alert—what could be up there awaiting them? In the distance he saw a jeep with three men sitting in it, not moving. Whitman signaled for those behind him to halt while he went cautiously forward to check on the situation.

As he reached the jeep, he discovered a scene of horror. "A quick look at the man sitting in the back . . . shows he has a bullet hole in his forehead," Whitman said. The two men in front were also dead. Running back to his captain who had halted with the rest of the group, Whitman reported on what he saw. Capt. J. O. Smith "agreed with me—try to find a way off the road so we won't have to go around that deadly curve."

With the entire Seventh Army held up and higher headquarters wondering what was causing the delay, Whitman got ten men to volunteer for a scouting mission to find a safer route. Within minutes the group scrambled back, one soldier wounded in the leg. They reported that they had found a new route—through a railroad tunnel.

To Whitman, that was as dangerous as the blind curve. "We go through the tunnel expecting to be fired on from the other end," he said, "or at least

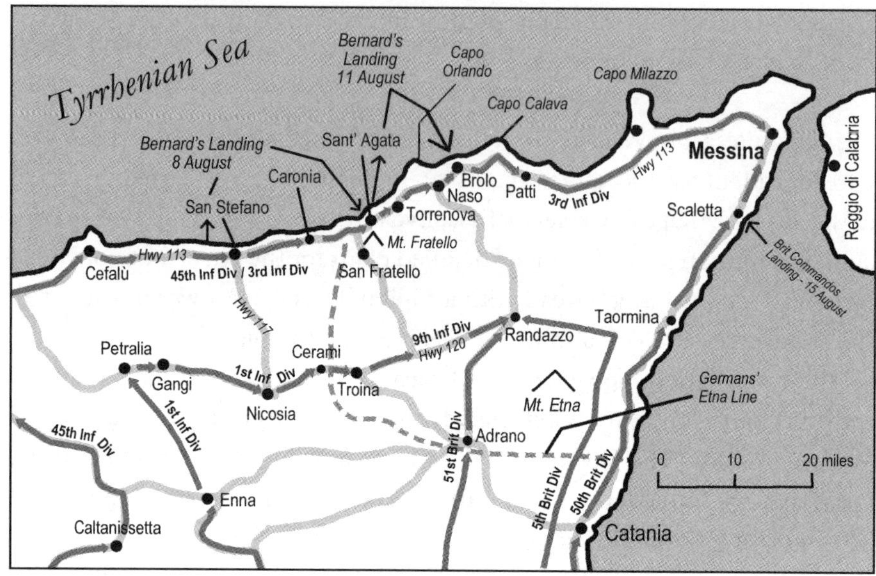

Map 13.1 ▪ The northern coast of Sicily, where the Germans tried but failed to prevent Seventh Army from reaching Messina

when we emerge from the far end." To everyone's surprise the tunnel was filled with Italian women and children taking refuge from the war. There were even beds and furniture and other household items inside. "The Germans really goofed," he said. "They really missed the great opportunity to hold us back with heavy casualties by not holding that railroad tunnel."[22] After its harrowing journey through the railroad tunnel, Whitman's Company B, along with Company C, were assigned to attack the Germans dug in on top of a high, craggy peak along the road to Santo Stefano di Camastra that the GIs called Bloody Ridge.

A history of the war described Bloody Ridge: "An almost perpendicular hill . . . held in force by the Germans. Their machine guns projected from every ravine and crevice on all sides of the height. The Americans stormed it one hot summer day. The first assault on the hill was thrown back; so was the second. The third attack, made late in the afternoon, finally forced the Germans off the hill, but at high cost. American soldiers fell in the greatest numbers since the start of the campaign."[23]

Whitman said,

> Across the Tusa River—which was dry—and up the rugged slopes drove our company and Company C. Neither company could get but part way up due to intense German fire. Their machine guns were cleverly concealed and camouflaged in the rocky hillsides in front of us, and they used flashless powder. They were most difficult to locate.
>
> In front of my platoon was a blown bridge, off to the left was a railroad, then the sea. I had two heavy machine guns from Company D which I placed near the coast road. Imagine—I and my thirty men held the left flank of the entire Seventh U.S. Army!
>
> To the left down the road was the Kraut anchor point, Santo Stefano. Every hour or so they would pound our ridge with artillery and mortars. We held our positions and were ordered back across the riverbed after dark. For four days we sat on our ridge and fired everything we had at the slopes of Bloody Ridge.

Capt. J. O. Smith had about thirty men up on the ridge, and Whitman had about the same number. It wasn't long before the Germans attacked the Company B positions.

> They smothered us with mortar shells and came at us. They knocked out one of our machine guns and wiped out most of the gun crew. We stopped them but we lost more men doing it.
>
> We captured a German half-track personnel carrier, some rifles and carbines, and a large Nazi flag which was in the half-track. If their attack had been a little stronger, they could have overrun us because our strength in manpower was getting very low. . . . We now had about fifty or sixty men in the entire company [an infantry rifle company's usual strength was about two hundred men] and some of these were about worn out, either physically or mentally or both.

Whitman said his battalion commander was relieved of command because he reported that 1st Battalion was in no shape to continue fighting unless it could get some rest and replacements. "As it was," Whitman continued, "it took the entire 157th Regiment of our division to finally take Bloody Ridge. We furnished them with what supporting fires we could as they struggled up the rocky slopes; they lived a life of hell and suffered heavy casualties. They were under aerial strafing attacks [by the Luftwaffe] daily, and the German long-range artillery shells skimmed the crest of the ridge causing the men to instinctively duck."[24]

Bloody Ridge was expensive real estate that the 45th Division truly paid for in blood. It also led to the capture of Santo Stefano. The Thunderbirds had given everything—emotionally and physically—that soldiers could give. On 31 July the 45th was pulled off the line and allowed to rest for a few days, their place at the front taken by the 3rd Infantry Division. Patton would tell the 45th Division's survivors, "You are one of the best—if not *the* best—divisions in the United States Army."[25]

■ ■ ■

The great achievement of Operation Husky took place on 24–25 July 1943 far from the battlefield. At that time, a majority of the Fascist Grand Council, meeting in Rome, approved nineteen to seven (with one abstention) a no-confidence vote against Mussolini, effectively ending his twenty-six-year reign as Italy's dictator. This stunning development must have shaken Hitler who, despite having had to send troops to bail his Axis partner out of his difficulties in North Africa and Greece and then bolster him in Sicily, still depended on the Italian armed forces to at least put up some form of resistance.

William Shirer wrote, "Reports soon reached Hitler that the Italian army was 'in a state of collapse,' as he put it to his advisors at OKW [Oberkommando der Wehrmacht, the German Army High Command]."[26] With the outcome of the massive battle at Kursk about to turn in the Red Army's favor, it was one more bit of bad news that Hitler did not need to hear.

On 25 July, after the council's vote, the diminutive King Victor Emmanuel III summoned Mussolini to the palace, announced that he was removing him as prime minister, then had him arrested by the Carabinieri. Marshal Pietro Badoglio, the aging former chief of the Italian general staff who had once used poison gas on Ethiopian tribesmen, was made prime minister, then disingenuously broadcast to the nation that Italy would remain loyal to Germany while secretly planning to exit the war.

If Badoglio and the king had any hope or expectation that the Germans would withdraw from Italy and thus spare it from the destruction of war, they were sadly mistaken. Hitler decided to occupy the country—twenty-two more months of fighting would ravage the kingdom.[27]

■ ■ ■

When he received word of Mussolini's ouster, Winston Churchill cabled Alexander: "The only thing that really matters at this moment is the great battle you are about to fight as head of 15th Army Group. Important as the battle would have been in ordinary circumstances, its effect will be redoubled now. No one can tell what the consequences far beyond the battlefield may be. This is a decisive moment in the war and your armies may strike a resounding blow. I thank God you are there and that all is in your hands. Strike hard and home."[28]

■ ■ ■

At his daily military situation conference on 26 July, Hitler, ever the micro-manager, specified the order in which the German forces should be evacuated from Messina: "First the paratroops, second the Göring [Panzer] Division . . . last the 29th Panzer Grenadier Division. . . . The parachute division is, of course, the most important because it is the most valuable." He also discussed plans for the German army to seize and occupy Rome—including the Vatican—in the wake of Mussolini's sacking and the likelihood of Italy declaring her neutrality.[29]

■ ■ ■

Palermo was a shattered city. There was no water, no lights, no operating sewers. Magnificent stone buildings that had stood for centuries were little more than toppled husks. The streets were filled with abandoned cars and carts, the scattered furniture and household items of the residents, and the occasional dead horse. The stench of death was cloying.

Col. Charles Codman, Patton's aide, recorded his impressions of the ruined capital: "Took a tour around Palermo today. . . . Street after street of crumbled houses. Whole blocks of shapeless rubble; parlor, bedroom, and bath exposed . . . by the fantastic projectile that strips away the façade and leaves intact the hat on the bureau, the mirror on the wall, the carafe on the night table. . . . The new experience is adjusting to the fact that all this beautifully executed chaos is the result of our *own* bombs, our *own* planes, our *own* gunfire. It is pretty lovely."[30]

Throughout the city, desperate, ragged Palermitani picked through the rubble, looking for food and begging the GIs for scraps. Even Patton was touched by their plight. "I feel very sorry for the poor things [children]. Wherever you pass them, they beg for food, but I suppose they are natural beggars. . . . I feel sorry for them."[31] While the civilians searched and begged for food, Patton's staff went searching for a building suitable to serve as Seventh Army headquarters; of course, only the Royal Palace would do.

The exterior of Palermo's Royal Palace (also known as the Palazzo del Normanni, or Norman Palace), while large and imposing, looks more like an ordinary, aging municipal building. But the treasures inside! Arched arcades circle the inner courtyard, where an impressive fountain splashes. Endless hallways were decorated with faded tapestries and Renaissance paintings in heavy gilded frames leading to endless rooms, dazzling ceilings, gorgeous chandeliers, glowing tile mosaics covering floors and walls, ornate balustrades, broad marble staircases, and an elaborately frescoed chapel that rivaled anything in Vatican City. It was truly a residence fit for a king—and a conquering general. Here Patton made his headquarters and his bed—the same one in which the kings of Sicily once slept.[32]

■ ■ ■

A sizeable contingent of American women—Army nurses—also soon arrived in Palermo. Among them was 2nd Lt. Bernice Heath, a member of the 59th Evacuation Hospital. After three years of training in Cincinnati, Ohio, she was accepted into the U.S. Army Nurse Corps, sent to Camp Kilmer, New Jersey, and then shipped overseas—first to Casablanca, Morocco, then to Bizerte, Algeria, and finally to Sicily.

"Back in Casablanca, we were stationed in General Patton's headquarters," she recalled. "I remember that he made the rounds of the hospital. He was a large man. You knew he was a man of authority."

The 59th Evacuation Hospital was established in the Renaissance buildings at the University of Palermo, which also served as Seventh Army headquarters. "Our unit had forty-eight nurses, forty male officers, and maybe two hundred enlisted men," Heath said.

> Whenever there was intensive fighting, we would have all these casualties coming in. It was sort of overwhelming at times, but we all kept working. We tried to stay calm. Of course, we saw things that we'd rather not see, but we never let it get us down.
>
> Sometimes we'd be on duty sixteen or seventeen hours. If you're scrubbed up in the middle of a surgical case, you can't say, "It's five o'clock—time for me to quit." We had air raids almost every night in Palermo. But we treated 10,600 patients.[33]

Another nurse with the 59th was Gertrude Lynn, who worked in the officers' ward. "We were injecting penicillin at the time for a lot of these wounded soldiers that we were caring for. One day General Patton came by, all spit and polish, really sharp man. And he inquired about the penicillin. At that time it was only used on Army people; civilians were not allowed to have it. We also used a great deal of sulfa powder that the doctors put on the wounds after surgery."[34]

■ ■ ■

Near the end of July, 1st Division medic Allen Towne was riding in a convoy along a twisting mountain road near Gangi when a German tank suddenly appeared, seemingly out of nowhere. "We were on one side of a deep ravine and the tank was firing at trucks of our convoy winding up the mountain on the other side of the ravine," he said.

While the convoy was stopped, the tank's gunner bracketed one of the American trucks with two shells; the third shell was right on the money. "I saw the driver ditch the truck and jump out," said Towne. "He was lucky because it was an ammunition truck. It started burning, and the cargo kept exploding like firecrackers. When the tank was finally knocked out, the truck was pushed off the road by a bulldozer and we continued on our way."[35]

■ ■ ■

Patton was growing concerned that the stubborn enemy defense along the north coast was creating too much of a delay; if his men had to battle for each and every roadblock, mountain pass, and blown bridge, Montgomery's Eighth Army would reach Messina well before he could. He had messaged the 45th's Middleton, "This is a horse race in which the prestige of the U.S. Army is at stake. We must take Messina before the British. Please use your best efforts to facilitate the success of our race."[36]

However, in his diary he wrote that "Middleton looked tired and his attacks have lacked drive"; he told the commander that he was going to give the Thunderbirds a rest and have Truscott's 3rd Division take over the advance. Middleton didn't like the idea but realized Patton was right. Patton was also concerned about the performance of Terry Allen and Ted Roosevelt and their 1st Infantry Division; he resolved to relieve the two leaders as soon as practical. Bradley and Eisenhower both concurred with his decision.[37]

■ ■ ■

Palermo may have been in American hands, but the Luftwaffe had not given up its attacks. In late July Rear Adm. Lyal A. Davidson's Task Force 88, made up of the cruisers *Philadelphia* and *Savannah* and the destroyers *Gherardi*, *Jeffers*, *Knight*, *Murphy*, *Nelson*, and *Trippe*, was providing fire support for American troops along the northern coast. On the afternoon of 31 July, while the task force was pounding German targets at Santo Stefano, a flight of eleven Junkers Ju-88 Stuka dive-bombers attacked *Philadelphia* and *Murphy*; the latter's gunners shot down two Stukas, while a bomb missed *Philadelphia* by fifteen yards.[38] Enemy aircraft would continue to be a nuisance to American shipping and Palermo, but Patton was pleased with the cooperation he received from the admiral: "We have a fellow named Davidson with us here who is swell and willing to fight."[39]

Charles Codman wrote to his wife, "We had quite a show from the palace window last night. It was very noisy but colorful in the extreme. The high-water mark—and perhaps the most beautiful as well as satisfactory sight I have ever beheld—was a flaming enemy bomber spattering itself and its occupants against the side of a mountain. God, it was gorgeous."

The next day Codman accompanied Patton as he visited another field hospital and pinned forty Purple Hearts on recuperating men. Codman said that "the Boss," as he called him, asked one injured soldier, "Where did you get it, boy?"

"In the chest, sir."

"Well, it may interest you to know that the last German I saw had no chest—and no head either. . . . Get well quickly—you want to be in on that final kill."

Codman was well acquainted with his boss' tough, blustery persona, and also his tender side. "The last guy he decorated was unconscious, oxygen mask, probably won't live," Codman continued. "The boss pulled one of those quick switches of his—took off his helmet, knelt down, pinned the medal on the pillow, whispered in the guy's ear—stood up at attention. Elementary if you like, but I swear there wasn't a dry eye in the house, and—as you know—hospital doctors, nurses, and interns are not the most impressionable people in the world."[40]

The following day the destroyer *Buck* sank an enemy submarine that was menacing six Liberty ships that she was escorting. And for the next several days the cruisers *Savannah* and *Philadelphia*, along with several destroyers, continued to pound German positions, roads, and railway lines along the northern coast in preparation for the next move.[41]

■ ■ ■

Patton had one more card to play in his conquest plan: the remainder of Manton S. Eddy's 9th Infantry Division. With the battle-worn 1st Division seemingly on its last legs, Patton decided to bring in his one remaining fresh division. The 9th's 39th RCT, commanded by Colonel Paddy Flint, who had been in Terry Allen's West Point class of 1912, had landed between Licata and Gela on 18 July and pushed northwest to Marsala, then cross-country toward Palermo. Other elements of the 9th—the 47th and 60th RCTs—traveled in five passenger ships and seven Liberty ships, escorted by six destroyers of Destroyer Squadron 17, from Mers el Kébir, Algeria, to Palermo, arriving on 1 August to a hot welcome.[42]

"At approximately 0415 on Sunday August 1, 1943," wrote *New York Times* correspondent Harold Denny, "enemy planes raided the harbor for an hour and 45 minutes. During the raid the 9th lost neither personnel nor equipment, but an undetermined number of enemy planes was shot down. That morning the unloading of ships began and division units went into bivouac east of Palermo. During the next few days concentration of the division east of Nicosia was completed." The division's entry into Palermo was a brief affair—the 9th was ordered to keep going to an assembly area at Cerami, a mountain town west of Troina.[43]

■ ■ ■

Also on 1 August Patton, realizing that all of his army deserved a big pat on the back, issued General Order Number 10, which was distributed to all American units under his command. It read:

> Soldiers of the Seventh Army:
>
> Landed and supported by the navy and air force, you have, during 21 days of ceaseless battle and unremitting toil, killed and captured more than 87,000 enemy soldiers. Captured and destroyed 361 cannon, 172 tanks, 928 trucks and 190 airplanes—you are magnificent soldiers!
>
> General Eisenhower . . . and General Alexander have both expressed pride and satisfaction in your efforts. Now, in conjunction with the British Eighth Army, you are closing in for the kill. Your relentless offensive will continue to be irresistible. The end is certain and very near. Messina is our next stop![44]

Patton mused over how to overcome the opposition on the north shore—he wanted something big, dashing, spectacular—and decided to leapfrog the enemy by making a series of amphibious "end runs" eastward along the coast. But, even with Hewitt gone, he found the Navy less than enthusiastic. "We are having a good deal of trouble in getting the Navy to go in for amphibious operations east of San Stefano," he said. "They appear to have no idea of the value of time or the need for improvisation. If they can't get everything they want, they say they can't move. I think this is the result of many years during which all officers who lost a ship were tried [by court-martial]. It is true that they have had two destroyers smashed by bombs and really think they should pull out, but we have had many thousands of men hit."[45]

Using his powers of persuasion, Patton convinced Admiral Conolly and Admiral Davidson to provide the lift and gunnery support; CruDiv 8, consisting of the *Philadelphia* and *Savannah,* plus destroyers and landing craft, were detailed to execute the operation. A motor torpedo boat squadron was also selected to support and screen the landings from any enemy naval incursion.

Now, which Seventh Army unit would be chosen to make this maneuver? The 1st Infantry Division and the just-arrived 9th Infantry Division were too far south of the coast, and the 45th Division needed rest. Only Truscott's 3rd was available; it had spent a week recuperating in Palermo. So by midnight on 1 August the 3rd finished relieving the 45th and was bivouacked west of Santo Stefano di Camastra, ready for its next assignment. D-Day for the amphibious operation was set for 7 August.[46]

■ ■ ■

Patton wrote in his journal on 2 August, "Inspected all sick and wounded at the . . . hospital. Pinned on some forty Purple Hearts on men hurt in an air raid. One man was dying and had an oxygen mask on, so I knelt down and pinned the Purple Heart on him, and he seemed to understand although he could not speak."[47]

In a letter to Beatrice on 2 August, Patton wrote that Alexander had paid him a visit.

> Alex is always good company and much interested in ruins. I showed him my palace. . . . There is a parliament room 140 feet long by 60 broad, with all the labors of Hercules in fresco on the walls at one end and on the ceiling. Someone is being roasted at the other end, Venus is having a time with someone, and in the middle there is a three-headed horse and a lot of soldiers.
>
> The middle part of the palace was built before 1000 A.D. and there is a chapel in it built by a Norman duke in 1040. The old Monsenieur [*sic*]

who runs it told me that it was reserved for royalty but insisted on having a mass for me, so I went all alone. . . . I decided to kneel all the time. It was not too bad as I had a royal red *prie-dieu*.

We are going to pull a stunt [the 3rd Division's amphibious end run] on the enemy pretty soon—long before you get this that may become quite famous.[48]

But first, a town called Troina, perched on a mountain top, would have to be taken.

■ 14 ■

ROUGH ROAD TO MESSINA

Dear George . . . You are doing a grand job.

—Franklin D. Roosevelt

Getting to Messina was harder than anyone thought. For the British, they were stalled between Catania and Messina. For the Americans, they would face three more major battles on the way there: Sant' Agata, Brolo, and Troina.

On the island's north shore, the retreating enemy—primarily Germany's recently arrived 29th Panzer Grenadier Division commanded by *Panzertruppe* Gen. Walter Fries—had blown bridges and left thousands of mines in its wake to delay the advance of the Americans.[1]

■ ■ ■

The issue of lack of Allied air support again raised its ugly head. On 1 August a forty-eight-plane Luftwaffe raid hit Palermo and ships anchored offshore. The destroyer *Mayrant* (DD 402), which had suffered previous damage, was caught in a four-hour downpour of red-hot debris after a bomb blew up a nearby train loaded with nine hundred tons of ammunition. One of the president's sons, Lt. Franklin Roosevelt Jr., was an officer aboard the *Mayrant* and helped save a wounded sailor's life.

For several days the enemy continued to pound the Palermo area with air raids—something the Allied air forces did little about. According to Samuel Morison, "Adequate air cover was never provided to the ships operating along this coast. Northwest African Tactical Air Command did furnish combat air patrols from its newly occupied Sicilian fields but under conditions that greatly limited its usefulness to the Navy. The Air Force reserved the right to withdraw combat air patrols without warning, and it refused to permit naval vessels to communicate directly with the planes, lest some naval commander attempt to control them.

"Consequently, there could be no coordination between ships and planes in an enemy air attack. The Luftwaffe evidently got on this strange state of affairs, for it adopted the tactic of sending a decoy plane ahead of a strike. The decoy would lead the entire combat air patrol away in pursuit, while the attack, which had been detected by ships' radar but could not be communicated to friendly planes, struck in. Fortunately the anti-aircraft gunners in Task Force 88 became very expert, through abundant experience; beating off enemy air attacks without benefit of [combat air patrol] became almost daily routine."

Three days later the Luftwaffe paid a return visit to Palermo. Raiders swept in and were greeted by intense anti-aircraft fire and driven off—but not before their bombs struck the destroyer USS *Shubrick* in the forward engine room, killing nine crewmen; eight others suffered burns so severe that they later died. Enemy air forces would continue attacking Palermo sporadically up through 23 August.[2]

■ ■ ■

On 4 August Patton received jocular plaudits from the commander in chief, President Franklin Roosevelt: "Dear George, . . . You are doing a grand job. . . . It was suggested . . . that after the war I should make you the Marquis of Mt. Etna. Don't fall into the crater!"[3]

Patton also received a gushing cable from Eisenhower congratulating him on his army's drive thus far. "The Seventh Army has already made a name for itself that will live in American history," Ike wrote. "Within the next few days it will add immeasurably to the lustre of its fame. I personally assure you that if we speedily finish off the Germans in Sicily, you need have no fear of being left there in the backwater of the war."[4]

Ike's effusive praise raised Patton's spirits to the zenith and wiped away the earlier self-doubts and the sense that his superior was disappointed in him. If there was a cloud higher than cloud nine, Patton certainly felt he had reached it. His mood was further elevated when, the very next day, he received the oak leaf cluster for his Distinguished Service Cross. There were, however, unseen events on the horizon about to knock him from his pedestal.[5]

■ ■ ■

Messina—Patton's obsession and the glittering prize that beckoned like a siren's song—still needed to be taken before the British could get there. Patton gave that mission to his most trusted unit: Truscott's 3rd Infantry Division.

The 3rd was still battling the Germans in the Caronie Mountains, and Lucian Truscott was informed on 3 August that Patton had arranged for the Navy, four days hence, to lift one of his battalions in an operation along the coast behind enemy lines. Although he did not think one battalion would be enough, Truscott gave the mission to Lt. Col. Lyle W. Bernard's 2nd Battalion, 30th RCT, and attached to it Batteries A and B of the 58th Field Artillery Battalion, one platoon of tanks from the 753rd Tank Battalion, and one engineer platoon. Plans were drawn up to depart from Santo Stefano and land at Sant' Agata di Militello, a decent-sized coastal town a few miles behind the Germans' coastline anchor at Caronia, while the rest of the division, traveling overland, would attempt to break through to Brolo.

Admiral Davidson's naval Task Force 88 would provide two cruisers (the *Philadelphia* and *Savannah*), six destroyers, two LSTs, seven LCTs, and one LCI on the night of 7–8 August. The LST could hold eighteen Sherman tanks or 160 troops, while the LCT, which came in several sizes, could haul four Shermans. An LCI could carry an entire infantry company—two hundred men.[6]

Patton soon got word that there was resistance to the amphibious "end run" operation; Truscott, Bradley, and Davidson's chief of staff were all calling for a postponement because the Marnemen weren't quite ready. But Patton was having none of it. After driving to Truscott's command post, he burst in, "giving everybody hell from the Military Police at the entrance right on until he came to me," Truscott said. "He was screamingly angry as only he could be, 'Goddammit, Lucian, what's the matter with you? Are you afraid to fight?'

"General, you know that's ridiculous and insulting. You have ordered the operation and it is now loading."

Patton's dander was still up: "General Truscott, if your conscience will not let you conduct this operation, I will relieve you and put someone in command who will."

Truscott replied, "General, it is your privilege to reduce me whenever you want to."

"I *don't* want to," Patton said, "I got you the DSM [Distinguished Service Medal] and recommended you for major general, but your own ability really gained both honors. You are too old an athlete to believe it's possible to postpone a match."

Truscott retorted, "You are an old-enough athlete to know that sometimes they are postponed."

"This one won't be," Patton shot back. "The ships have already started."

"This is a war of defile," Truscott replied, "and there is a bottleneck delaying me in getting my guns up to support the infantry. They—the infantry—will be too far west to help the landing."

Patton smiled, "Remember Frederick the Great: '*L'audace, toujours l'audace.*' I know you will win and if there is a bottleneck, you should be there and not here."

Truscott said, "I will tell you one thing—you will not find anyone who can carry out orders which they do not approve of as well as I can."

Then Patton cooled off. "Dammit, Lucian, I know that. Come on, let's have a drink—of your liquor." Shortly thereafter Patton departed "in his usual good spirits," Truscott said.[7]

■ ■ ■

Despite a two-hour delay, the operation was launched from beaches west of Santo Stefano, and everything proceeded smoothly. The shelling by one of the destroyers of the coastal highway held by the 29th Panzer Grenadier

Division destroyed a key bridge and caused a traffic jam of German vehicles trying to escape the area.

Shrugging off attacks by enemy aircraft, the Navy kept firing. The official report of the campaign said, "This operation was successful in breaking the enemy line anchored at Mount Fratello and ending the resistance in that area. Twelve hundred prisoners were captured without any casualties to our forces."[8]

Patton wrote to Beatrice, "We pulled a landing operation the other night. No opposition. When we got to an orchard, there were 400 Germans asleep. It was butt and bayonet for a while. It was too dark to shoot. We won."[9]

■ ■ ■

Whether the Seventh Army would beat Montgomery to Messina was still an open question—except in Patton's mind. He wrote to General Leslie McNair, head of Army Ground Forces back in Washington, "We have been very fortunate in our operations so far, and I am betting that we get to Messina first in the current horse race."[10]

Everything was going perfectly. Seventh Army had the enemy on the run, Italian soldiers were surrendering in droves, Palermo had fallen, his army was overcoming opposition along the northern coast, and Montgomery was still struggling south of Messina. What could possibly go wrong?

The truth of the old biblical expression, "Pride goeth before destruction," suddenly derailed Patton's joy. In quick succession, two incidents occurred that would overshadow and tarnish Patton's—and Seventh Army's—accomplishments to date.

The first came on 3 August when the general was visiting the 15th Evacuation Hospital at Nicosia, some sixty miles southeast of Palermo, where he would talk privately to the brave men of II Corps wounded in battle, pin medals on them, and say a few prayers with and for them.

While making the rounds with Maj. Gen. John P. Lucas and a group of medical officers, he came upon twenty-eight-year-old Pvt. Charles H. Kuhl, a rifleman assigned to Company L of the 1st Division's 26th RCT; Kuhl was sitting slumped on a stool. A doctor had written on his medical chart, "Psychoneurosis anxiety state, moderately severe. Soldier has been twice before in hospital within ten days. He can't take it at the front, evidently. He is repeatedly returned [for duty]."[11]

Kuhl later wrote, "I thought I had lost my nerves. . . . I was sitting in the [receiving] tent when it happened—waiting to be admitted—when General Patton and his guard walked in. I don't remember for sure but I would say there were about twenty-five or thirty soldiers in there."[12]

Lt. Col. Perrin H. Long, an Army doctor who witnessed what happened next, said that Patton "came into the tent with the [medical unit's] commanding officer and other medical officers. The general spoke to the various patients in the receiving tent and especially commended the wounded men. Then he came to Private Kuhl and asked him what was the matter. The soldier replied, 'I guess I can't take it.'"[13]

Patton became enraged and kicked Kuhl in the backside, yelling to the staff, "Don't admit this son of a bitch," then screamed at the private, "You're going back to the front, you hear me, you gutless bastard? You're going back to the front!"[14]

Doctor Long said, "The general immediately flared up, cursed the soldier, called him all types of a coward, then slapped him across the face with his gloves and finally grabbed the soldier by the scruff of his neck and kicked him out of the tent."[15]

After Patton stormed out, Kuhl was examined and found to have a body temperature of 102.2 degrees; further tests revealed that he was suffering from malaria.[16]

■ ■ ■

Still boiling, Patton returned to his headquarters and dashed off an order to all Seventh Army units:

> It has come to my attention that a very small number of soldiers are going to the hospital on the pretext that they are nervously incapable of combat. Such men are cowards and bring discredit on the Army and disgrace to their comrades who they heartlessly leave to endure the danger of a battle which they themselves use the hospital as a means of escaping.

> You will take measures to see that such cases are not sent to the hospital but are dealt with in their units. Those who are not willing to fight will be tried by Court-Martial for cowardice in the face of the enemy.[17]

When word of the slapping incident filtered back to Eisenhower, he was livid. Had he not, just a week earlier, commended Patton on his outstanding leadership—and now *this*? It was difficult enough trying to hold this fractious coalition together and keep Patton and Montgomery from doing battle with each other, but an officer striking an enlisted man was intolerable, a court-martial offense. Since Ike could not afford to lose arguably his most aggressive commander, he chose to write Patton a private letter of reprimand—without even informing Marshall—in an effort to keep the incident quiet.[18]

But the Kuhl incident was not the last time that Patton would physically assault a hospitalized soldier.

■ ■ ■

While he was still battling the Germans standing in his way, Truscott stewed over the impending amphibious end run along Sicily's northern coast. On 8 August it got underway. Bringing Bernard's assault team to Sant' Agata was Adm. Davidson's Task Force 88. No one knew what kind of reception Fries' 29th Panzer Grenadier Division would offer.[19]

When the Yanks landed later that morning, they found the Germans frantically trying to escape, but their route had been blocked by the guns of the *Philadelphia* and *Savannah*. Upon landing, Bernard's men and the tankers took the rear of the German column under fire and decimated it, killing 250 of the enemy and capturing another 1,200. A quantity of German tanks and vehicles was also destroyed. A swarm of enemy planes attacked the *Philadelphia* but were driven off by naval anti-aircraft guns and the unusual appearance of Allied warplanes.[20]

■ ■ ■

On 11 August a second amphibious maneuver by Bernard's battalion and supporting forces landed behind the enemy lines at Brolo, about four miles east of Cape Orlando.

Truscott said, "That day of August 11th I will never forget. Bernard's battalion was already somewhat reduced in strength from previous losses, and probably did not number more than 650. [The usual strength of an infantry battalion was about 800 men.] We knew that the beach at Brolo was none too good, and that the exits inland were difficult—through an olive grove and up steep banks onto the coastal highway.

"Bernard's objective was not far behind the German lines from Cape Orlando south through Naso, and it was expected that the German reaction would be even more violent than in the previous landing at Sant' Agata, for the Germans' one route of escape was along the foot of Mount Cipolla where Bernard was to pull the drawstring of the bag.

"No other battalion was within Bernard's objective, and those miles were across inconceivably difficult terrain with a bitterly defending enemy. We knew that Bernard's battalion would be hard pressed to maintain for many hours. We committed every element in the Division, including a Ranger Battalion just recently attached, to fight their way through to Bernard's battalion. . . . Every gun and tank was emplaced as far forward as we could get them. The aim was not merely to defeat an enemy and take an objective; it was to aid comrades who were in danger. The urgency of the situation was impressed on all, and by daylight the whole Division was in movement."

As the day wore on, the Germans, rather than fleeing, turned and began counterattacking Bernard's men in force, including with tanks. Truscott could only listen to messages pouring in to his command post's radio. Each hour brought more distressing news—the naval fire support had ceased and no Allied warplanes had appeared. Requests for artillery fire became more frequent and frantic. No reinforcements had arrived. "All of us felt a sense of desperation," said Truscott.

At 1610 hours another call came from Bernard: "Where is reinforcing infantry? Need doughboys badly. Another counterattack on. Ammo very short." Then: "Being counterattacked by battalion from west. Must have Navy and Air on [coordinates] 702504 immediately or we are lost." Then the radio went silent until late that night.

It was later learned that rescuing units had arrived and stopped the Germans in the nick of time. Truscott said, "We lost seven of the eight guns we put ashore and three of the four tanks which landed. . . . We took only a handful of prisoners, but the roads were littered with German dead and with destroyed tanks and vehicles. Our losses from this small force totaled 167.

"Early the next morning I saw Bernard when he came down off the mountain which his little force had held so gallantly. I could only say, 'Thank God, Bernard, for I am certainly glad to see you.' Bernard's reply was even more heartful: 'General, you just don't know how glad I am to see *you*.'"[21] The battle for Brolo would be the enemy's last stand of any strength against the Americans along the coast prior to his complete evacuation at Messina.[22]

■ ■ ■

A third amphibious leapfrog landing was planned. On 16 August the end of the Sicilian campaign was even more clearly in sight, and Patton wanted so badly to capture Messina—and headlines—before Montgomery did that he could taste it. Ordering another "end run" amphibious operation, he arranged for Davidson's Task Force 88 to transport elements of the 45th Division's 157th RCT eastward beyond Brolo and provide them with fire support. But the Germans were withdrawing toward Messina faster than Seventh Army could outflank them.

Truscott had to threaten to stop the 3rd Division's pursuit of the Germans in order to get Keyes to call Patton and explain that the 157th's landing was not practical and could lead to a friendly fire disaster. Patton gave in and told General Middleton that there was to be no firing upon landing. To further ensure a safe landing, Truscott sent two officers from his staff to meet the incoming waves of Thunderbirds and assure them that the beach was already in friendly hands. The landing came off without a disaster.[23]

■ ■ ■

Simultaneously with this action, the even more desperate battle of Troina was taking place. Overshadowing the battles, however, one question loomed like a barrage balloon: What should be done about Patton and his temper?

15

CAPTURING A TOWN, LOSING A COMMANDER

You are to be congratulated for a truly great performance.

—**Terry de la Mesa Allen**

Compared to the British Eighth Army's struggle up the island's east coast, the American drive up the center of Sicily was like a stroll in the park. That is, until the Seventh Army—or more specifically, Terry Allen's 1st Infantry Division—reached Troina, high upon a mountain some twenty miles west of Mount Etna, Europe's largest active volcano.

Eisenhower wrote, "As the Seventh Army approached the western slopes of the Mount Etna highlands, fighting became more and more severe. The Battle of Troina, conducted largely by the 1st Division, was one of the most fiercely fought smaller actions of the war."[1] But first would come the battle for Nicosia, twelve miles to the west.

Capt. James L. Pence and his Company A, 16th RCT, were approaching Nicosia, a town of about ten thousand people that has been described as looking like "a stairway to the sky." He said, "Enemy resistance of the II Corps front had stiffened and was increasing. A German motorized division [the 29th Panzer Grenadier] faced the 45th Infantry Division on the left, or north, flank of II Corps. The 1st Infantry Division on the right flank was opposed by a German panzer division [the Hermann Göring]. Remnants of the 26th and 28th Italian Divisions also were known to be in this area."

Pence was frustrated by the enemy's rearguard delaying actions. Intelligence correctly surmised that preparations were being made by the enemy to organize an outpost line of resistance just west of the Santo Stefano–Mistretta-Nicosia road, with the main defensive position—the Etna Line—farther to the east.

"The terrain in this area was particularly well suited to the delaying tactics that the enemy was employing," he said. "A series of rocky ridges and mountains afforded the enemy numerous excellent defensive positions. The road net was extremely limited, canalizing communications along the two east-west highways in the corps zone. This inadequate road net also severely restricted the mobility and maneuverability of the fighting troops."[2]

Correspondent Richard Tregaskis, following the 1st Division, wrote, "We moved on to Hill 841 without resistance and also, noticeably, without breakfast or water. We paused to look out on . . . the usual clusters of gray buildings. It soon became apparent why the Germans had offered a considerable fight for this high ground. We could look directly over the road winding through Sperlinga and from there to Nicosia, and even see such details as the movement of carts in the streets."

Tregaskis watched from a safe distance the 1st Division's 18th RCT advance toward Nicosia. "We heard the sound of 'burp guns,'" he said, "and the crunching of mortar shells from the direction of Nicosia. A smudge of dirty black smoke puffed from one section of Nicosia. The troops of the 18th Infantry . . . were probably fighting in the town itself." After a short while the sound of firing died down. Nicosia had fallen.

Hitching a ride in a jeep with a couple of grimy, shell-shocked German POWs sitting on the hood, Tregaskis and correspondent John Hersey then headed back westward for the town of Gangi, draped over the top of a hill like a beige cloak, where Terry Allen had his forward command post. Allen showed them a map with two arrows converging on Nicosia, then described the two-pronged tactics his division had used to squeeze the enemy out of the town. "Had we kept up a frontal attack," Allen told the reporters, "it would have meant just a bloody nose for us on every hill. . . . This was about as stubborn as any resistance we've encountered so far. The fall of Nicosia probably means that the Germans will have to retire to their next road-net at Troina; Troina is the last road-net center before Mount Etna."[3]

As matters turned out, by the morning of 28 July Nicosia had been abandoned by the enemy—but not before the 18th RCT took a haul of prisoners. Medic Allen Towne noted, "The 18th captured 700 Italian soldiers along with a few Germans." Those who survived retreated to Troina while continuing to lob harassing artillery fire at the Yanks.[4]

■ ■ ■

After leaving Nicosia, Captain Pence led his men east on rocky trails toward Troina, then called a halt for the night; the men slept for two hours on hard ground. As dawn broke Pence was awakened by one of his platoon leaders: "Hey, Captain—come over here and have a look."

About two hundred yards away on top of a ridge outside of Troina, Pence said, "Germans could be seen all along the ridge. They had apparently just awakened and were walking about, stretching, indulging in horseplay, and attending to their personal needs. One shot put an end to their dawn activities, at least on the side of the ridge facing [my] company." After a brief firefight, Company A secured the enemy position and took one hundred prisoners.[5]

Perched atop a mountain that dominated Highway 120, Troina was a natural defensive stronghold that elements of three enemy divisions had chosen well to defend. Like so many of the mountaintop towns scattered all over Sicily, Troina was nothing special—just a collection of stone and stucco buildings crowded together and looking as if they had been there since the dawn of time.

But Troina, home to 1,200 hardy mountain folk, was special in a military sense. One road, Highway 120, coming from Nicosia and Cerami, entered it from the northwest; two roads left it from the east—one that eventually reached Catania to the southeast and the other that stretched northeastward to Randazzo, snaked around Mount Etna, and then went on to Taormina on the east coast. The 15th Panzer Grenadiers, under Lieutenant General Eberhard Rodt, left behind as a rear guard, knew that if they could stall the Americans long enough, more of their countrymen could be evacuated from the island to Italy itself and live to fight another day. The 15th Panzer Grenadiers, augmented by elements of Giacomo Romano's 28th Aosta Infantry Division and Ottorino

Schreiber's 26th Assietta Infantry Division, would give new meaning to the word "tenacious."[6]

Terry Allen didn't know exactly what he would find at Troina. The same faulty intelligence that had plagued him during the 1st Division's landing at Gela bit him again at Troina. Aerial surveillance had been virtually nonexistent, radio communication between mountain peaks was spotty, and, aside from a few men with binoculars scanning the terrain ahead, no one seemed to know how many of the enemy were there.[7]

The struggle for the town began on 31 July when the 39th RCT of the 9th Infantry Division took Cerami, two road miles west of Troina, with very little resistance. Allen and Bradley, who was at the 1st Division command post to observe the action, both agreed that the 39th and the attached 4th Tabour of French Moroccan Goumiers (a feared battalion of some nine hundred men who were no strangers to atrocities), along with tanks from the 2nd Armored Division, should be allowed to have first crack at Troina.[8]

Allen Towne recalled the Goumiers: "The Goums were a native French Moroccan unit. They were from the Atlas Mountain and were used to this type of terrain. A few of them were wounded and passed through our aid station during the next few days. They spoke French and I believe they were a Free French unit. They seemed to be excellent soldiers and did a lot of night fighting. Their specialty was to infiltrate enemy lines. We were told they used knives at night to kill the enemy sentries. They would then cut off their ears and bring them back as proof of their success."[9]

There wasn't supposed to be much opposition in Troina; civilians and POWs assured the Americans that only a handful of enemy soldiers remained in the town. But it was a trap. As the 39th RCT and 4th Tabour approached Troina early on the morning of 1 August, they were saturated by a fearsome, daylong barrage of mortars and artillery, completely halting their attack. It was now the Big Red One's turn again; Allen called on the 16th and 18th RCTs to lead the way.[10]

Looking up at the collection of stone houses, Terry Allen's men were disheartened. They had just spent the past three weeks fighting uphill in stifling heat and humidity against a determined enemy who showed no signs of quitting. Their casualties had been heavy, and new replacements were slow in learning the art and science of close-quarter combat. But intelligence thought that the town was free of any serious German opposition. Intelligence was dead wrong.[11]

War correspondent Jack Belden would call the fight for the town "the toughest battle in Sicily."[12] Allen Towne echoed that sentiment, recalling, "The battle was the toughest and most significant of the Sicilian campaign. Troina was situated on the top of a 3,600-foot peak and was an important road junction. . . . The enemy occupied the high ground north, west, and south of Troina, and used the town as an observation post and as an artery of supply and communication. It was very important for the Germans to hold Troina as long as possible in order to protect their withdrawal over the Straits of Messina. This was their only route of escape to the mainland of Italy."[13] The Germans were determined to block the Americans' advance toward Messina for as long as possible.[14]

By the time the battle for it was over, "Troina" was a curse word as foul and obscene as any that ever came out of any 1st Division GI's mouth.

■ ■ ■

On the battle's opening day Sgt. Gerry H. Kisters of the 2nd Armored Division's Company B, 91st Reconnaissance Squadron, was part of a ten-man detachment near Gagliano, southwest of Troina, advancing ahead of the leading elements of 1st Division troops. Their advance was stymied when they encountered a large crater in the highway.

Kisters and Lt. Orsell C. Price, the officer leading the group, "went up to look over the high ground commanding the road. They practically stepped on a German machine-gun nest and captured the crew before they realized what had happened. Then, another machine gun, higher on the slope, opened fire on them. Kisters left Lieutenant Price with a tommy gun to guard the prisoners." Kisters then took off with a carbine to get the second machine-gun crew.

"Crawling half of the sixty feet to the German gun position, Kisters was hit three times in each leg by snipers he never saw, and finally stopped. The terrain was rocky. Moving from cover to cover, he shot three of the Germans in the gun crews. The fourth got up and started to run. 'I'd just got a bead on him when a sniper hit me in the right arm and paralyzed it. I knew I was done shootin' so I called to Price. He made the German prisoners come up to me, and they carried me down. . . . I guess the snipers could still have fired on us, but they must have not wanted to hit their own men. Or somethin'."

For his brazen act of bravery, Kisters received the Medal of Honor; his citation reads, "Despite the wounds, he continued to advance on the enemy, and captured the second machine gun after killing three of its crew and forcing the fourth member to flee." But he played down any heroism on his part. He told *Yank* in his aw-shucks style, "The shape I was in after all those snipers got to me, it was just as dangerous to move backwards as forwards. So I moved forwards." Kisters survived his wounds and was given a battlefield commission; he died in 1986 at age sixty-seven.[15]

■ ■ ■

On the morning of 2 August, as the 1st Division troops left their line of departure and started uphill toward Troina, another barrage fell on them like a steel tidal wave—and then another and another. Unable to advance or retreat, the men took cover behind any rock they could find. Royal Air Force Spitfires were called in for airstrikes but seemed not to make a dent in the defenders' determination.

As one historian wrote, "The siege of Troina raged on, exposing both the attackers and defenders to dire conditions. Food, water, and ammunition for the Americans could only be brought up during the night by mules. During the day, a summer sun scorched the men who burrowed into whatever protection they could find while the near-incessant shelling exploded about them. Mines bedeviled movement."[16]

Not content with simply bombarding their foes from long range, the Germans also struck out with combat patrols against the 18th RCT that disrupted any American attempts to climb the heights.[17] At least twenty-four counterattacks hit the Yanks.[18]

As the 1st Division's 16th RCT moved out from its assembly area at Cerami, just west of Troina, at 0300 hours on 3 August a swarm of German artillery shells crashed down upon it, sending the men to ground—not just for a few hours but for two days. It seemed to the GIs that every shell in the Wehrmacht's arsenal had been shipped to Sicily and was personally being used against them.

Also adding their voices to the fight were German snipers, well hidden among the buildings, as well as mortars and machine guns. There was no easy path to Troina; minefields were everywhere. Some sixty 1st Division men were caught in an ambush and mowed down; another sixty were taken prisoner. That afternoon Company F reported that, after starting out with nearly two hundred soldiers, it was down to one officer and thirty-five men; Company G had just forty men left.

Had it not been for the timely intervention of six battalions of Brig. Gen. Clift Andrus' 1st Division Artillery, more airstrikes by Spitfire pilots, and a seventy-two bomber raid, the Big Red One would have been ground into the Bloody Red One.[19]

■ ■ ■

Two days later another Medal of Honor was conferred for actions at Troina. On Monte Basilio, overlooking the town, Pvt. James W. Reese of the 26th RCT, 1st Infantry Division, was a crewman on a 60-mm mortar squad that was hit by one of the Germans' artillery barrages. He directed the other members of his squad to withdraw to safety while he stayed at the tube and continued to drop rounds into it. With his last round he scored a direct hit on a German machine-gun position; he then picked up a rifle and advanced in the open toward the enemy.

According to Reese's posthumous Medal of Honor citation, "Despite a heavy concentration of machine-gun, mortar, and artillery fire, the heaviest experienced by his unit throughout the entire Sicilian campaign, he remained at this position and continued to inflict casualties upon the enemy until he was killed." Reese became the first of sixteen Big Red One soldiers in World War II who would receive the U.S. armed force's highest military decoration for extraordinary acts of valor. He was also one of 267 1st Division men killed in the twenty-seven days from the Gela invasion through the battle for Troina.[20]

■ ■ ■

Badly coordinated air support plagued the Americans' entire Sicily operation. On 5 July dive-bombers from the U.S. XII Air Support Command were supposed to have plastered Troina; they hit Oliver Leese's XXX Corps headquarters far to the east instead. "What have we done to deserve such a bombing?" an irate Leese reportedly yelled at Maj. Gen. Edwin J. House, the commander of the XII Air Force.[21]

Under the cover of darkness late on 5 August, the Germans began pulling out of Troina, leaving behind shattered buildings, destroyed vehicles, and the bodies of their comrades. The Germans had suffered heavily from Allied artillery and warplanes; the 15th Panzer Grenadiers, who had garrisoned the town, lost an estimated 1,600 men. But with their twenty-four counterattacks, they had stalled the 1st Division drive. German prisoners admitted that they had been under strict orders to fight to the last man. The German high command had decided that their forces in Troina had done all they could do and, to spare them from total annihilation, pulled them out and sent them to Messina.[22]

The next day at 0300 hours, as the ragged remnants of the 16th RCT climbed cautiously up toward the wrecked town, they were accidentally struck by a U.S. Air Force aerial bombing mission; many were killed or wounded. The Yanks found Troina empty of German troops, but they discovered that most of the residents had survived, having burrowed into the deepest recesses of their sturdy stone houses. The civilians emerged with cheers and flowers and *vino* for their liberators.[23]

■ ■ ■

Omar Bradley had promised that, once Troina was in American hands, Terry Allen and the Big Red One would get a rest and be relieved by the bulk of Manton Eddy's 9th Infantry Division that had arrived in Palermo's harbor on 1 August. Allen never saw the next blow coming.

As heavy as the Americans' casualties had been, the battle of Troina brought the worst news of all. Terry Allen—and Teddy Roosevelt Jr. too—had long displeased Omar Bradley and now, with Patton's blessing, was Bradley's perfect opportunity to get rid of the two of them and bring in a disciplinarian who would ride herd on the proud but unruly division. Using the excuse that Allen had delayed his final assault on Troina with his entire division and thus had allowed the Germans to withdraw, Bradley, as II Corps commander and Allen's immediate superior, decided to sack him.

While it seems absurd that anyone would be fired for being too successful, such appears to be the case with Terry Allen. Bradley noted in his memoirs, "By now Allen had become too much of an individualist to submerge himself without friction in the group undertakings of war. The 1st Division, under Allen's command, had become too full of self-pity and pride. To save Allen both from himself and from his brilliant record, and to save the division from the heady effects of too much success, I decided to separate them. Only in this way could I hope to preserve the extraordinary value of that division's experience in the Mediterranean war, an experience that would be of incalculable value in the Normandy attack."

Bradley also knew that he couldn't let Allen go without also sacking Roosevelt. "Allen, I realized, would feel deeply hurt if he were to leave the division and Roosevelt were to remain. He might have considered himself a failure instead of the victim of too much success. By the same token, Roosevelt's claim to the affections of the 1st Division would present any new commander with an impossible situation from the start. Any successor of Allen's would find himself in an untenable spot unless I allowed him to pick his own assistant commander. Roosevelt had to go with Allen for he, too, had sinned by loving the division too much."

Realizing that his decision would shock them both, Bradley called the two generals into his command post in Nicosia to break the bad news. "The relief came as a severe blow to them," Bradley admitted. "But though it was one of my most unpleasant duties of the entire war, I had to do it. Fortunately, they rebounded like good soldiers. Allen returned to Europe with a superbly trained 104th Division which he led to the Elbe [River]. And Roosevelt returned to England to win a Medal of Honor on the Normandy assault [with the 4th Infantry Division at Utah Beach]. There at the age of fifty-six he made his fourth H-hour landing on a hostile shore."[24]

Although Bradley claimed that the decision to relieve Allen and Roosevelt was his alone, Patton was the real instigator—at least a week before the battle for Troina. On 31 July he wrote in his diary, "I got Ike's permission to relieve both Allen and Roosevelt. . . . There will be a kick over Teddy but he has to go: brave but otherwise no soldier. I telegraphed Allen's and Roosevelt's relief to Bradley and sent him a personal note suggesting that he postpone it until the 1st Division is relieved by the 9th [Division]."

Replacing Allen and Roosevelt were Maj. Gen. Clarence Huebner—Alexander's former deputy chief of staff—and Col. (later Brig. Gen.) William G. Wyman. Those two officers would lead the division to triumph a year later in Normandy and beyond.[25]

Crestfallen, Allen told his wife Mary Fran in a letter that he and Roosevelt had both been relieved of command: "I just received orders today which were a great surprise and the actual meaning of which I do not exactly know. Ted R. and I have both been relieved from the division and have been directed to report to the American commander in chief [Eisenhower] at Algiers. . . . Needless to say I will be overjoyed at the prospect of any assignment which means a return home and the opportunity to be with you again, my dear, even though my actual start [back to the U.S.] may be a bit delayed and the distant future may involve another combat assignment."[26]

In another letter to Mary Fran, Allen noted, "Patton was most kind and cordial and thoroughly appreciative of the division. . . . He put us up overnight at the Royal Palace [in Palermo]. . . . It was some contrast to the battlefield bivouac that we had been living in for the past thirty days." Allen then met with Eisenhower who showered him with appreciation and dangled the possibility of a corps command in front of him, depending on the Army's wants and needs.

Eisenhower told Allen that he had "the longest, most arduous and most successful combat record of any general officer in this war and could carry a great deal of prestige." Ike then awarded him the Distinguished Service Medal.[27]

■ ■ ■

The first the men knew of Allen's sacking was on the afternoon of 6 August when he and Huebner both appeared at the 16th RCT's command post. After introducing Huebner and telling the men that a change of command had been made, Allen said, "The battle of Troina was by far the toughest battle we've had—far tougher than any in Africa. I'm proud of the tenacity of the

16th . . . the indomitable defiance displayed by all of you, the spirit each man has shown and is still showing. You are to be congratulated for a truly great performance."[28]

When the rest of the division got the news, it was like a bomb going off. The men felt shocked, stunned, hurt, and angry over what they regarded as an unjust firing of their two beloved leaders. Lt. Joe Dawson, Company G, 16th Regiment, spoke for the majority of 1st Division GIs when he said, "We had the most wonderful leader in Terry Allen, whose absolute capacity to inspire an *esprit de corps* as no other man I've ever known and was loved by everybody in the division because of he being a soldier's soldier."[29]

On 7 August, the day after he got the ax, Terry Allen wrote a letter to the men from whom he had just been separated: "To all members of the Fighting First: In compliance with recent orders, Major General Clarence Huebner, who fought in this division with great distinction during the last war, has been designated as Division Commander. I feel most fortunate to have been your commander during the preceding year. You should be proud of your combat records. . . . You have lived up to your battle slogan: 'Nothing in Hell must stop the First Division.'"[30]

Even American journalist and war correspondent Quentin Reynolds got on the Terry Allen bandwagon. In a letter to Terry's wife, he wrote, "Never in my life have I seen a man so worshipped as Terry was and is—not only by his men in the First but by every war correspondent who had ever come in contact with him. As far as I am concerned, Terry Allen is the greatest leader of men and the greatest tactical general in our army. We were all sick when he was sent home. . . . It looks as if you and I are in love with the same fellow."[31]

Joe Dawson slowly came around to being a huge Clarence Huebner fan:

> General Huebner realized that he faced a problem. He was smart enough to take some people into his confidence and say, "I've got to become the commander of the 1st Division and it's going to be tough because I've got to follow a man who has been outstanding, but I've got to . . . stamp myself as being *the man*." And what did he do? He did it the most incredible way I ever could possibly conceive. We were battle-seasoned veterans by that time [but] Huebner insisted on everybody from the division staff down to

> the lowest private to re-learn how to hand salute, and the manual of arms, and the close-order drill—things that we said, "Why, those are superficial nonentities. We're combat men, we're veterans." And we hated him at first [but] I came to love him just like everybody else did when we learned who he was and what he was and how great a man he really was. But that first time was something to behold.[32]

■ ■ ■

The bloody, bruised, and battered 1st Infantry Division, now under new leadership, was not required to take part in the final ten days of the battle for Sicily. Thinking that they had done more than enough and that perhaps they were on their way home, the survivors began packing their gear and getting ready to leave the island. Little did they know that the Army had another invasion in store for them: Operation Overlord. Instead of going home, they would soon be going to England to prepare for the next invasion—Normandy, France.[33]

The battle of Sicily still needed to be won, however. And another Patton slap was on the horizon.

▪ 16 ▪

A FALL FROM GRACE

I ought to shoot you myself, you goddamned whimpering coward.

—**George S. Patton Jr.**

On 10 August, a week after Private Kuhl was slapped and five days after Troina was taken, Patton was on his way to visit Omar Bradley when he stopped off at the 93rd Evacuation Hospital near Santo Stefano on the northern coast. There he said that he

> talked to 350 newly wounded. One poor fellow who had lost his right arm cried; another had lost a leg. All were brave and cheerful. The 1st Sergeant of C Company, 39th Infantry, was in for his second wound. He laughed and said that after he got his third wound he was going to ask to go home. I had told General Marshall some months ago that an enlisted man hit three times should be sent home.
>
> In the hospital was one louse. He was unhurt but told me that he was unable to take it—just a coward. I gave him hell and slapped his face with my gloves. Companies should deal with such men and if they shirk, try them for cowardice.[1]

This time the soldier slapped was twenty-one-year-old Sgt. Paul G. Bennett, a member of the 17th Field Artillery Regiment, who was sitting on the corner of a bunk and shaking with convulsions. Omar Bradley quoted from a report by a doctor who was present:

> Patton asked, "And what's happened to you?"
>
> Bennett: "It's my nerves, sir. I can't stand the shelling any more."
>
> George raised his voice. "Your nerves, hell," he shouted, "you're just a goddamned coward."
>
> The soldier cried and George slapped him. "Shut up," he said. "I won't have these brave men here who've been shot see a yellow bastard crying."
>
> George struck the man again. His helmet liner fell off and rolled across the dirt floor.
>
> Patton called to the receiving officer, "Don't you admit this yellow bastard. There's nothing the matter with him. I won't have the hospitals cluttered up with sonsabitches who haven't the guts to fight."
>
> Then turning to the patient, he said, "You're going back to the front lines—you may get shot and killed, but you're going back to the fight. If you don't, I'll stand you up against a wall and have a firing squad kill you on purpose."[2]
>
> At this point Patton even pulled out one of his ivory-handled revolvers and stuck it in Bennett's face, yelling, "I ought to shoot you myself, you goddamned whimpering coward."[3] As he left the hospital, Patton growled at Col. Donald E. Currier, the hospital commander, "I won't have these cowards hanging around our hospitals. We'll probably have to shoot them some time anyway, or we'll raise a breed of morons."[4]

Patton could have omitted mentioning the incident in his diary that day but he chose not to: "At [the 93rd] evacuation hospital . . . saw another alleged nervous patient—really a coward. I told the doctor to return him to his company and he began to cry so I cursed him well and he shut up. I may have saved his soul if he had one."[5]

Shocked at Patton's tirade and physical violence against a patient, Currier wrote a detailed secret report of the incident and sent it to his superior. It would finally reach Eisenhower on 17 August—the same day that Patton rolled triumphantly into Messina.[6]

■ ■ ■

After the incident at the 93rd Evacuation Hospital, Patton drove on to Bradley's headquarters and proudly told his II Corps commander how he had treated the "louse." A horrified Bradley noted in his memoirs,

> Canny a showman as George was, he failed to grasp the psychology of the combat soldier . . . a man who lives each day with death tagging him at the elbow and lives in a world of dread and fear. . . . Since conflict was to be the inevitable lot of all mankind, George reasoned that man should resign himself to it and indeed welcome it as a manly challenge. Exhilarated as he was by conflict, he found it inconceivable that men, other than cowards, should want no part of war.
>
> At the same time he could not believe that men could break under an intense mental strain as a result of the hardships endured in war. To him it was axiomatic that those who did not wish to fight were cowards. If one could shame a coward, George said, one might help him to gain his self-respect. I cannot believe that George was intentionally brutal in striking the soldier he called a coward. Patton simply sought to purge that soldier of "cowardice" by shaming him.[7]

For his part, John P. Lucas saw nothing especially remarkable about the incident. After the war he wrote, "There are always a certain number of such weaklings in any Army, and I suppose the modern doctor is correct in classifying them as ill and treating them as such. However, the man with malaria doesn't pass his condition on to his comrades as rapidly as does the man with cold feet, nor does malaria have the lethal effect that the latter has."[8]

■ ■ ■

"The battalion chaplain brought me the news," said Lt. Col. Joseph Couch, commander of Bennett's unit, the 1st Battalion, 17th Field Artillery.

> He was a grave and honest man and not one given to exaggeration, yet for several agonizing minutes I refused to believe him. Or it seemed that some member of the unit with a warped sense of humor was carrying a joke a bit too far.

The chaplain's report was: "General Patton slapped Sergeant Bennett in the hospital." It simply could not be true! He explained that Bennett had just returned to duty after a siege of malaria. He had been slapped three days ago but had made no complaint except to the chaplain.

I had served with this regular Army soldier from Georgia for more than two years on maneuvers and in combat and knew him to be a brave and dedicated man. It had been a severe loss to the unit when he had contracted malaria about two weeks before while we were pursuing German forces across Sicily. . . . At this time in Sicily malaria was taking a heavy toll in our forces, particularly among combat troops.

Investigation of the matter with the battery commander and with Sergeant Bennett indicated that the chaplain had reported accurately. There was no doubt about it: Lieutenant General George S. Patton, while on a tour of a nearby U.S. military hospital, had accused Bennett of malingering and, without waiting for an explanation, had slapped him several times across the face as he lay on his hospital cot.

Through one nearly sleepless night I tried to decide what to do with this disturbing news. As battalion commander I could hardly ignore it, but as a junior lieutenant colonel I could not confront a lieutenant general; a written report would go directly to General Patton, or at least to a member of his loyal staff. In my quandary I went to see my group commander, a wise and older colonel. His firm admonition was to do nothing. I bit my lip and took his advice.[9]

■ ■ ■

In a 9 August letter to Beatrice, Patton reflected on all that had been accomplished up until now. "I have lived a long time in the last thirty days, but I feel very humble. It was the superior fighting of the American soldier, the wonderful efficiency of our mechanical transport, the work of Bradley, Keyes, and the Army staff that did the trick. I just came along for the ride. . . . I certainly love war."[10]

■ ■ ■

Lt. Bill Whitman did not share Patton's sentiments. Near the middle of August he recalled being again confronted by war's grim reality: "We moved back to a bivouac along the coast road near Cefalù. It was night when we moved into the area and tripped over the bodies of dead Americans of the 3rd Division who had fought in that area previously . . . dead Americans who were being buried in mattress covers in a long trench that had been scooped out by a bulldozer. I had also seen one of my friends, Captain Butler, a rifle company commander in our 2nd Battalion, go into one of those mattress covers. At that moment I knew that I really hated war with a purple passion!"[11]

■ ■ ■

After Hitler's 20 July order for German and Italian forces to prepare to abandon Sicily, the evacuation operation code-named *Lehrgang* (Lesson) began on 1 August. Although on a smaller scale than the British/French evacuation at Dunkirk in May and June of 1940, it was no less dramatic and well carried out.

The move was brilliantly orchestrated by Kriegsmarine captain Gustav Freiherr von Liebenstein, a veteran of World War I. He and his men utilized fourteen landing craft and eleven Siebel ferries—flat-bottomed troop and supply boats that had a capacity of fifty tons, could carry 150 to 200 men, and could move fully loaded at a speed of seven knots. The Axis made the day-and-night crossings of the strait in only thirty minutes.

Lehrgang managed to transport 950 vehicles, 21 tanks, 22 artillery pieces, over 100 tons of ammunition, and 1,370 tons of other equipment, along with tens of thousands of German and Italian soldiers from both Messina and Taormina over the next couple of days. A heavy Allied air raid on Messina on the night of 11–12 August suspended the ferries heading across the strait to Reggio di Calabria. When the planes had gone, the evacuation resumed with renewed vigor.

This end phase of Husky has been criticized for allowing so many Axis forces to slip out of Sicily almost unscathed, but the Allies defended their lack of aggression by pointing out that the enemy had heavily fortified both sides of the strait with some five hundred artillery pieces (including anti-aircraft guns) as well as a strong combat aircraft presence in Italy.

The Germans and Italians could not believe that the Allies, with all their air and naval power, seemed to be doing so little to stop them. By the time the ferrying operation was concluded, approximately 110,000 troops—40,000 Germans and 70,000 Italians—would cross to the toe of the boot of Italy—to live and fight another day.[12]

■ ■ ■

Following Lt. Col. Lyle Bernard's desperate amphibious capture of Brolo on the northern coast, the 3rd Infantry Division was closing in on Messina, but as of 12 August it still had many treacherous miles to go. Using hundreds of mules that it had commandeered from civilians to haul its supplies, the 30th RCT was winding its way over narrow paths barely wide enough for a man and a mule. Once they reached Highway 113, the coast road between Palermo and Messina, and passed through small villages clinging to the sides of spectacular cliffs, Truscott's men were stopped dead in their tracks as they approached Cape Calavà.

The retreating Germans, Truscott said, "had blown 150 feet of roadway into the sea a hundred feet below. Days would have been required to blast another road from the cliff. . . . Already the 15th Infantry and the Ranger Battalion were beyond the Cape without artillery or tanks, and with only infantry weapons." Reaching them quickly was imperative.[13]

To war correspondent Ernie Pyle, who accompanied the 3rd Division, Husky was "an engineer's war." The combat engineers, those masters of construction and destruction, had their hands full while both leading and following the infantry divisions. The Germans had blown bridges that needed to be repaired and emplaced mines that needed to be dug up and disposed of.

Pyle noted, "The mine detector and bulldozer were the two magic instruments of our engineering. . . . In the American sector alone [the Germans] destroyed nearly 160 bridges. They mined the bypasses around the bridges, they mined the beaches, they even mined orchards and groves of trees that would be logical bivouacs for our troops."[14]

Col. Leonard Bingham, commanding officer of the 3rd Division's 10th Engineer Battalion, was called forward to restore Highway 113. The official report of the campaign states, "By hanging 'a bridge in the sky' the engineers were able to permit a jeep carrying General Truscott to cross the wooden structure eighteen hours after starting work. Six hours later, after a bit of shoring here and there, heavier vehicles began to cross."[15]

Ernie Pyle described the feat:

> Around dusk of the day before, the engineers had told me they'd have jeeps across the crater by noon of the next day. It didn't seem possible at

> the time . . . [but] the first jeep rolled cautiously across the bridge at high noon, to the very second.
>
> In that first jeep were General Truscott and his driver, facing a 200-foot tumble into the sea if the bridge gave way. The engineers had insisted they send a test jeep across first. But when he saw it was ready, the general got in and went. It wasn't done dramatically but it was a dramatic thing. It showed that the Old Man had complete faith in his engineers. I heard soldiers speak of it appreciatively for an hour.

Truscott's crossing over the rickety structure was followed by a line of jeeps and foot soldiers as part of the division's spearhead. When this initial group had crossed, the engineers went about strengthening the span so that it could hold heavier traffic.

Pyle's praise for the engineers was fulsome. He wrote admiringly, "The tired [engineers] began to pack their tools in trucks. Engineer officers who hadn't slept in thirty-six hours went back to their olive orchard to clean up. They had built a jerry bridge, a comical bridge, a proud bridge, but above all the kind of bridge that wins wars. And they had built it in one night and half a day. The general was mighty pleased."[16]

On 14 August the 3rd Division reached the town of Patti, where it continued to drive the Germans back. When the Marnemen reached Cape Milazzo, they captured, according to Truscott, "a huge ammunition dump, several batteries of artillery, more than 150 undamaged vehicles, several thousand gallons of gasoline and oil, huge stocks of lumber, several long-wave transmitters, and a complete radio direction finder."[17]

■ ■ ■

At about this same time Bill Whitman had a memorable meeting with General Patton on Highway 113. During a lull in the fighting, Whitman was ordered by his company commander to take a jeep and head for the rear to obtain ammunition, rations, water, mail, and miscellaneous supplies. "We came to a blown-out bridge with a bypass around it which our engineers had made," Whitman remembered.

> There was only enough space for one vehicle at a time to use the bypass. As we reached the middle of it, we came radiator to radiator with a

command car heading east. Both vehicles stopped, front bumper to front bumper.

There in the back seat of the car were Generals Patton and Bradley. Patton, who was sitting in the back on Bradley's right, stood up and shouted in his high-pitched voice, "Lieutenant, you are going to the *rear*, and I am going to the *front*. Therefore *my* business is more important than *yours*. Now back up that goddamn jeep and get the hell out of the way."

I yelled at my driver, who sat staring at all those stars, "For Christ's sake, *back this son-of-a-bitch up and let's get the hell out of here!*" We did.[18]

■ ■ ■

Eisenhower was also anxious to have Messina in the bag but worried that too many of the enemy were allowed to escape; it must be said that he, as Allied commander of the Husky campaign, did little to halt the escape. "By the time the Seventh and Eighth Armies had closed up into their final assault against the Mount Etna bastion," he wrote, "the Germans saw that the game was up and began the evacuation. . . . Our bombers operated against this line of escape but the narrowness of the strait allowed the enemy to get out most of the badly battered German garrison during hours of darkness."[19]

Ike's aide, Harry Butcher, wrote that the home front couldn't understand how so many of the enemy were permitted to depart Sicily. "No one seems to emphasize the bitter truth, which is that troops do not have that mysterious power . . . to walk across the water. We still have to rely on landing craft and, unfortunately, we didn't have enough to continue to supply Sicily and conduct two other large-scale operations at the same time."[20]

And Samuel Morison was quoted as saying, "The Navy was frightened; the Straits smelled too much of the Dardanelles [scene of the disastrous World War I amphibious operation at Gallipoli]."

Many postwar critics of Husky felt that the Seventh and Eighth Armies should have landed initially at Messina, rather than having to battle their way for a month across the island to get there. Husky expert British Major Hugh Pond noted, "The reluctance of the Navies to go anywhere near the narrows was amazing enough during the campaign, but it was even worse when it resulted in the completely successful evacuation by the enemy not only of the troops, but also the majority of tanks, guns, and other heavy equipment. . . .

[The Sicily evacuation] was one of the outstanding maritime retreats of the war, in a class with Dunkirk and Guadalcanal. Better than Dunkirk, in fact, where the British Expeditionary Force was forced to destroy or abandon most of its equipment."[21]

The II Corps commander, Omar Bradley, said, "Like George [Patton], I too was anxious to get into Messina before the British . . . for by now the speedy capture of Messina was unimportant. However rapidly we pushed into that city, we could not cut the enemy's escape route across to Italy."[22] Patton, however, did not think a speedy capture of Messina was unimportant, nor was he willing to share the glory with the British. Luckily, unlike Troina, there was no desperate, fight-to-the-death scenario for Messina. The capture of the city was almost a let-down.

"Cautiously, under a butter-colored moon, U.S. 3rd Division patrols reconnoitered the last eight miles to Messina," wrote *Time* magazine correspondent Jack Belden. "The stony Sicilian landscape flashed now and then with snipers' fire. The road was edged with the menace of mines, booby traps, and demolition chasms. But clearly the stubborn, skillful, beaten enemy had pulled out. At 5:30 a.m., August 17, Lieutenants Jeff McNeely and Ralph Yates led patrols into Messina. The Battle of Sicily, thirty-eight days after it had begun, was over."[23]

At dawn on that day Truscott met up with Darby and his 3rd Ranger Battalion occupying a ridge overlooking the prize; both units sent patrols into the city.[24] Just as Truscott's men had been the first to enter Palermo, so they, and the Rangers, were the first to enter Messina. Truscott recalled, "I was on the heights above Messina looking down on the town and across to the toe of Italy. At 0700 one patrol brought out the *Podesta* [comparable to a mayor] and several civic functionaries to make the civil submission of the city. At 0800 another patrol brought the senior Italian military authority to surrender the city. Colonel Michele Tomaselle presented to me the Beretta pistol which he carried."

The formal surrender was delayed until General Patton arrived, which happened at about 1000 hours. Earlier that morning Patton, Lucas, and Hap Gay had climbed into a Piper Cub reconnaissance plane at Palermo's Bocca di Falco airport and flew to the 3rd Division's command post located in a farmhouse at Falcone, where they met Keyes. They then motored to the top of a hill overlooking bomb-damaged Messina and joined Truscott and Darby.

"General Patton finally arrived," said Truscott, "with his characteristic flurry: 'What in the hell are you all standing around for?' I assured him that we were only awaiting his arrival."[25] Looking down from the heights, Patton observed, "Messina is the worst mess I have seen. It is really smashed."[26] Best of all, there was no sign of the British.

With that, the entourage drove down the hill into the city, chased by a barrage of German artillery shells from across the strait. Some of the men riding behind the vehicle carrying Patton and Truscott were wounded.

Truscott recalled, "Just after we arrived in the city, a British armored patrol entered it from the west. General Montgomery had no doubt been anxious to beat General Patton into Messina, for he had landed a patrol a few miles down the coast for the purpose of being there before us. The race to Messina was ended."[27]

According to Patton, "In the town of Messina we met three British tanks and a few men who had arrived at 10:00 under the command of a general. It is very evident that Montgomery sent these men for the purpose of stealing the show. They had landed from one LCT about fifteen miles south and had come directly up the road. I think the general was quite sore that we got there first, but . . . the race was clearly to us."[28]

The British commander of the 4th Armoured Brigade, Brigadier J. C. Currie, shook Patton's hand and said, "It was quite a jolly good race and I congratulate you."[29]

■ ■ ■

The end of the Sicilian campaign could not have come soon enough for the Rangers, who were completely worn out. An exhausted Bill Darby wrote, "The night Messina fell my Rangers bivouacked in a cemetery there. German batteries across the Straits were blasting the city, some shells hitting the cemetery and knocking caskets out of the walls [of the mausoleums]. Skeletons were all around, and the smell of death curled the hairs of the Rangers' nostrils, but the exhausted 3rd Battalion slept on."

Darby and 3rd Ranger Battalion commander Lt. Col. Herman Dammer were fitfully sleeping when a motorcycle roared up to their resting spot in the cemetery; the courier had a message. "We were to hasten back to Palermo for final preparations for an assault somewhere in Italy. I looked from Colonel Dammer to the messenger. I'm afraid my eyes said clearly that I would like to throw him into one of the empty caskets and seal it in the wall."

The tired, dust-covered 3rd Rangers were assembled and hurried back to join the 1st and 4th Rangers. "Our clothes were in tatters, shoes worn thin, and most equipment ready for salvage," said Darby. "Only our weapons were in tiptop shape. We would need these in Italy."[30]

■ ■ ■

Time magazine's Jack Belden wrote,

> By midmorning the U.S. Seventh and the British Eighth Armies had entered Messina in force. . . . For the soldiers who had fought so bitterly a few days previously in the barren mountains to the west, the finale in Sicily seemed an anticlimax. In Messina the doughboy was lost; there was no one to fight. Private Hays Cathey stood in the street, hardly knowing what to do. "That's all there is, there ain't no more," he commented. Then, he sat on a debris-littered curbstone, opened a tin of cheese and disregarded everything.
>
> But for Messina's civilians the fall of the city was a relief. Two hundred of them came out in their rags and gave a feeble cheer. When the enemy guns started shelling from the mainland, they scurried out of town. It is unlikely that many will come back for a long time. There is nothing for them to come back to. Of all the wrecked cities of Sicily none is so thoroughly wrecked as Messina. From one end of the town to the other, I have not seen a building that has not been damaged.
>
> Hardest hit are the railroad and dock areas. In the harbor a sunken liner's funnels still stick out of the water. The remains of one or two ferries clutter the slipways. Concrete piers have been cut in two. Railway cars are smashed. The scene recalls the earthquake of 1908, when 91 percent of Messina's buildings were destroyed and 78,000 of its residents perished.
>
> This is what [the Allies] did in the island that the Germans had called "one huge impregnable fortress": Defeated 300,000 enemy troops. Thereby they eliminated the Italian Sixth Army, of which more than half deserted, most of the remainder being killed, wounded or captured. Of 75,000

Germans, perhaps 40,000, led by one-armed General Hans Valentine Hube, escaped to the Italian mainland. Estimated Allied casualties: 22,000.[31]

■ ■ ■

Montgomery graciously cabled Patton: "The Eighth [Army] sends its warmest congratulations to you and your splendid Army for the way you captured Messina and so ended the campaign in Sicily."

Other plaudits soon arrived. Alexander wrote, "Your country will be very proud of you and so am I to have the honour of having under my command such magnificent troops." Marshall wrote, "You have done a grand job of leadership." President Roosevelt messaged, "All of us are thrilled. . . . My thanks and enthusiastic approbation." Even Admiral Hewitt, busily getting ready for Operation Avalanche, took time to send his cheers: "The Navy is proud to have been able to participate."[32]

Only Eisenhower's congratulations were conspicuous by their absence; he had just received the report about Patton's second slapping incident.

■ ■ ■

With Husky concluded, Ike was in Algiers finalizing plans for the invasion of Italy when the report reached his desk. Ike's naval aide, Capt. Harry Butcher, wrote,

> This forenoon [17 August] General T. J. Davis, the [Attorney General], phoned me to get on the interoffice phone so he could talk confidentially. When I did, he said that Brigadier General Fred Blesse, the Surgeon General, had received a report from one of his medical officers in Sicily which was most alarming and implicated General Patton.
>
> T. J. thought General Ike should see Blesse as soon as possible to get the full story, rather than to have it go through lower levels and create a great deal of talk. Blesse came in around noon and showed Ike the report, the gist of which was that Patton had visited evacuation hospitals and had rousted out certain patients by the "scruff of the neck," presumably suspicious they were laggards.
>
> Whatever the cause, Ike said afterwards he would have to give Patton a jacking up. . . . Ike added that the medical report showed that many

American soldiers had marched over the rough terrain until they had literally worn the skin off their feet.[33]

■ ■ ■

Ike did indeed give Patton a "jacking up." Patton's lack of self-control had become a maddening distraction. He noted, "I felt that Patton should be saved for service in the great battles still facing us in Europe, yet I had to devise ways and means to minimize the harm that would certainly come from his impulsive action and to assure myself that it would not be repeated. . . . I wrote him a sharp letter of reprimand in which I informed him that repetition of such an offense would be cause for his instant relief."

In his letter he said,

> I am attaching a report which is shocking in its allegations against your personal conduct. I hope you can assure me that none of them is true, but the detailed circumstances communicated to me lead to the belief that some ground for the charges must exist.
>
> I am well aware of the necessity for hardness and toughness on the battlefield. I clearly understand that firm and drastic measures are at times necessary in order to secure the desired objectives. But this does not excuse brutality, abuse of the sick, nor exhibition of uncontrollable temper in front of subordinates. . . . I must seriously question your good judgment and your self discipline as to raise serious doubts in my mind as to your future usefulness.
>
> No letter that I have been called upon to write in my military career has caused me the mental anguish of this one, not only because of my long and deep personal friendship for you but because of my admiration for your military qualities, but I assure you that conduct such as described in the accompanying report will not be tolerated in this theater no matter who the offender may be.

Ike then required Patton to personally apologize "to the two men he had insulted . . . to all the personnel of the hospital[s] present at the time of the incident[s] . . . and the officers and representative groups of enlisted men of each of his divisions to assure them that he had given way to impulse and respected their positions as fighting soldiers of a democratic nation."[34]

Eisenhower immediately met with three senior war correspondents who had heard rumors about the slapping incidents and asked them to keep the story under wraps; should word leak out, Patton might have to face a court-martial, and Ike couldn't afford to lose him. The correspondents agreed to keep the matter quiet—for the time being.[35]

■ ■ ■

Deeply shamed and mortified by Ike's letter, Patton replied to his superior, "I want to commence by thanking you for this additional illustration of your fairness and generous consideration in making your communication [of the complaint] personal [rather than official].

"I am at a loss to find words with which to express my chagrin and grief at having given you, a man to whom I owe everything and for whom I would gladly lay down my life, cause for displeasure with me. I assure you that I had no intention of being either harsh or cruel in my treatment of the two soldiers in question. My sole purpose was to try and restore in them a just appreciation of their obligations as men and soldiers."[36]

Eisenhower accepted Patton's apology and hoped that the two incidents would fade away, but in November they would resurface with even more potentially serious consequences.

■ ■ ■

After the fall of Messina, Lt. Col. Joseph Couch, commanding Sgt. Paul Bennett's unit, the 1st Battalion, 17th Field Artillery, said,

> We then returned to our bivouac near Termini Imerese, and I hoped that the slapping incident would be soon forgotten by all except Sergeant Bennett.
>
> But it was not to be forgotten. The day after we returned to bivouac, a full colonel, resplendent in the well-pressed uniform of a staff officer, roared up to battalion headquarters . . . and snapped out a command to fetch Sergeant Bennett. His brief, icy explanation was that "General Patton wants to see him." Bennett was hustled off with scarcely time to button his shirt. On his face was the look of a man en route to the gallows.

> Bennett returned before nightfall to tell us that General Patton had apologized to him in person. The entire incident had a bizarre, Alice-in-Wonderland air about it. In a few days the incident was a major news item. When he was finally named, the soldier struck by Patton was identified as Sergeant [*sic*] Charles H. Kuhl; Paul Bennett was not mentioned. General Patton had slapped two hospitalized soldiers that day [*sic*] but somehow the news had been modified. We were greatly relieved, for neither Sergeant Bennett nor his battalion commander wished to achieve such notoriety.[37]

■ ■ ■

In his diary on 21 August Patton wrote that he had had Bennett report to him at his headquarters and explained to him "that I had cussed him out in the hope of restoring his manhood, that I was sorry, and that if he cared, I would like to shake hands with him. We shook."

But the act must have irritated Patton to his core. "It is rather a commentary on justice when an Army commander has to soft-soap a skulker to placate the timidity of those above," he inscribed in his diary.[38]

The next day he wrote, "I had in all the doctors and nurses and enlisted men who witnessed the affairs with the skulkers. I told them about my friend in the last war who shirked, was let get by with it, and eventually killed himself. I told them that I had taken the action I had to correct such a future tragedy."

Patton then had Private Kuhl report to him. "He was one of the two men I cussed out for skulking," he recorded in his diary. "I told him why I did it, namely, that I tried to make him mad with me so he would regain his manhood. I then asked him to shake hands, which he did."[39]* (Herman Kuhl, the

---

* Kuhl said, "After the incident, I was admitted [to the hospital] and that is when they found out I had malaria. I was flown back to Africa to recuperate. Then I was brought back to Palermo, Sicily, for the General to apologize. . . . He was a very rough and tough General. I will say he got what he went after no matter what. Personally I don't like him as a man but still don't have any hard feelings against him." "Charles H. Kuhl: The George S. Patton Slapping Incident," https://www.alexautographs.com/auction-lot/the-george-s-patton-slapping-incident-charles-h-k_FA24C55823. After the war, Kuhl tried to remain out of the spotlight, telling anyone who asked that it was no big deal. But in one interview he said, "At the time it happened, [Patton] was pretty well worn out. . . . I

private's father, wrote to his congressman, stating that he forgave Patton for the incident and requesting that he not be disciplined.[40])

■ ■ ■

Shortly before beginning his apology tour to the units, Patton wrote two letters of appreciation, the first to Lyal Davidson for the conduct of Task Force 88, which had carried out the amphibious landings along the north coast:

> My dear Admiral Davidson:
>
> Please accept for yourself and for the officers and men of your force the sincere and heartfelt appreciation and admiration the Seventh Army feels for your constant, gallant, and generous assistance. Everything that we have asked from you, you have more than granted. The gunfire support that you have provided has been of inestimable value, and it is my considered opinion that the three landing operations, carried on by you, were of critical importance in the rapid and successful advance on Messina.
>
> It is our hope that in future operations we shall again have the pleasure of being associated with you and your men.
>
> Most sincerely,
> G. S. Patton Jr.,
> Lieut. General, U.S. Army, Commanding[41]

The second was General Order 18, directed to the soldiers of the Seventh Army:

> Born at sea, baptized in blood, and crowned with victory, in the course of thirty-eight days of incessant battle and unceasing labor, you have added a glorious chapter to the history of war.
>
> Pitted against the best the Germans and Italians could offer, you have been unfailingly successful. The rapidity of your dash, which culminated in the capture of Palermo, was equaled by the dogged tenacity with which you stormed Troina and captured Messina.

---

think he was suffering a little battle fatigue himself." Kuhl retired to a relatively peaceful life as a janitor in Indiana; he died at age fifty-five. Axelrod, *Patton: A Biography*, 116.

> You have killed or captured 113,350 enemy troops. You have destroyed 265 of his tanks, 2,324 vehicles, and 1,162 large guns. . . . But your victory has significance above and beyond its physical aspect—you have destroyed the prestige of the enemy.
>
> Your fame shall never die.[42]

And neither, or so it seemed, would the two slapping incidents. To Patton, of course, they were trivialities, no more important than chewing out a sergeant for not wearing a tie—winning the war was the supreme thing. But in the wake of the avalanche of criticism long after the events, Patton had fallen into a deep depression.[43]

■ ■ ■

Between 24 and 30 August Patton visited each American division on Sicily where he expressed his remorse—of a fashion—in front of large numbers of troops. Near the end of his ten- or fifteen-minute speech to various units, he said, "In my dealings with you I have been guilty on too many occasions, perhaps, of criticizing and of loud talking. I am sorry for this and wish to assure you that when I criticize and censure I am wholly impersonal. . . . For every man I have criticized in this Army, I have probably stopped, talked to, and complimented a thousand, but people are more prone to remember ill usage than to recall compliments. Therefore, I want you officers and men who are here to explain to the other soldiers, who think perhaps that I am too hard, my motives and to express to them my sincere regret."

Then he switched focus:

> In the Sicilian campaign we lost some 1,500 of our comrades, killed in action. I do not grieve for their death because I thank God that such men have lived. But I do say to you all that it is our sacred duty to see that each of our dead comrades is escorted through the Pearly Gates by a large, a very large number of enemy dead. It is up to us now and hereafter to produce these escorts for our heroic slain.
>
> You know that I have never asked one of you to go where I feared to tread. I have been criticized for this, but there are many General Pattons

and there is only one Seventh Army. I can be expended but the Seventh must and will be victorious.[44]

■ ■ ■

For those soldiers who were predisposed to hate Patton, the slapping incidents added more fuel to their already smoldering fires. A sergeant in the 1st Infantry Division named John J. Moglia said that 50,000 soldiers on Sicily "would have gladly shot the general on sight—had generals not been out of season."[45]

On 27 August the entire 1st Infantry Division was summoned to hear an address by the Seventh Army commander. The division was trucked to a treeless hill and ordered to sit under the broiling sun. Medic Allen Towne remembered, "Our division had no love for Patton because our first experience with him had been in southern Tunisia when he took over II Corps. He had decided to instill discipline and had ordered us all to wear ties and leggings while the division was fighting in the African desert. This did not sit well with the men."[46] They were also still angry about the removal of Allen and Roosevelt.

Clarence Huebner, the 1st Division's commanding general, noted, "I assembled 18,000 men and Patton made a speech, a very good speech, in which he explained that he was sorry. But when he was finished, not one man clapped or said anything. There was no applause. They knew Patton was wrong."[47]

Allen Towne said,

> The division band played while everyone was assembling. Then, an honor guard, made up of a spruced-up infantry platoon, performed a formal rifle drill. I wondered why we were there. We had been on alert because it was thought that the surrender of Italy was imminent. There was a tentative plan to land a U.S. division at the Rome airport and help bring about an earlier end to the war. Rumor had it that the 1st Division would be doing this. Did it mean the rumors were true, that we were to be airlifted to Rome? We knew that the Italians wanted to get out of the war. Or was it possible that some of us might go home? After all, we had been overseas for more than a year.
>
> Finally, General Patton was introduced by General Andrus [commander of the 1st Division Artillery]. Patton came forward wearing his

> pearl-handled [*sic*] revolvers and his helmet liner with the three stars, He started his speech by saying, "You are part of the Seventh Army that was born at sea and baptized in the blood of our filthy enemy. We have killed many of them and will have the opportunity to kill more. That is what our job is. We are here to kill the enemy."
>
> It was a real blood-and-guts speech. When he finished, there was complete silence. There was no applause. Nothing at all. My reaction, which was probably shared by everyone, was, *What is this all about? Why are we here listening to this?* Most of us thought the speech was in bad taste. There were very few men who just wanted to kill the enemy. We would rather that they surrender so we could all go home.
>
> It was not until weeks later that we found out what the speech was all about. I read in an old issue of *Newsweek* that Patton had slapped a 1st Infantry Division soldier in a field hospital for being a coward. The man was in the hospital because he had an anxiety state breakdown, probably brought on by malaria. Patton had been ordered by General Eisenhower to apologize to the men of the 1st Division. That speech was supposed to be an apology.[48]

■ ■ ■

Not everyone felt animosity toward their commander. Maj. Ted Conway of the 60th RCT of the 9th Division recalled,

> We were assembled in a large olive orchard. . . . General Patton arrived in that famous command car of his with the two metal flags on either side. . . . We all stood at attention and put on our helmets and the bugler sounded "Attention" and General Patton mounted a platform in front of 3,000 troops.
>
> General Patton had a rather high, squeaky voice, and as he started to address the regiment he said, "Take seats," so we sat down on our helmets—it was a practice of those days, to keep us out of the mud or the dust . . . and General Patton started to give us what we knew was to be his apology. But he never got past his first word, which was "Men!" and at that point the whole regiment erupted. It sounded like a football game—a touchdown had been scored because the helmets (steel pots) started flying through the air, coming down all over—raining steel helmets and the men just shouted

"Georgie, Georgie,"—a name which he detested. He was saying—we *think* he was saying—"at ease, take seats," and so on. Then he had the bugler sound "Attention" again, but nothing happened. Just all these cheers.

So finally General Patton was standing there and he was shaking his head and you could see big tears streaming down his face and he said, or words to this effect, "The hell with it," and he walked off the platform. At this point the bugler sounded "Attention" and everybody grabbed the nearest available steel helmet, put it on, being sure to [fasten] the chin strap (which was a favorite Patton quirk) and as he stepped into his command car and again went down the side of the regiment, dust swirling, everybody stood at attention and saluted to the right and General Patton stood up in his command car and saluted, crying. . . . He was our hero. We were on his side. We knew the problem. We knew what he had done and why he had done it.[49]

■ ■ ■

The victory in Sicily was a major triumph, the biggest war story at the time in the United States and around the world. In a feature article about Truscott, *Life* magazine reported, "In seventeen days the [3rd] Division fought its way over a ninety-mile stretch of mountains and staged two waterborne landings behind retreating German lines to capture Messina. It was a phenomenal drive which another general interpreted by saying, 'What Truscott did in Sicily was to turn his infantry into cavalry.'"[50]

Time magazine correspondent Jack Belden wrote, "Sitting at his desk in North African Headquarters, surrounded by the press, 'Ike' Eisenhower, a ready, salty speaker, groped hard for the right tribute to his men. There was so much to praise: the courage of the airborne troops; the skill of the pilots and sailors; the resourcefulness of the engineers who rebuilt roads and bridges; the endurance of the infantrymen who hiked the skin off their soles. For a good five minutes the General groped. When he found the words they were unquotable. But for quotation he said: 'They did everything the finest armies in the world could have done.'"[51]

Patton, too, felt justifiably proud of Seventh Army and his own accomplishments in the Sicily campaign. But he was about to face the most serious crisis of his Army career.

17

THE SLAPS HEARD 'ROUND THE WORLD

I don't think [Patton] will be used in combat any more.

—Drew Pearson

The thirty-eight-day battle for Sicily had ended—and so had the lives of 2,811 American soldiers, sailors, and airmen. An additional 6,471 had been wounded, and 686 were missing or captured. The British had suffered, too, with 2,721 men killed, 7,939 wounded, and 2,183 missing. Malaria was just as problematic, with 11,590 British and 9,892 Americans becoming casualties of the disease.

Heavier losses, however, were suffered by the Axis forces. The Italians had 4,325 men killed, a staggering 40,655 missing (most probably by desertion), and 116,681 captured. The Germans lost 4,678 killed, 13,500 wounded, and 5,500 taken prisoner. The loss of matériel—tanks, trucks, artillery pieces, and warplanes—was almost incalculable.[1]

But the war was not yet over—not by a long shot. More battles and more invasions were on the horizon. To get the American divisions back up to fighting trim, and to train raw replacements that were now flooding in to the 1st, 3rd, 9th, 45th Infantry, 82nd Airborne, and 2nd Armored Divisions, a new regimen of training was instituted in various parts of conquered Sicily. The remarkable American war machine was just getting cranked up.

■ ■ ■

George Patton was a man who loved action and hated inertia; he saw the war going on without him as an outrageous, intolerable situation. With the end of the Sicily campaign, he became an army commander without an army to command. A new force—the Fifth United States Army—had been created, with Lt. Gen. Mark W. Clark at its helm, a fact that irritated Patton to no end. A fleet commanded by Vice Adm. H. Kent Hewitt—another galling episode—would transport Fifth Army to Salerno and provide fire support.

Before sailing off to lead his 3rd Division ashore at Salerno, Lucian Truscott told Patton what Eisenhower had said about him: that he was "'the only general who can inspire men to conquer.' That was nice of Ike, but I wish he would give me a chance to do some more conquering."[2]

Patton could only sit and watch from afar. He remained in Palermo through autumn and into winter, wondering what fate had in store for him. Although worried that the two slapping incidents had wrecked his chances for another command, he recalled Ike promising that he would not be left in the backwater of the war. Yet here he was, very much in said backwater, floating aimlessly. He wrote to Beatrice on 30 August, "Apparently I will join the Army of the unemployed for a while, so don't worry about me. I seem to either fight like hell or do nothing."[3]

In early September Patton flew back to Algiers to visit a training camp for the 34th and 36th Infantry Divisions getting ready for Avalanche. "A day or two in Algiers almost kills me," he grumbled in his diary. "No one there seems interested in the war, and one cannot escape the feeling that the so-called Allied Headquarters is a British headquarters commanded by an American [Eisenhower]. . . . It is felt inadvisable, from an inter-Allied standpoint, to give any credit to the Seventh Army."[4]

But there was nothing for him—just a hint that he might get an army to lead after the initial invasion of France if it proved to be successful. Already Bradley had gotten an army group for Overlord, but Seventh Army went temporarily inactive. At the War Department Patton was seen—thanks in large part to the slapping incidents—as too hot-tempered, too mercurial, too prone to make hasty, poor judgments. Patton biographer Martin Blumenson noted, "Yet whatever faults Patton embodied, he was too valuable to discard. His prestige, reputation, proficiency, and genius would be utilized—but at a level no higher than the command of a field army."[5]

■ ■ ■

Many—perhaps most—of the GIs who had fought in Sicily assumed or at least hoped that they had done enough in this war and would soon be going home. Such was not to be. Those who had survived Husky had learned lessons in combat that would be valuable for upcoming operations. They were "in for the duration," as the phrase went. But until their new assignments could be worked out, most of the troops remained in Sicily. The Army tried to make their stay comfortable without losing their combat edge.

First Division medic Allen Towne recalled that his unit was trucked south to Palma di Montechiaro, halfway between Gela and Agrigento, and set up camp between an almond grove and the beach. "It was a very pleasant location," he said, and the men were at last able to clean up, enjoy some recreation, and just take life easy. Medical duties were resumed; new equipment had to be received and inventoried, and vaccinations had to be administered, as malaria and other diseases such as typhus, yellow fever, and tetanus were still a major problem; even civilians were treated. Besides millions of mosquitoes, there were swarms of centipedes that liked to crawl nightly under the blankets with the soldiers.

For recreation there was swimming in the sea, movies, USO shows featuring Bob Hope and Frances Langford, and sightseeing trips to other parts of the island. One day in August Towne and other members of his unit were given a visit to Agrigento, one of the ancient Greek cities in Sicily, full of temples and catacombs. He said, "We had lunch there at a former German officers' mess, and they still had Hitler's picture on the wall. We were served by the same Sicilians who had served the Germans. I suppose war was just an interlude for them, and they did not care who was in control.

"On the whole, the two months spent resting in Sicily were somewhat enjoyable, but the time dragged and most of us were bored. A lot of us did not feel topnotch. Perhaps we all had a touch of malaria or some other tropical disease we had picked up in Africa or Sicily. . . . We called it 'the Sicilian Crud.'"[6]

■ ■ ■

Reflecting on the just-concluded campaign, Dwight Eisenhower said, "The results of the Sicilian campaign were more far-reaching that the mere capture of the enemy garrison. . . . the bombastic Mussolini was thrown out. . . . Mussolini's place as Premier was taken by old Field Marshal Pietro Badoglio," who publicly announced that the war—and Italy's participation in it—would continue while behind-the-scenes maneuvering was underway for Italy to go neutral so as to avoid—or so it was hoped—continued destruction and Nazi Germany's occupation and retribution.

To bring about the total capitulation of Italy, Ike said, "Then began a series of negotiations, secret communications, clandestine journeys by secret agents, and frequent meetings in hidden places that, if encountered in the fictional world, would have been scorned as incredible melodrama. Plots of various kinds [such as the landing of a large airborne force near Rome] were hatched only to be abandoned because of changing circumstances." Italy formally surrendered on 8 September 1943—just hours before Operation Avalanche (and the two British invasions) hit her shores.[7]

On 9 September, just two months after Husky had been launched, Mark Clark's Fifth U.S. Army came ashore under heavy fire at Salerno. Darby's Rangers played a vital role in sealing off Chiunzi Pass at the north end of the beachhead to prevent any German troops from rushing down from Naples. The 36th Infantry Division received its baptism of fire and was nearly pushed back into the sea until Clark's floating reserve, the 45th Division, arrived to save the beachhead. It would take nine more months and considerable bloodshed before Rome would be captured.[8]

Even the fall of Rome on 4 June 1944 was seen as anticlimactic; two days later the Normandy invasion wiped the Italian campaign off the front pages of newspapers back home and around the world. Italy became "the forgotten front."[9]

■ ■ ■

Patton remained based in his luxurious Palermo palace throughout the autumn of 1943, watching his subordinate commanders and staff officers—Lucas,

Keyes, Truscott, Middleton—head off to other combat assignments. Patton fretted that the war was passing him by and that the two slapping incidents had destroyed his military career.[10]

Then on 17 September, like a celestial messenger, Ike appeared in Palermo and announced to Patton that he would get an army; just which one he was not yet at liberty to say. A grateful Patton told Ike that he would "serve under the Devil to get in the fight."[11] While the details were being worked out, Patton busied himself with more trips to Cairo (which he described as "disgusting"), Karnak, Benghazi, Tobruk, El Alamein, Corsica, Carthage, Jerusalem, and other destinations that fed his fascination with history.[12]

Patton confided in his diary on 6 October that he wished "something would happen to Clark," presumably so that he could take command of Fifth Army and get back in the war. He also posted several entries with barely disguised glee about the difficulties that Clark and Fifth Army were having in Italy.[13]

■ ■ ■

On 20 October 1943 the 1st Infantry Division left Palma di Montechiaro in southwest Sicily and headed for the harbor at Augusta, where transports were waiting to take them to their next destination: England. There they would spend over half a year getting ready for Overlord. Many of those who had survived North Africa and Sicily would not survive Normandy—or the eleven months of combat that followed until Victory in Europe Day.[14]

But first General Patton, who still had a few more months of enforced idleness to endure, wanted Clarence Huebner's departing 1st Division to see him in all his glory one last time—and maybe show him a little love.

Col. Stanhope Mason, chief of staff to Huebner, recalled,

> In the harbor of Augusta, with all transports loaded and ready to sail for England when the British Navy gave the order, we received aboard ship an official notification that General Patton would see us off by cruising around through the anchored convoy in an open launch. Though not mentioned in the dispatch, it took no great imagination that General Patton wanted to be seen by all the departing troops. General Huebner correctly sensed

this implied wish. Huebner . . . was comparatively new at our Division Headquarters, so he had not acquired a feel for their grudge against Patton.

General Huebner told me to issue orders that, at the hour specified for the Patton visit, troops would line the rails and give the Commanding General a cheer as he traversed the waters of the harbor. Even at that brief time of having served as his chief of staff, he expected and listened rationally to opinions and recommendations that I felt he should consider.

In this case I recommended that he *not* have the troops line the rails—and I filled in all the background which led me to believe the troops would neither applaud nor cheer. Sure, they would obey orders and man the rails but Patton would sail around amidst a silence that would both disappoint and displease him; that he, General Huebner, would be greatly embarrassed if I was right in my surmise. Huebner gave it careful thought but came to the conclusion that I was overly apprehensive. He knew soldier thinking and he wasn't wrong often as to their reaction. This time he was completely wrong.

The order to man the rails for the Patton send-off was issued. It included a veiled suggestion as to how (applause, cheering) the troops should show appreciation of the Army Commander's visit to say *bon voyage* to the departing division. At the appointed time, General Patton, beribboned and impressive, stood majestically in the center of the open launch as it cruised through the anchored ships. Silence was total. Every ship had its rails solidly lined with soldiers as deep as space permitted. But not a cheer was heard. No applause. Nothing but sepulchral silence.

When the cruise-around ceremony was finished, when General Patton via launch had exited the scene, I headed back to our tiny shipboard office space where I would be face-to-face with a very much-disconcerted boss. I, therefore, was rapidly schooling myself, in my own mind, to avoid at all costs, any major display of an "I-told-you-so" frame of mind.

I found General Huebner quiet, thoughtful, with mixed emotions running all the way from anger and chagrin to a deeply felt embarrassment. I was relieved to see that he intended to let bygones be bygones, holding no one to blame for a regretful outcome of what was in reality a well-intentioned gesture. For my part, I also regretted this ill will being so evident at a time when Patton was most in need of a morale boost.

> On the other hand, it must be admitted that his former and generally known slurs on the men of the 1st Division gave them ample cause to be resentful. In brief, he brought it on himself.[15]

Patton did not mention this "silent treatment" in his diary or memoirs, nor did his aide, Colonel Codman.

■ ■ ■

Patton's spirits received a slight boost later in October when "Beetle" Smith confirmed what Ike had said: that he would have a chance to command an army for the invasion of Normandy. But that seemed eons away, and it was just an unofficial rumor anyway.[16]

On 17 November, as Clark's Fifth Army slogged its way side by side with the British Eighth Army northward through Italy's southern Apennine Mountains, Patton wrote in his diary, "I have seldom passed a more miserable day. I have absolutely nothing to do and hours of time in which to do it. From command of 240,000 men, I now have less than 5,000. . . . well, pretty soon I will hit bottom and then bounce," he predicted confidently.[17]

Patton had virtually forgotten about the two slapping incidents that had occurred in early August, and assumed everyone else had, too. But such was not the case.

■ ■ ■

The slapping incidents were little known back in the United States, but they suddenly moved front and center in November thanks to the newspaper columnist and syndicated radio commentator Drew Pearson, and they provoked a wave of anger against Patton—three months after they took place and after Patton had apologized to the troops.

Back in August Pearson had charged in a broadcast that U.S. Secretary of State Cordell Hull was anti-Soviet and wished to see Russia bled white in the fighting with the Germans. Hull responded by calling the charges "monstrous and diabolical falsehoods," and President Roosevelt came to Hull's defense, denouncing Pearson as a "chronic liar."

Previously a staunch Roosevelt supporter, Pearson felt that his reputation had been sullied by the president's remarks. If he could find a sensational "news scoop," thought Pearson, his readers and listeners would forget that FDR had insulted him.

Pearson's scoop came from a friend working in the Office of Strategic Services who had heard the slapping story whispered in the halls of the War Department. The friend suggested that if Pearson broke this sensational, exclusive news story, his reputation as a truth-dealing journalist would be restored.

And so, on 21 November, Pearson blew the lid off the open secret. The other war correspondents who had been in Sicily at the time of the two incidents had held to a "gentleman's agreement" to not release what they knew about the story—just as they had also not released Ike's secret announcement to them in advance of Operation Husky.

But Pearson, who had not been in the war zone, did not feel bound by any such agreement and put the information—replete with errors, half-truths, and exaggerations—out to his readers and listeners. He accused the Army of a cover-up, telling his audience,

> A great mystery has surrounded the whereabouts of General "Blood and Guts" Patton.* His pearl-handled [*sic*] revolver, his picturesque language, made headlines in the Tunisian campaign but he has not been heard of since. Here is the reason:
>
> General Patton was going through a hospital in Sicily and inquired what was the matter with a [combat-] fatigue patient. A fatigue patient is one suffering from shellshock or nerves. General Patton apparently used his own judgment as to the soldier's illness, ordered him up out of bed, and when he didn't get up right away, pulled him up and struck him, knocking him down.

Pearson conflated the details of the two slapping incidents and quoted an anonymous (possibly nonexistent) source who said that Patton could no longer expect to receive any important battlefield command. "I don't think he [Patton] will be used in combat any more," Pearson said, apparently quoting the source.

---

* There was no "mystery." With the Sicilian campaign finished Patton had been given some much-needed time off by Ike. And it was preposterous to assert that Patton "hadn't been heard from since Tunisia"; he had been in the news almost every day since Husky began.

The broadcast ignited a firestorm. A United Press news release reported, "Radio commentator Drew Pearson said tonight in his broadcast that Lieutenant General George S. Patton, commander of the U.S. Seventh Army in the Sicilian campaign, had been 'severely reprimanded' by General Eisenhower for mistreating an American soldier suffering from shock, or a nervous ailment, in a hospital in Sicily. The War Department said it had 'no information and no comment.'"[18] Pearson's words created indignation across America. Congressmen and newspaper editors called for the general's dismissal and punishment—perhaps even a court-martial.

The aftereffects of the negative publicity continued to eat at Patton. To forget his troubles he busied himself with more sightseeing trips to Naples and Pompeii, but he couldn't help but feel useless while the war went on without him. In his diary on 24 November he wrote, "If the fate of the only successful general in this war depends on the statement of a discredited writer like Drew Pearson, we are in a bad fix. . . . [But] I am perfectly certain that this is not the end of me."[19]

■ ■ ■

The slapping incidents refused to go away. An article in the 6 December 1943 issue of *Time* stated,

> On November 21 crusading Drew Pearson, once called a liar by the President, let his nationwide radio audience in on a secret that scores of U.S. correspondents had shared with thousands of U.S. soldiers since August. George S. Patton, the General who does not believe in nerve difficulties, had some himself. For slapping a hospitalized soldier, Pearson disclosed that the General had been "severely reprimanded" by General Eisenhower.
>
> Next day, at 5:30 p.m., a spokesman for Allied Headquarters in Algiers issued to appalled newspapermen a masterpiece of "public relations" technique: "General Patton has never been reprimanded at any time by General Eisenhower." Every single word of the denial was true. The sum total was not. In Army language, a reprimand is "an official rebuke administered as a punishment," following strictly defined rules of disciplinary procedure. To those millions of Americans whose English is not false-bottomed, the denial could mean only that Patton was beyond reproach.

On November 23, at 10:30 a.m., a high officer in General Eisenhower's command [chief of staff Walter Bedell Smith] admitted that such doubletalk had been intentional. Now the spokesman said he was "a little ashamed" of having told the U.S. people the day before . . . "not the complete truth." The complete truth was what the Senate Military Affairs Committee demanded next day from War Secretary [Henry L.] Stimson. But the administration of truth in theaters of war, said Secretary Stimson stiffly, is up to the commanding generals.

There were two different problems, confusingly interwoven: "Blood and Guts" and Truth and Confidence. On the Senate's list of promotions was Patton (to the permanent rank of Major General). On the people's mind was, as grass-root William Allen White's *Emporia Gazette* stated in plain singletalk, the question whether they can "believe the reports and statements of our leaders . . . in this war." The people did not shout for General Patton's scalp.

There were editorial shouts and much dinner-table clamor—and humorists in the Army's . . . Pentagon Building in Washington sang: "Pistol-Packing Patton Laid that Private Down." But *PM*'s honest editor John P. Lewis admitted that his mail was running almost 5-to-1 against the paper's high-blood-pressure cry for a court-martial . . . The prevailing Congressional opinion was that Patton, exactly like any other soldier, should stay where his superiors considered him most effective.

But on the more basic matters of truth and confidence, a wave of popular discomfort penetrated deep from the editorial columns. That "the Army has been caught in a barefaced misstatement of fact" (as the *Cleveland Plain Dealer* put it), was bound to have repercussions far beyond the personal fate of the Problem General.[20]

■ ■ ■

One of the reasons that Pearson's "scoop" caused a furor was his allegation that the Army in general, and Eisenhower in particular, had attempted to "cover up" the whole story. There might have been a ham-handed effort to manage the negative news, but Eisenhower said it wasn't intentional.

In *Crusade in Europe*, Ike wrote, "I called in to see me a group of reporters who had brought me the story of the occurrence. I explained to them in detail the action I had taken and the reasons for it. I read them the letter I had written to Patton and extracts from [his reply]. This, so far as I was concerned, closed the incident."

Eisenhower stressed that there had been no attempt at censorship:

> On the contrary, my staff and General Patton were told that under no circumstances was there to be any effort to suppress the story. These specific instructions, which I issued personally to a group of newspapermen, covered "indirect pressure" as well as direct censorship, They were flatly told to use their own judgment.
>
> However, the aftermath connected with this episode temporarily strained our usually splendid relationship with the press. When, months later, the story finally reached Washington via the gossip route, a great public uproar immediately followed its broadcast by a commentator.

Ike held another press conference in which his chief of staff Walter Bedell Smith was told to fill in any details but to "tell the full truth. Eisenhower said,

> During this later conference a question was posed concerning disciplinary action against Patton, and [Smith] replied that no reprimand had been administered, which was technically correct, since the reprimand had not been recorded in the official files. But it was factually wrong. [After the conference a reporter] called me on the phone to protest what he called "the shabby treatment of the press." Instantly I issued orders for correction.
>
> But the damage was done and the story already in America; and this only ten minutes later! [Smith] ruefully regretted his error.

Ike learned his lesson: "In dealing with [the press] we plainly had to be right the first time."[21]

■ ■ ■

Public opinion was largely on Patton's side. Beatrice sent him favorable newspaper clippings, and friends wrote to offer their support. Retired generals also weighed in on the matter. Former Army chief of staff Charles P. Summerall told his friend Patton that he was "indignant about the publicity given a trifling incident," adding that "whatever [Patton] did" he was sure it was "justified by the provocation. Such cowards used to be shot, now they are only encouraged. . . . Only those who carry the responsibility of winning battles know the difficulty of making men fight and so far you have excelled all others in this accomplishment. . . . The country would suffer a calamity in not having your continued leadership. . . . Your place is already made in history."[22]

Maj. Gen. Kenyon A. Joyce, another Patton friend, called Drew Pearson a "sensation monger" and stated that "niceties" should be left for "softer times of peace."[23]

One notable dissenter, former mentor and General of the Armies John J. Pershing, publicly condemned Patton's actions, an act that left him "deeply hurt" and caused him to vow to never speak to Pershing again.[24] In the wake of the cascade of criticism long after the events, Patton sank into a deep depression. It was Thanksgiving 1943 but Patton said, "I had nothing to be thankful for, so I did not give thanks."[25] By mid-December 1943 the government had received around 1,500 letters related to Patton, with many calling for his dismissal and others defending him or calling for his promotion.

To lift his spirits Patton made a list of his accomplishments going back to North Africa: "My command so far has disposed of 177,000 Germans, Italians, and French—killed, wounded, and prisoner, of which they have killed and wounded 21,000. Our average loss has been one man for 13½ of the enemy. It would be a national calamity to lose an Army commander with such a record."[26]

■ ■ ■

There was still no word on any further assignment for Patton, but he closely followed the events in Italy; Clark's Fifth U.S. Army and the British Eighth Army, now under Oliver Leese, were stalemated along the formidable Gustav Line running the width of Italy and anchored by the heights of Monte Cassino. High-level meetings involving Roosevelt, Churchill, and Stalin had taken place in Cairo and Tehran that would decide the future direction of the war and its immediate aftermath.[27]

After the Tehran Conference Roosevelt and Eisenhower visited Patton in Sicily. "Everyone was most affable to me," Patton said. "Eisenhower was very nice also, and said he felt I would soon get orders to go to UK and command an Army." Patton was hoping for something definite, but it was not yet forthcoming.[28]

In mid-January 1944 Patton got the news that he would receive command of an army forming in England—but that he would be serving under the command of his former friend and subordinate Omar Bradley (whom he once called "a man of great mediocrity"). There was also some talk at higher headquarters of reconstituting Seventh Army with Patton in command of the invasion of southern France (Operation Anvil/Dragoon), but it was just talk.[29]

■ ■ ■

Patton finally received his marching orders in late January and flew off to Prestwick, Scotland, to confer with Eisenhower, who was again the Supreme Commander of Allied Forces. Bradley had gotten command of First U.S. Army, and Patton would get not a fighting command, but the First U.S. Army Group, a fictitious organization designed to deceive the Germans into believing that he would lead the Allies' invasion of France across the Straits of Dover/Pas de Calais rather than the intended target of Normandy.

Patton was at first feeling let down but soon began to see the value in the deception plan code-named Operation Fortitude. The ruse worked perfectly, and the Normandy invasion—Operation Overlord—successfully penetrated the continent. Patton would then get the Third U.S. Army—a real force—and blaze a trail across France, Belgium, Luxembourg, and into Germany, Austria, and Czechoslovakia by the time the war ended on 8 May 1945. His successes in North Africa and especially in Sicily had paved the way for him to reach the heights of martial glory that he had always assumed that fate would bestow upon him.[30]

Postscript

On Sunday, 9 December 1945, seven months after the war in Europe ended, Patton was on a pheasant-hunting trip in Germany with his old chief of staff Maj. Gen. Hap Gay and was preparing to fly back to the United States the next day on Ike's personal plane. He was in good spirits, anxious to spend Christmas at home with Beatrice, their daughters Little Bea and Ruth Ellen, son-in-law John Waters (who had been a POW in North Africa), and their son George, a West Point cadet. It was to have been his first time home and with the family in years.

While riding with Gay in the back seat in his 1938 Cadillac staff car on a street in northeast Mannheim, Germany, they slammed into an Army truck that made a sudden turn in front of them. Patton was thrown forward and hit his head, resulting in fractured vertebrae and paralysis. Rushed to a U.S. Army hospital in Heidelberg, he remained conscious for days. "I'll try to be a good patient," he told his medical team.

Beatrice flew over immediately, arriving on 11 December in a plane made available to her by Ike. Cheered by her presence, Patton appeared to be improving despite being in traction and a body cast, and plans were made to return him to the United States. But on 21 December he declined suddenly and died.

The sixty-year-old George Smith Patton Jr., a general both loathed and loved, was buried in the American Military Cemetery in Hamm, Luxembourg, beneath a simple white marble cross set in the middle of the graves of Third Army men he had commanded. As Geoffrey Keyes said, "I know George would want to lie beside the men of his army who have fallen."[31]

On the day after Patton died, his friend Lt. Gen. Geoffrey Keyes issued Seventh Army General Orders 635:

> With deep regret, announcement is made of the death of General George Patton Jr. . . . Probably no soldier had has a greater compliment paid him than that given General Patton by his most powerful and skilled opponents. He was termed the ablest American field commander faced by the German Army on any front.
>
> The entire Allied world now pays tribute to the man who deserves more than a lion's share of the credit for the victories of our arms in the bitter European struggle just ended.
>
> Seventh Army has lost a great friend, a gallant warrior, and inspiring leader. Our country has lost a great and fearless citizen. May we comfort ourselves with the thought that he died as he loved to live—ever fighting![32]

EPILOGUE

ANALYSIS AND ASSESSMENT

More than eighty years on, Operation Husky still has its supporters and detractors. There seems to be no middle ground.

One historian called the operation "unique in that several new designs of landing craft [the LST, LCT, and LCI] were first tried under warlike conditions and adverse weather. The new amphibious vehicle, the DUKW, proved its worth and made itself indispensable. Experience with this newcomer and others, such as the tank pontoons, was invaluable for the planning of future amphibious assaults."[1]

Samuel Morison praised Husky's scope: "This was a very bold plan. No amphibious operation on so broad a front—practically eight reinforced divisions landing abreast—had ever been tried before, nor was it ever tried again, even in Normandy, where the initial assault force was less than this strength."[2]

Husky has also been roundly criticized by military experts, armchair generals, and Monday-morning quarterbacks for its numerous failures, which included the disastrous American and British airborne assaults; the insufficient Allied air cover throughout the campaign; the internecine fighting between the British and Americans who were trying to achieve a common goal; and the allowing of 110,000 German and Italian soldiers to escape to the Italian mainland almost undisturbed, along with much of their equipment.[3]

Historian James Holland pointed out, "Another criticism has been that the Allied approach was over-cautious; but it has to be remembered that Husky was planned at a time when it was not at all clear what the strength of the defence would be, and on the back of a stiff battle in Tunisia in which Italian units for the most part had fought well."[4]

Ranger veteran and author Col. Robert W. Black pointed out the major failing:

> Unfortunately, Operation Husky never envisioned that the real prize was not terrain, but the destruction of German and Italian forces on the island. Because of questionable planning and usage on the part of the land, air, and sea forces of the Allies and the consummate skill of the Germans, that destruction did not occur.
>
> The Allies had the power to close the Straits of Messina and did not get it done. With German assistance, the Italians were able to evacuate 70,000 men, 300 vehicles, and 100 pieces of artillery. The Germans successfully evacuated 39,569 men, including 4,444 wounded, and saved 9,605 vehicles, including forty-seven tanks, ammunition, fuel, and other critical supplies that were taken to the Italian mainland.[5]

It was true. No one—not Marshall, Eisenhower, Alexander, Patton, Montgomery, Hewitt, Cunningham, Bradley, or any of the rest of the cast of characters in this drama—seemed to grasp the importance of pinching off the escape route between Messina and Calabria. There was a great hesitation on the Allies' part to risk their air and naval assets in trying to force the well-fortified strait. This failure needlessly allowed the enemy to keep on fighting on the mainland of Italy for another twenty-one months.

British military historian Shelford Bidwell also took both Patton and Montgomery to task for allowing tens of thousands of enemy soldiers and their vehicles and weapons to slip across the Strait of Messina: "Without either consultation or permission from OKW, Kesselring flew to Sicily, ordered the German commander to form a strong defensive perimeter around Messina, collect as many troops in it as possible, German and Italian, and prepare to cross the straits into Calabria. . . . That the vainglorious Patton could not even dent the German defence at Messina, that Montgomery's mysterious indolence led to the Eighth Army's failure to pursue a beaten opponent, and that the inactivity of the Allied navies and air forces all contributed to Kesselring's success does not detract from his feat in organizing a German Dunkirk."[6]

For Lt. Bill Whitman, the Allies' failure to prevent the evacuation forever loomed large; he would have to face some of these same units again in Italy. "There has been something which has puzzled me over the many years [since the war]," he said in 1990. "With Allied control of both the air and the sea, why did we permit the successful escape of the Axis forces from the island? . . . I am still puzzled why we could not stop 125,000 [*sic*] men, weapons, and equipment from crossing two and a half miles of water in six days, when we controlled sea and air? Why?"[7]

Chief of Naval Operations Adm. Ernest J. King took a dim view of the entire enterprise, saying that Sicily was "merely doing something for the sake of doing something."[8]

Other historians have also been highly critical of the decision to invade Sicily in the first place. Samuel W. Mitcham Jr. and Friedrich von Stauffenberg, for example, pointed out: "It is undoubtedly true that the Allies made a mistake by going into Sicily. In May 1943, after the fall of Tunisia, there was probably still time to launch an invasion of northwestern Europe in the summer or early fall of 1943, as George C. Marshall advocated."

The two authors also noted, "If the Allies *had* to invade a Mediterranean island in the summer of 1943, their target should have been Sardinia," because it was much less strongly defended than Sicily and was roughly the same distance from Tunisian air bases. Had Sardinia been taken, "When the major Allied landings on the Italian mainland came, they could have taken place 100 miles *north* of Rome instead of 100 miles *south* of it."

Mitcham and Stauffenberg concluded, "Finally, it must be noted that the capture of Sicily was a burden, not a blessing, to the Allies. Impoverished before, [Sicily] was now devastated as well, and its port and communications infrastructure had to be completely rebuilt," and Allied troops needed to be stationed there to act as an occupying force.

The Germans, of course, were happy that the Allies did not attempt other options. General Heinrich von Vietinghoff, commander of the German Tenth Army in Italy, said that the Allies missed an opportunity by not invading the toe of Italy before the Sicilian campaign was finished, claiming that it could have been accomplished "without special difficulty."[9] (Just where the Allies could have obtained the additional divisions required for such an operation, he did not say.)

And Albert Kesselring noted, "The Axis command was mighty lucky, helped above all as it was by the methodical procedure of the Allies. The absence of any large-scale encirclement of the island or a thrust up the coastline of Calabria gave us long weeks to organize the defense areas with really weak resources. The slow advance of the main attack and the remarkable dissipation of [the Allies'] forces over the island allowed the Axis command to bring sufficient reinforcements to the defense areas as they were threatened. The enemy failure to exploit the last chance of hindering the German forces crossing the Straits of Messina, by continuous and strongly coordinated attacks from the sea and air, was almost a greater boon to the German command than their failure immediately to push their pursuit across the Straits on 17 August." Kesselring also felt that the three-week lull before the Allies invaded southern Italy "was again a gift to the Axis" and gave the Germans time to organize their defenses, which would stymie the Allied advance for almost two years.[10]

Curiously, the viewpoint that the Allies should have gone straight for the strait and avoided the month-long slog across the island ignores several factors. Those who hold that view apparently assume that the hundreds of Italian and German fighters and bombers spread out at air bases across Sicily and southern Italy would have remained grounded, while the still-sizeable Italian fleet, although never terribly aggressive, would have remained passive and holed up at their naval bases at Spezia and Taranto.

Hugh Pond contended that "the true reason for turning a blind eye to Messina was the quarter of a million Empire troops who lie buried at Gallipoli."[11] The tragic slaughter of Australian and New Zealand troops in World War I while storming the Turkish coast in the Dardanelles Strait was a nightmare that haunted Churchill, who had been First Lord of the Admiralty and was responsible for the operation, and many other British officers and men for the rest of their lives.

■ ■ ■

To be sure, Operation Husky leaves us with many "should haves" and "what ifs." A battle once fought cannot be refought, but the lessons learned from failures and successes can be applied to future operations. Much of what was learned from Husky was applied to Overlord.

While critics may be correct in their disparagements of the tactics of Husky, and even the choice of Sicily as the target, the overriding strategic accomplishment of the operation should not be ignored: the removal of Mussolini from power and the withdrawal of his nation from an active role in the Axis's prosecution of the war. Italy may have been Hitler's weakest partner, but its capitulation was a blow from which Nazi Germany would never recover; ultimate defeat was only a matter of time.

■ ■ ■

Despite its many failings, the Sicily campaign was a victory—pure and simple. Husky showed that, when properly coordinated, a ground army and a naval force could work closely together to achieve battlefield success. And it gave Eisenhower his second opportunity to lead a coalition force in a large-scale, multi-faceted amphibious invasion and no doubt contributed to his being selected as the Supreme Commander of the Allied Expeditionary Force slated for the Normandy invasion and the campaign into the heart of Nazi Germany.

Husky also brought George S. Patton Jr.—colorful, controversial, contentious, and courageous—to the fore, vindicating his belief in the fighting abilities of the American soldier, and forever enshrining his name in the pantheon of great military leaders.

After Messina fell, Eisenhower's naval aide Harry C. Butcher wrote, "Patton's great progress gives Ike a warm glow, as there are many Army officers who could not see through Patton's showmanship and boisterousness to discern his fine qualities of leadership on which Ike banked so strongly. In addition, the success of the Seventh Army lets Americans hold their heads high among the British and other Allies who may have been bit skeptical after the Kasserine affair."[12]

One of the finest tributes to Patton was voiced in December 1943 by John J. McCloy, the assistant secretary of defense. Patton related that McCloy said he had "in his makeup certain chemicals no other general had; that I was a great fighter and an inspiring leader. . . . I was not to worry about what was said about me as that would hurt my efficiency. He also said that I look and act like a general and that no one else we have does. . . . You have color, personality, and size. Men like to follow a man they can respect."[13]

■ ■ ■

In the end, although the execution of Husky was far from perfect from both American and British perspectives, it broke new ground for amphibious operations in terms of its size and scope. It thrust green American troops into full battle with their Axis foes and taught them how to fight and defeat a well-armed and determined enemy. It introduced new instruments of war—the LST, LCT, LCI, and DUKW—that made invading a hostile shore, if not exactly easy, at least efficient and achievable. It solidified the necessity for naval, ground, and air assets to work together as a team and not as rival services. It established Eisenhower and Patton, despite their personal flaws, as two of America's finest military leaders.

Husky also proved that a deception plan, even one as improbable as Mincemeat, was an important component in an operation's overall strategy. Mincemeat's success did much to set the stage for Operation Fortitude that was implemented before Overlord and fooled the Germans into believing that the landings would take place far from where they actually occurred.

It showed that both the U.S. Navy and Royal Navy were capable of great things: delivering huge numbers of invasion troops and the tons of supplies necessary to sustain them for weeks on an enemy-held island, then providing those troops with floating artillery platforms that could destroy attacking enemy forces, such as was demonstrated at Gela. And it demonstrated that navies could also evacuate mass casualties as well as prisoners of war.

Husky, it could be said, was the dress rehearsal for Operation Overlord. Had Husky failed, the Allies would have had to seriously rethink their strategy for invading the Nazi-occupied European continent—a far more formidable task. But Husky did not fail, and the lessons learned from it paved the way for the overwhelming success of Overlord eleven months later.

As Admiral Hewitt said in his after action report, "The brilliant achievements of the Allied forces in this conquest, launched on a magnitude which heretofore had never been attempted, were due principally to the singleness of purpose which all forces demonstrated. The appreciation of each others' problems produced an inter-service spirit of co-operation and common endeavor which welded the naval and military forces into a single team possessed with the resolute will to win."[14]

NOTES

Introduction

1. Martin Blumenson, *Sicily: Whose Victory? Ballantine's Illustrated History of World War II, Campaign Book No. 3* (New York: Ballantine, 1969), 45; Ezio Costanzo, *La Guerra in Sicilia 1943: Storia Fotografica* (Catania, Sicily: Le Nove Muse Editrice, 2009), 66.
2. George S. Patton, diary entry, 5 July 1943, George S. Patton Papers, Library of Congress.
3. Patton, diary entry, 9 May 1943.
4. Martin Blumenson, *The Patton Papers* (Boston: Da Capo Press, 1974), 46.
5. Michael Haskew, "How George S. Patton Vanquished Pancho Villa's Lieutenants," *Military Heritage*, May 2015.
6. "Message to Seventh Army at Sea," 7 July 1943, Patton Papers.
7. Patton, diary entry, 9 July 1943.

Backstory

1. Reflections of author's visits to Sicily.
2. "*Mare Nostrum*? Mussolini Looks Out on the Mediterranean," *New York Times*, 27 April 1930.
3. John Grigg, *1943: The Victory That Never Was* (New York: Hill & Wang, 1980).
4. The Churchill Project, "Were "Soft Underbelly' and 'Fortress Europe' Churchill Phrases?" 1 April 2016, www.winstonchurchill.hillsdale.edu/soft-underbelly-fortress-europe.
5. Mark W. Clark, "Address of 1 June 1970," in *The Heroic Memory: The Memorial Addresses to the Rt. Hon. Sir Winston Spencer Churchill Society, Edmonton, Alberta*, ed. Ronald I. Cohen (Edmonton: Churchill Statue and Oxford Scholarship Foundation, 2004).
6. Anthony Saunders, *Hitler's Atlantic Wall* (Gloucestershire, UK: Sutton, 2001).
7. Grigg, *1943*.
8. Basil H. Liddell Hart, *History of the Second World War* (New York: G. P. Putnam's Sons, 1970), 437–38.

9. Grigg, *1943*, 69, 73–75.
10. Grigg, *1943*, 69; Liddell Hart, *History of the Second World War*, 435–39.
11. Liddell Hart, 435–39; Patton, diary entry, 21 January 1943; Samuel E. Morison, *History of United States Naval Operations in World War II*, vol. 9, *Sicily-Salerno-Anzio, January 1943–June 1944* (Boston: Little, Brown, 1953), 8–9.
12. Liddell Hart, *History of the Second World War*, 435; Grigg, *1943*, 69.
13. Patton, diary entry, 21 January 1943.
14. Patton, diary entry, 20 January 1943.
15. Omar N. Bradley, *A Soldier's Story* (Chicago: Rand McNally, 1951), 119; Ben Macintyre, *Operation Mincemeat: How a Dead Man and a Bizarre Plan Fooled the Nazis and Assured an Allied Victory* (New York: Harmony, 2010); Liddell Hart, *History of the Second World War*, 437–38; Robert F. McEniry, "The WWII Bombing of Pantelleria Island: A Test of Air Power," *WWII History*, November 2009; Wesley F. Craven and James L. Cate, eds., *The Army Air Forces in World War II*, vol. 2, *Europe—Torch to Pointblank: August 1942 to December 1943* (Washington, DC: Office of Air Force History, 1983), 427–30.
16. McEniry, "Bombing of Pantelleria Island."
17. Patton, diary entry, 4 October 1942.
18. George S. Patton, letter to Frederick Ayer, 20 October 1941, Patton Papers collection, LOC.
19. Patton, diary entry, 28 September 1941.
20. Blumenson, *The Patton Papers*, 88.
21. Dwight D. Eisenhower, *Crusade in Europe* (Garden City, NY: Doubleday, 1948), 82; Kevin Hymel, *Patton's War: An American General's Combat Leadership*, vol. 1, *November 1942–July 1944* (Columbia: University of Missouri Press, 2021), 37.
22. Michael Korda, *Ike: An American Hero* (New York: HarperCollins, 2007), 329; Hymel, *Patton's War*, 37; Eisenhower, *Crusade in Europe*, 82.
23. Hymel, *Patton's War*, 37.
24. Patton, letter to Beatrice Patton, 3 December 1942; Patton, diary entry, 11 December 1942.
25. Patton, diary entry, 10 July 1943.
26. Hymel, *Patton's War*, 23.
27. Patton, letter to Beatrice Patton, 3 December 1942.
28. Blumenson, *The Patton Papers*, 410.
29. Patton, diary entry, 21 January 1943.
30. Patton, diary entry, 6 March 1943.
31. Patton, diary entry, 18 January 1944.
32. Patton, diary entry, 15 January 1943.
33. Patton, diary entry, 16 January 1943.
34. Patton, diary entry, 18 January 1944.
35. Patton, diary entry, 13 June 1943.

36. Patton, diary entry, 14 February 1943.
37. Blumenson, *The Patton Papers*, 231.
38. Patton, diary entry, 17 July 1943.
39. Patton, letter to Beatrice Patton, 6 March 1943.
40. Patton, diary entry, 29 April 1943.
41. Patton, diary entry, 21 October 1942.
42. Patton, diary entry, 22 October 1942.
43. Patton, diary entry, 22 October 1942.
44. Patton, diary entry, 24 October 1942.
45. Patton, diary entry, 23 October 1942.
46. H. Kent Hewitt, *The Memoirs of Admiral H. Kent Hewitt*, ed. Evelyn M. Cherpak (Newport, RI: Naval War College Press, 2004), 169–73.
47. Blumenson, *The Patton Papers*, 173–77.
48. Patton, letter to Beatrice Patton, 1 April 1943.
49. Bradley, *A Soldier's Story*, 58.
50. Patton, diary entry, 30 October 1942.
51. Bradley, *A Soldier's Story*, 58.
52. Patton, diary entry, 8 April 1943; Bradley, *A Soldier's Story*, 62–63.

Chapter 1. Getting Ready

1. Eisenhower, *Crusade in Europe*, 187.
2. Hewitt, *Memoirs*, 198.
3. Carlo D'Este, *Bitter Victory: The Battle for Sicily 1943* (New York: Harper, 1988),118; Hugh Pond, *Sicily* (London: William Kimber, 1962), 38–39.
4. Pond, *Sicily*, 39.
5. Patton, letter to Beatrice Patton, 23 April 1943.
6. Patton, letter to Beatrice Patton, 5 May 1943.
7. Patton, diary entry, 29 April 1943.
8. Patton, letter to Beatrice Patton, 10 May 1943.
9. Patton, diary entry, 4 May 1943.
10. Eisenhower, *Crusade in Europe*, 155–56.
11. Patton, diary entry, 9 May 1943, 9 June 1943.
12. Patton, diary entry, 26 May 1943.
13. Pond, *Sicily*, 41.
14. Eisenhower, *Crusade in Europe*, 169–70.
15. Eisenhower, 166–71.
16. Bradley, *A Soldier's Story*, 118–19.
17. H. Kent Hewitt, "Naval Aspects of the Sicilian Campaign," *Proceedings*, July 1953.
18. DUKW is a General Motors designation: *D* (put in service in 1942), *U* (utility amphibious vehicle), *K* (front-wheel drive), *W* (dual rear-driven axles). Ian V. Hogg and John

Weeks, *The Illustrated Encyclopedia of Military Vehicles* (London: New Burlington Books, 1988), 308–9.

19. Harry W. Edwards, *A Different War: Marines in Europe and North Africa* (Washington, DC: Marine Corps Historical Center, 1994), 22–23; “DUKW,” https://truck-encyclopedia.com/ww2/us/GMC_DUKW.php.
20. “USS LST 393,” www.lst.393.org.
21. Frank A. Blazich Jr., “Bridging the Gap from Ship to Shore,” *Naval History* 35, no. 4 (August 2021).
22. Hewitt, *Memoirs*, 202.
23. Edwards, *A Different War*, 23.
24. Hewitt, *Memoirs*, 202.
25. Morison, *Sicily-Salerno-Anzio*, 81; Patton, diary entry, 30 June 1943; Hewitt, *Memoirs*, 201–2; Patton, diary entry, 9 May 1943, 30 June 1943.
26. S. W. C. Pack, *Operation Husky: The Allied Invasion of Sicily* (New York: Hippocrene Books, 1977), 59.
27. Because of a shortage of naval transports, most of the 9th Division would be held in Seventh Army reserve in Algeria until 1 August, when it would come ashore at Palermo. One regiment—the 39th—would land between Licata and Gela on 18 July and push northwest to Marsala and then cross-country to Palermo. See 9thinfantrydivision.net.
28. Patton, letter to Beatrice, 13 June 1943.
29. Charles Scheffel with Barry Basden, *Crack! and Thump: With a Combat Infantry Officer in World War II* (Llano, TX: Camroc Press, 2007), 100.
30. Charles R. Codman, *Drive* (Boston: Little, Brown, 1957), 94.
31. Stanley P. Hirshson, *General Patton: A Soldier's Life* (New York: HarperCollins, 2002), 373.
32. Harley Reynolds, *How I Survived Three First Wave Invasions* (Minneapolis: Mill City Press, 2008), 84–85.

Chapter 2. The Airborne

1. James M. Gavin, *On to Berlin: Battles of an Airborne Commander* (New York: Viking, 1978), 18.
2. Eisenhower, *Crusade in Europe*, 173.
3. Gerard M. Devlin, *Paratrooper! The Saga of U.S. Army and Marine Parachute and Glider Combat Troops During World War II* (New York: St. Martin's Press, 1979), 226.
4. James C. Bonta, “The Invasion of Pantelleria, 11 June 1943: Personal Experience of a Company Executive Officer, Company A, 907th Air Base Security Battalion” (Fort Benning, GA: Infantry School, 1949–50), https://mcoecbamcoepwprd01.blob.core.usgovcloudapi.net/library/DonovanPapers/wwii/STUP2/A-F/Bonta%20James%20C.%20CPT.pdf.

5. Craven and Cate, eds., *The Army Air Forces in World War II*, 427–30.
6. Devlin, *Paratrooper!* 220.
7. Gavin, *On to Berlin*, 18.
8. Gavin, *On to Berlin*, 22.
9. William B. Breuer, *Air Drop Sicily: Allied Airborne Strike, July 1943* (Novato, CA: Presidio Press, 1983), ix.
10. Gavin, *On to Berlin*, 18–19.
11. Barbara Fauntleroy, *The General and his Daughter: The Wartime Letters of General James M. Gavin to His Daughter Barbara*, ed. Gayle Wurst (New York: Fordham University Press, 2007), 38.
12. Gavin, *On to Berlin*, 18–23.
13. Breuer, *Air Drop Sicily*, 41.
14. Eisenhower, *Crusade in Europe*, 173.
15. Gavin, *On to Berlin*, 23.
16. Francis T. Miller, *The Complete History of World War II* (New York: Home Education Guild, 1945), 668.
17. Gavin, *On to Berlin*, 24.
18. Pond, *Sicily*, 62.
19. Vincent P. O'Hara, *Struggle for the Middle Sea: The Great Navies at War in the Mediterranean Theater, 1940–1945* (Annapolis, MD: Naval Institute Press, 2009), 215.
20. Pond, *Sicily*, 22.
21. "Gela Beachhead Counterattack of 1943," www.comandosupremo.com/gela-1943.
22. John L. La Monte and Winston B. Lewis, *The Sicilian Campaign: 10 July–17 August 1943* (Washington, DC: Naval Historical Center, 1993), 56–61; Johannes Steinhoff, *Messerschmitts Over Sicily: Diary of a Luftwaffe Fighter Commander* (Mechanicsburg, PA: Stackpole Books, 2004), 134.
23. Shelford Bidwell, "Kesselring," in *Hitler's Generals*, ed. Correlli Barnett (New York: Grove Weidenfeld, 1989), 278–79.
24. Albert Kesselring, *The Memoirs of Field-Marshal Kesselring* (New York: Skyhorse, 2016), 161.
25. Gavin, *On to Berlin*, 24.
26. "Douglas M. Bailey, 463rd Parachute FA Bn.: The Landing in Sicily," www.secondworldwar.nl/douglas-m-bailey-landing-in-sicily.php.
27. Breuer, *Air Drop Sicily*, 60–61.
28. Breuer, 68.
29. Pond, *Sicily*, 65.
30. Otis L. Sampson, *Time Out for Combat* (privately published, 2005), 50–58.
31. Lt. Col. George Merz, USAF (Ret.), "A Very Special Report from Operation Husky," interview by 1st Lt. Lewis E. Johnston, AUS (Ret.), https://amcmuseum.org/history/a-very-special-report-from-operation-husky/.

32. Gavin, *On to Berlin*, 24, 36.
33. Devlin, *Paratrooper!* 226.
34. Sampson, *Time Out for Combat*, 55–58.
35. D'Este, *Bitter Victory*, 244.
36. D'Este, 248.

Chapter 3. Ladbroke

1. Scott McGaugh, *Brotherhood of the Flying Coffin: The Glider Pilots of World War II* (Dublin, Ireland: Osprey, 2023), 54.
2. Samuel W. Mitcham Jr. and Friedrich von Stauffenberg, *The Battle of Sicily: How the Allies Lost Their Chance for Total Victory* (New York: Orion Books, 1991), 72; "Arthur Royall—Operation Ladbroke," https://war-experience.org/index.php/?s=Arthur%20Royall.
3. Pond, *Sicily*, 50–53; Pack, *Operation Husky*, 40–41, 47–56, 70.
4. McGaugh, *Brotherhood of the Flying Coffin*, 54–55.
5. Pond, *Sicily*, 50–52, 69.
6. Pond, 51.
7. John C. Warren, *Airborne Missions in the Mediterranean 1942–1945*, USAF Historical Studies no. 74, Maxwell Air Force Base, AL, 1955, 23–24.
8. McGaugh, *Brotherhood of the Flying Coffin*, 54–57.
9. Breuer, *Air Drop Sicily*, 40–42; Pond, *Sicily*, 52; James Holland, *Sicily '43: The First Assault on Fortress Europe* (New York: Penguin/Random House, 2020), 276–77.
10. Flint Whitlock, *If Chaos Reigns: The Near-Disaster and Ultimate Triumph of the Allied Airborne Forces on D-Day, June 6, 1944* (Philadelphia: Casemate, 2011), 63–74.
11. "Arthur Royall—Operation Ladbroke."
12. Harry Jost, "Airborne Operations in Sicily, July 1943," Infantry School, Fort Benning, GA, 1948–49, https://mcoecbamcoepwprd01.blob.core.usgovcloudapi.net/library/DonovanPapers/wwii/STUP2/G-L/JostHarryF%20%20CPT.pdf.
13. "Arthur Royall—Operation Ladbroke."
14. McGaugh, *Brotherhood of the Flying Coffin*, 60–71.
15. Bradley, *A Soldier's Story*, 126–27.
16. Jost, "Airborne Operations in Sicily."
17. Pack, *Operation Husky*, 86–87.

Chapter 4. Rangers Lead the Way

1. William O. Darby and William H. Baumer, *Darby's Rangers: We Led the Way* (San Raphael, CA: Presidio Press, 1980), 85.
2. "Caltanissetta," www.italyheritage.com/regions/sicilia/caltanissetta/gela.htm; "Gela," www.sicily-visitor.com/places/gela.php; www.worldhistory.org/Gela.

3. Darby and Baumer, *Darby's Rangers*, 85–86.
4. Darby and Baumer, 1–2; "William O. Darby," https://encyclopediaofarkansas.net/entries/william-orlando-darby-2414/.
5. Ralph G. Martin, "Invasion of Sicily," *Yank*, 13 August 1943.
6. Morison, *Sicily-Salerno-Anzio*, 68–69.
7. Darby and Baumer, *Darby's Rangers*, 85.
8. Darby and Baumer, 86–87; Albert N. Garland and Howard M. Smyth, *United States Army in World War II: Mediterranean Theater of Operations, Sicily, and the Surrender of Italy* (Washington, DC: U.S. Army Center for Military History, 1965), 136.
9. Robert W. Black, *The Ranger Force: Darby's Rangers in World War II* (Mechanicsburg, PA: Stackpole, 2009), 131.
10. Darby and Baumer, *Darby's Rangers*, 85–88.
11. "Gela Beachhead Counterattack of 1943."
12. Darby and Baumer, *Darby's Rangers*, 85–88.
13. Garland and Smyth, *Mediterranean Theater of Operations*, 147–62.
14. Darby and Baumer, *Darby's Rangers*, 87–88.
15. James B. Lyle, "The Operations of Companies A and B, 1st Ranger Battalion, at Gela, Sicily, 10–11 July 1943," Advanced Infantry Officers Course, Infantry School, Fort Benning, GA, 1948–49.
16. Pond, *Sicily*, 87; Black, *The Ranger Force*, 132.
17. Pond, 87; Morison, *Sicily-Salerno-Anzio*, 97.
18. Darby and Baumer, *Darby's Rangers*, 88.
19. Lyle, "Operations of Companies A and B."
20. LaMonte and Lewis, *The Sicilian Campaign*, 62–68, 81–82.
21. Darby and Baumer, *Darby's Rangers*, 88–89; Ian Westwell, *Spearhead: U.S. Rangers "Leading the Way"* (Surrey, UK: Ian Allen Publishing, 2003), 30.
22. Lyle, "Operations of Companies A and B."
23. Darby and Baumer, *Darby's Rangers*, 88–89.
24. Hymel, *Patton's War*, 151, 153.

Chapter 5. The Big Red One Arrives

1. USS Landing Craft Infantry National Association, "LCI Facts," usslci.org/facts.
2. H. Kent Hewitt, "Action Report—Western Naval Task Force: The Sicilian Campaign, Operation Husky, July-August 1943," *United States Naval Administrative Histories of World War II*, https://www.history.navy.mil/content/history/nhhc/research/library/online-reading-room/title-list-alphabetically/s/the-sicilian-campaign-operation-husky.html, 2–3.
3. Carlo D'Este, *Patton: A Genius for War* (New York: HarperCollins, 1995), 504; Morison, *Sicily-Salerno-Anzio*, 64; Kevin Hymel, "Patton's War for Sicily's Beaches," *WWII Quarterly*, Winter 2022.

4. Gerald Astor, *Terrible Terry Allen: Combat General of World War II—The Life of an American Soldier* (New York: Ballantine, 2003), 6–90.
5. Astor, 88–89.
6. Bradley, *A Soldier's Story*, 109–10.
7. Allen N. Towne, *Doctor Danger Forward: A World War II Memoir of a Combat Medical Aidman, First Infantry Division* (Jefferson, NC: McFarland, 2000), 61.
8. Bill E. Faust, *Memoir* (Carlisle Barracks, PA: U.S. Army Heritage Center Foundation, 1982).
9. Bradley, *A Soldier's Story*, 109–10.
10. Astor, *Terrible Terry Allen*, 159.
11. Astor, 188–89.
12. Bradley, *A Soldier's Story*, 143.
13. Astor, *Terrible Terry Allen*, 103–4.
14. Blythe Foote Finke, *No Mission Too Difficult: Old Buddies of the 1st Division Tell All About World War II* (Chicago: Cantigny First Division Foundation, 1995), 129.
15. Towne, *Doctor Danger Forward*, 65–66.
16. Reynolds, *How I Survived Three First Wave Invasions*, 57–59.
17. "First Pictures of Sicily Invasion," *Life*, 2 August 1943.
18. "Sicily Invasion Goes Well," *Life*, 26 July 1943.
19. John W. Baumgartner, Al De Poto, William Fraccio, and Sam Fuller, *The 16th Infantry: 1861–1946* (Du Quoin, IL: Cricket Press, 1999), 37–38.
20. Finke, *No Mission Too Difficult*, 130–31.
21. Baumgartner et al., *The 16th Infantry*, 37–38.
22. Hewitt, "Action Report," 3.
23. Morison, *Sicily-Salerno-Anzio*, 101.
24. Morison, 85–86, 89.

Chapter 6. Here Come the Thunderbirds

1. George A. Fisher, *The Story of the 180th Infantry Regiment* (Privately published, 1947), 19–21.
2. D'Este, *Bitter Victory*, 264.
3. Blumenson, *The Patton Papers*, 231; "Remembering a Veteran: Colonel Troy H. Middleton, 4th Division, AEF," roadstothegreatwar-ww1.blogspot.com/2021/05/remembering-veteran-colonel-troy-h.
4. Flint Whitlock, *The Rock of Anzio: From Sicily to Dachau—A History of the 45th Infantry Division* (Boulder, CO: Westview Press, 1998), passim; D'Este, *Bitter Victory*, 264n.
5. Raymond S. McLain, "Diary of the Sicilian Campaign," https://www.45thdivision.org/Veterans/McLain_Sicily.htm, 2–3.
6. Kenneth D. Williamson, *Tales of a Thunderbird in World War II* (Privately published, 1994), 69–70.

7. Ed Speairs, interview by author, 19 January 1995.
8. Brummett Echohawk with Mark R. Ellenbarger, *Drawing Fire: A Pawnee, Artist, and Thunderbird in World War II* (Lawrence: University Press of Kansas, 2018), 15–16.
9. David Israel, *The Day the Thunderbird Cried: Untold Stories of World War II* (Privately published, 2005), 98–99.
10. Don Robinson, *News of the 45th* (New York: Grosset & Dunlap, 1944), 61–77.
11. Bill Whitman, *"Scouts Out!"* (Los Angeles: Authors Unlimited, 1990), 8–9.
12. "Heroic Spotter Pilot," *Shipmate*, July/August 1983; "USS *Philadelphia*—CL-41—Handwritten Notes, Saturday, July 10, 1943," www.brigs.us/Phila/Handwritten-notes-7-10-43.
13. Rick Atkinson, *The Day of Battle: The War in Sicily and Italy, 1943–1944* (New York: Henry Holt, 2007), 116; Garland and Smyth, *Mediterranean Theater of Operations*, 100, 136; Fisher, *Story of the 180th Infantry Regiment*, 19–21; Samuel W. Mitcham Jr. and Friedrich von Stauffenberg, *The Battle of Sicily: How the Allies Lost Their Chance for Total Victory* (New York: Orion Books, 1991), 96.
14. Patton, diary entry, 13 July 1943.
15. Atkinson, *The Day of Battle*, 116, 120.
16. Blumenson, *The Patton Papers*, 276–77.
17. Pond, *Sicily*, 97–98.
18. Fisher, *Story of the 180th Infantry Regiment*, 19–23.
19. Eisenhower, *Crusade in Europe*, 173–74.
20. Whitman, *"Scouts Out!"* 13–14.

Chapter 7. Marnemen Hit the Beach

1. Westwell, *Spearhead*, 32; "Operation Husky: The Invasion of Sicily, 9 July–17 August 1943," https://www.history.navy.mil/browse-by-topic/wars-conflicts-and-operations/world-war-ii/1943/sicilian-campaign.html.
2. Will Lang Jr., "Lucian King Truscott Jr.," *Life*, 2 October 1944.
3. Lucian K. Truscott Jr., *The Twilight of the U.S. Cavalry: Life in the Old Army, 1917–1942* (Lawrence: University Press of Kansas, 1989), xv.
4. Lang, "Lucian King Truscott Jr."
5. Harvey Ferguson, *The Last Cavalryman: The Life of General Lucian K. Truscott Jr.* (Norman: University of Oklahoma Press, 2015), 183.
6. Lucian K. Truscott Jr., *Command Missions* (Novato, CA: Presidio Press, 1990), 196–98.
7. "443rd Anti-Aircraft Battalion," texasmilitaryforcesmuseum.org/36division/archives/443/44344.
8. Truscott, *Command Missions*, 212–13.
9. Garland and Smyth, *Mediterranean Theater of Operations*, 131; Morison, *Sicily-Salerno-Anzio*, 85.

10. Hewitt, "Action Report," 3–7; Garland and Smyth, *Sicily and the Surrender of Italy*, 129–31.
11. Robert J. Cressman, *The Official Chronology of the United States Navy in World War II* (Annapolis, MD: Naval Institute Press, 1999), 168.
12. Hewitt, "Action Report," 4–7.
13. Westwell, *Spearhead*, 32; Garland and Smyth, *Mediterranean Theater of Operations*, 129.
14. Pack, *Operation Husky*, 75.
15. Garland and Smyth, *Mediterranean Theater of Operations*, 125.
16. "LST-158," https://www.navsource.org/archives/10/16/160158.htm; Morten Jessen, "The Sinking of LST-158," https://airwarpublications.com/new-earticle-sinking-lst-158/.
17. Hewitt, "Action Report," 3.
18. Truscott, *Command Missions*, 214.
19. Audie Murphy, *To Hell and Back* (New York: Henry Holt, 1949), 1–4.
20. Hewitt, "Naval Aspects of the Sicilian Campaign."
21. Ernie Pyle, "Sicily Landing," in *The Army Reader*, ed. Karl Detzer (Indianapolis: Bobbs-Merrill, 1943), 439–41.

Chapter 8. D-Day at Gela

1. La Monte and Lewis, *The Sicilian Campaign*, 62–68, 81–82.
2. Baumgartner et al., *The 16th Infantry*, 39–40.
3. Garland and Smyth, *Mediterranean Theater of Operations*, 100, 136, 139.
4. Jonathan A. Woislaw, "The 1st Infantry Division in Sicily: A Case Study in Tactical Intelligence" (Master's thesis, U.S. Army Command and General Staff College, 2021).
5. Hewitt, "Action Report," 5.
6. Baumgartner et al., *The 16th Infantry*, 39.
7. Finke, *No Mission Too Difficult*, 130.
8. Morison, *Sicily-Salerno-Anzio*, 101.
9. Gavin, *On to Berlin*, 35–36; Garland and Smyth, *Mediterranean Theater of Operations*, 148–49.
10. Garland and Smyth, *Mediterranean Theater of Operations*, 162–63.
11. Garland and Smyth, 164.
12. Garland and Smyth, 148–49.
13. Garland and Smyth, 147–62; Morison, *Sicily-Salerno-Anzio*, 111–13.
14. Garland and Smyth, 150–52.
15. Donald M. Weller, "Naval Gunfire Support of Amphibious Operations: Past, Present, and Future," Naval Sea Systems Command, Naval Surface Warfare Center, Headquarters U.S. Marine Corps, Dahlgren, VA, 1977.

16. La Monte and Lewis, *The Sicilian Campaign*, 103; Garland and Smyth, *Mediterranean Theater of Operations*, 152–53.
17. Lyle, "The Operations of Companies A and B, 1st Ranger Battalion, at Gela, Sicily."
18. La Monte and Lewis, 86–87.
19. D'Este, *Bitter Victory*, 282–83.
20. Gavin, *On to Berlin*, 28–30.
21. Woislaw, "The 1st Infantry Division in Sicily."
22. Darby and Baumer, *Darby's Rangers*, 90.
23. Phil Nordyke, *Four Stars of Valor: The Combat History of the 505th Parachute Infantry Regiment in World War I* (Minneapolis: Zenith Press, 2006), 74–76.
24. Darby and Baumer, *Darby's Rangers*, 90.
25. Baumgartner et al., *The 16th Infantry*, 39.
26. Hewitt, "Naval Aspects of the Sicilian Campaign."
27. Garland and Smyth, *Mediterranean Theater of Operations*, 154.
28. Nordyke, *Four Stars of Valor*, 81.
29. Woislaw, "The 1st Infantry Division in Sicily."
30. "Gela Beachhead Counterattack of 1943."
31. Garland and Smyth, *Mediterranean Theater of Operations*, 165.
32. Nordyke, *Four Stars of Valor*, 74.
33. Breuer, *Air Drop Sicily*, 138; Nordyke, *Four Stars of Valor*, 91.
34. Baumgartner et al., *The 16th Infantry*, 39–40.
35. William B. Allmon, "USS *Murphy*: Long Service in Wartime," *WWII History*, July 2011.
36. Hewitt, "Action Report," 11.
37. Eisenhower, *Crusade in Europe*, 174.
38. Breuer, *Air Drop Sicily*, 139.
39. Fauntleroy, *The General and His Daughter*, 40.

Chapter 9. D-Day Plus One

1. Gavin, *On to Berlin*, 29–32.
2. Gavin, 29–32; Darby and Baumer, *Darby's Rangers*, 90; D'Este, *Bitter Victory*, 294; Holland, *Sicily '43*, 318.
3. La Monte and Lewis, *The Sicilian Campaign*, 91.
4. Baumgartner et al., *The 16th Infantry*, 40–41.
5. Morison, *Sicily-Salerno-Anzio*, 111; Astor, *Terrible Terry Allen*, 195–96.
6. Hewitt, Action Report, 5.
7. Whitman, "*Scouts Out!*" 13–15.
8. Garland and Smyth, *Mediterranean Theater of Operations*, 152.
9. Astor, *Terrible Terry Allen*, 196–97.
10. Baumgartner et al., *The 16th Infantry*, 40.

11. Astor, *Terrible Terry Allen*, 196.
12. Pond, *Sicily*, 91.
13. Hewitt, "Action Report," 18.
14. "Alexander Pete Suer," https://www.uswarmemorials.org/html/people_details.php?PeopleID=10744.
15. "Dan McIlvoy," www.ww2-airborne.us/units/505/505_memories.
16. Patton, diary entry, 10 July 1943.
17. Hymel, "Patton's War for Sicily's Beaches"; Astor, *Terrible Terry Allen*, 193.
18. Lyle, "The Operations of Companies A and B, 1st Ranger Battalion, at Gela, Sicily"; Astor, *Terrible Terry Allen*, 198.
19. George S. Patton Jr., *War As I Knew It* (Boston: Houghton Mifflin, 1947), 55–56.
20. Patton, diary entry, 11 July 1943.
21. Finke, *No Mission Too Difficult*, 129, 133–34; La Monte and Lewis, *The Sicilian Campaign*, 91.
22. Patton, *War As I Knew It*, 56–57. Actually, the *Robert Rowan* had a crew of 421; all of them managed to abandon ship before the explosion and were rescued by nearby vessels. Finke, *No Mission Too Difficult*, 134.
23. Patton, diary entry 11 July 1943.
24. Bradley, *A Soldier's Story*, 130.
25. Astor, *Terrible Terry Allen*, 200.
26. "Robert Craig," www.cmohs.org/recipient/robert-craig.
27. Truscott, *Command Missions*, 214.
28. Whitman, *"Scouts Out!"* 9–10.
29. "Gela Beachhead Counterattack of 1943."
30. Woislaw, "The 1st Infantry Division in Sicily"; Baumgartner et al., *The 16th Infantry*, 41.
31. Darby and Baumer, *Darby's Rangers*, 85–91; Westwell, *Spearhead: Rangers*, 29–34.
32. "Troops and Cargo Transported During World War II under U.S. Army Control," American Merchant Marine at War, http://www.usmm.org/armycargo.html.
33. Hewitt, "Action Report," 68.

Chapter 10. Disaster in the Sky

1. D'Este, *Patton: A Genius for War*, 445.
2. Gavin, *On to Berlin*, 67.
3. Pond, *Sicily*, 100; Blumenson, *The Patton Papers*, 280–82.
4. Patton, diary entry, 11 July 1943.
5. Morison, *Sicily-Salerno-Anzio*, 141.
6. Blumenson, *The Patton Papers*, 280–82.
7. Nordyke, *More Than Courage*, 47; Devlin, *Paratrooper!* 237.
8. Pond, *Sicily*, 105–6.
9. Pond, 104.
10. Fisher, *The Story of the 180th Infantry Regiment*, 28.

11. Reynolds, *How I Survived Three First Wave Invasions*, 57–59.
12. Bradley, *A Soldier's Story*, 133.
13. Breuer, *Air Drop Sicily*, 60–61.
14. Robert Uhrig, diary, 63–64, author's collection.
15. "Colonel Reuben Tucker," https://ww2-airborne.us/division/campaigns/sicily.html.
16. Pond, *Sicily*, 104.
17. Mark J. Alexander and John Sparry, *Jump Commander: In Combat with the 505th and 508th Parachute Infantry Regiments, 82nd Airborne Division in World War I* (Havertown, PA: Casemate, 2010), 86–87.
18. Williamson, *Tales of a Thunderbird in World War II*, 73–74.
19. Michael N. Ingrisano, *Valor Without Arms: A History of the 316th Troop Carrier Group, 1942–1945* (Hoosick, NY: Merriam Press, 1991), 23.
20. "Charles Keerans," https://militaryhallofhonor.com/honoree-record.php?id=203999.
21. Robert Dorr, "Friendly Fire's Deadliest Day," *America in WWII*, February 2010.
22. Spencer F. Wurst and Gayle Wurst, *Descending from the Clouds: A Memoir of Combat in the 505 Parachute Infantry Regiment, 82nd Airborne Division* (Drexel Hill, PA: Casemate, 2007), 67.
23. Lt. Col. George Merz, USAF (Ret.), "A Very Special Report from Operation Husky," interview by 1st Lt. Lewis E. Johnston, AUS (Ret.), https://amcmuseum.org/history/a-very-special-report-from-operation-husky/.
24. Avis D. Schorer, *A Half Acre of Hell: A Combat Nurse in World War II* (Lakeville, MN: Galde Press, 2002), 87–88.
25. Pond, *Sicily*, 105.
26. Harry C. Butcher, *My Three Years with Eisenhower: The Personal Diary of Captain Harry C. Butcher, USNR, Naval Aide to General Eisenhower, 1942 to 1945* (New York: Simon and Schuster, 1946), 362.
27. Patton, diary entry, 13 July 1943.
28. Eisenhower, *Crusade in Europe*, 174.
29. Pond, *Sicily*, 100.

Chapter 11. Massacre at Biscari

1. Morison, *Sicily-Salerno-Anzio*, 124; Hirshson, *General Patton: A Soldier's Life*, 354.
2. Edwards, "A Different War: Marines in Europe and North Africa."
3. Fisher, *The Story of the 180th Infantry Regiment*, 24; Morison, *Sicily-Salerno-Anzio*, 145.
4. Tom H. Kelly, "War Criminal Paroled: Horace T. West and the Final Chapter of the Biscari Massacre," *Army Lawyer*, no. 5, 2020.
5. Hirshson, *General Patton: A Soldier's Life*, 375.
6. Oklahoma National Guard Museum Facebook page, https://www.facebook.com/okngmuseum.
7. Whitlock, *The Rock of Anzio*, 34, 50.

8. D'Este, *Bitter Victory*, 317.
9. Whitlock, *The Rock of Anzio*, 34, 50; Hirshson, *General Patton: A Soldier's Life*, 174; "John T. Compton," www.findagrave.com/memorial/56307603/john-travers-compton.
10. Patton, letter to Beatrice Patton, 16 July 1943.
11. D'Este, *Bitter Victory*, 317.
12. Hirshson, *General Patton: A Soldier's Life*, 378–79; "Crimes of the Allies in Sicily and Naples in the Second World War," interview of Sicilian historian Giovanni Bartolone by Federico Dal Cortivo, www.leccecronaca.it/index.php/ 2012/10/29/i-crimini-degli-alleati-in-sicilia-e-a-napoli-nella-seconda-guerra-mondiale-il-ruolo-della-mafia-e-quello-della-massoneria.

Chapter 12. Reconnaissance in Force

1. Andrew J. Birtle, *Sicily: The U.S. Army Campaigns of World War II* (Washington, DC: U.S. Army Center for Military History, 1993), 10.
2. Bradley, *A Soldier's Story*, 159–60.
3. Patton, diary entry, 13 July 1943.
4. Blumenson, *The Patton Papers*, 286–88.
5. Patton, diary entry, 17 July 1943.
6. Kesselring, *The Memoirs of Field-Marshal Kesselring*, 164–65.
7. Hewitt, "Action Report," 12.
8. Blumenson, *The Patton Papers*, 293–94; Holland, *Sicily '43*, 428.
9. "British 8th Army Lands on Sicily," *Life*, 2 August 1943.
10. Guido Rossi, "Italian Fellas in Olive Drab: Exploring the Experiences of Italian American Servicemen in Sicily and Italy, 1943–1945" (Master's thesis, University of Southern Mississippi, 2017).
11. Robert P. Argentino, interview by James Zanella, Heinz History Center, Pittsburgh, PA, 8 October 2004, https://www.heinzhistorycenter.org/wp-content/uploads/2022/08/Argentine-Robert.pdf.
12. Rossi, "Italian Fellas in Olive Drab."
13. Towne, *Doctor Danger Forward*, 72–73.
14. Patton, letter to Frederick Ayer, 6 August 1943.
15. "Summary of Events," 17 July 1943, Patton Papers collection.
16. Patton, diary entry, 19 July 1943.
17. Fauntleroy, *The General and His Daughter*, 43.
18. Patton, diary entry, 19 July 1943.
19. Darby and Baumer, *Darby's Rangers*, 104–5.
20. Truscott, *Command Missions*, 222–23.
21. Truscott, 226.
22. Morison, *Sicily-Salerno-Anzio*, 186; Garland and Smyth, *Mediterranean Theater of Operations*, 236–37.

23. Towne, *Doctor Danger Forward*, 72–73.
24. Eisenhower, *Crusade in Europe*, 168–69.
25. Dan Kurzman, *The Race for Rome: How the Eternal City Was Saved from Nazi Destruction* (Garden City, NY: Doubleday, 1975), 84–85.
26. Miller, *The Complete History of World War II*, 670–71.
27. "Rome Claims Pope Deplored Bombing in Letter to Vicar," *Denver Post*, 22 July 1943; Kurzman, *The Race for Rome*, 84–85.
28. William L. Shirer, *The Rise and Fall of the Third Reich: A History of Nazi Germany* (New York: Simon & Schuster, 1960), 1294–95.
29. Garland and Smyth, *Mediterranean Theater of Operations*, 213–14.
30. Bradley, *A Soldier's Story*, 143.
31. Patton, diary entry, 20 July 1943.
32. Blumenson, *The Patton Papers*, 294.
33. Patton, letter to Beatrice Patton, 20 July 1943.
34. Patton, diary entry, 21 July 1943.
35. Patton, diary entry, 19 July 1943.
36. Darby and Baumer, *Darby's Rangers*, 104–5.
37. Patton, diary entry, 21 July 1943.
38. Patton, diary entry, 22 July 1943.
39. "Historical Record of the 2nd Armored Division, 22 April–25 July 1943," https://mcoecbamcoepwprd01.blob.core.usgovcloudapi.net/library/Documents/Hardcopy/paper/802AD_403.pdf.
40. Patton, letter to Beatrice Patton, 22 July 1943. In the letter he didn't say if he personally had shot the mule or if someone else did.
41. Gavin, *On to Berlin*, 45.
42. Fauntleroy, *The General and his Daughter*, 42–43.
43. Gavin, *On to Berlin*, 50–53.
44. Bill Mauldin, *Sicily Sketch Book* (Palermo, Sicily: I.R.E.S., 1943), 14.

Chapter 13. Palermo and Beyond

1. Truscott, *Command Missions*, 226–27.
2. "Lucian King Truscott, Jr.," *Life*, 2 October 1944.
3. Truscott, *Command Missions*, 227.
4. Patton's account of the capture of Palermo, 23 July 1943.
5. Morison, *Sicily, Salerno, Anzio*, 188.
6. Oliver North, *War Stories III: The Heroes Who Defeated Hitler* (Washington, DC: Regnery Publishing, 2005), 112.
7. Patton, *War As I Knew It*, 63; D'Este, *Bitter Victory*, 424.
8. "The Surrender of Palermo," *Life*, 23 August 1943.
9. Murphy, *To Hell and Back*, 13–15.
10. John Follain, *Mussolini's Island* (London: Hodder & Stoughton, 2005), 211.

11. Patton, diary entry, 23 July 1943.
12. Patton, diary entry, 22 July 1943.
13. Patton's account of the capture of Palermo, 23 July 1943.
14. Patton, letter to Eisenhower, 24 July 1943.
15. Eisenhower, *Crusade in Europe*, 175–76.
16. Holland, *Sicily '43*, 480.
17. Morison, *Sicily, Salerno, Anzio*, 195–96.
18. Janis Allen, ed., *We Shall Come Home Victorious: Stories of World War II Veterans* (Privately published, 2020), 153.
19. Whitman, "*Scouts Out!*" 26.
20. "Battle of Sicily," *Time*, 26 July 1943.
21. Echohawk, *Drawing Fire*, 139.
22. Whitman, "*Scouts Out!*" 26–29.
23. Miller, *The Complete History of World War II*, 679.
24. Whitman, "*Scouts Out!*" 26–29.
25. Whitlock, *The Rock of Anzio*, 67.
26. Shirer, *The Rise and Fall of the Third Reich*, 1294. After being arrested Mussolini was held in multiple locations before being confined in the Hotel Campo Imperatore at the Gran Sasso d'Italia ski resort in the Abruzzo Mountains east of Rome. A few days after the Allies launched Operation Avalanche, the 9 September 1943 invasion of southern Italy, Mussolini was rescued from his mountaintop prison by a daring German commando raid led by Colonel Otto Skorzeny and brought back to meet Hitler in Germany. Hitler intended to reinstall his Axis partner as the head of a puppet government to continue the fight. But on 28 April 1945 Mussolini and his mistress Clara Petacci were captured by Italian communist partisans and executed near Lake Como. Their corpses were taken to Milan, where they were abused by crowds, then strung up at a gas station.
27. "Armistice with Italy; September 3, 1943," The Avalon Project, Yale Law School, https://avalon.law.yale.edu/wwii/italy01.asp.
28. Nigel Nicolson, *Alex: The Life of Field Marshal Earl Alexander of Tunis* (London: Weidenfeld and Nicolson, 1973), 204.
29. Bidwell, "Kesselring," in *Hitler's Generals*, 228–31.
30. Codman, *Drive*, 110–11.
31. Patton, letter to Beatrice Patton, 20 July 1943.
32. Follain, *Mussolini's Island*, 215.
33. Bernice Heath, interview by Hermann J. Trojanowski, University of North Carolina at Greensboro, 2001, www.gateway.uncg.edu/islandora/object/wvhp%3A20835.
34. "Gertrude A. Lynn Talks About Her Experiences Serving in the U.S. Army Nurse Corps with the 59th Evacuation Hospital During World War II," Women's Overseas Service Oral History Project, Michigan State University, www.d.lib.msu.edu/wosl/103.

35. Towne, *Doctor Danger Forward*, 72–73.
36. Patton, letter to Middleton, 28 July 1943.
37. Patton, diary entry, 30 July 1943.
38. Hewitt, "Action Report," 14–15; "USS Philadelphia V (CL-41)," www.history.navy.mil/content/history/ nhhc/research/histories/ship-histories/danfs/p/philadelphia-v.html.
39. Patton, diary entry, 31 July 1943.
40. Codman, *Drive*, 111.
41. "USS Philadelphia V (CL-41)."
42. Morison, *Sicily, Salerno, Anzio*, 193.
43. Harold Denny, "Across the Mediterranean to Sicily: Battles, Recognition, Rest," in *Hitler's Nemesis: The 9th Infantry Division*, https://lonesentry.com/gi_stories_booklets/9thinfantry/index.html.
44. General Order #10, 1 August 1943.
45. Patton, diary entry, 5 August 1943.
46. Hewitt, "Action Report," 14; Morison, *Sicily, Salerno, Anzio*, 195–97.
47. Patton, letter to Beatrice Patton, 2 August 1943.
48. Eisenhower, *Crusade in Europe*, 175–76.

Chapter 14. Rough Road to Messina

1. Birtle, *Sicily*, 23.
2. Morison, *Sicily-Salerno-Anzio*, 192–94.
3. Franklin Roosevelt, letter to Patton, 4 August 1943.
4. Dwight Eisenhower, cable to Patton, 3 August 1943.
5. Blumenson, *The Patton Papers*, 312.
6. Morison, *Sicily-Salerno-Anzio*, 197–98.
7. Patton, diary entry, 10 August 1943; Truscott, *Command Missions*, 234–35.
8. La Monte and Lewis, *The Sicilian Campaign*, 144; Hewitt, "Action Report," 15.
9. Patton, letter to Beatrice Patton, 2 August 1943.
10. Patton, letter to Leslie McNair, 2 August 1943.
11. Hirshson, *General Patton: A Soldier's Life*, 392–93
12. "Charles H. Kuhl: The George S. Patton Slapping Incident," https://www.alexautographs.com/auction-lot/the-george-s-patton-slapping-incident-charles-h-k_FA24C55823.
13. Perrin H. Long, Lt. Col., Medical Corps, letter on the subject of "Mistreatment of Patients in Receiving Tents," 16 August 1943, https://members.tripod.com/msg_fisher/93evac-9.html.
14. Atkinson, *The Day of Battle*, 147.
15. Long, "Mistreatment of Patients."
16. Blumenson, *The Patton Papers*, 331.

17. Edwin Hoyt, *The GI's War: The Story of American Soldiers in Europe in World War II* (New York: McGraw-Hill, 1988), 242.
18. Korda, *Ike: An American Hero*, 408–9.
19. Morison, *Sicily-Salerno-Anzio*, 191.
20. Hewitt, "Action Report," 15; Morison, *Sicily-Salerno-Anzio*, 198–99.
21. Truscott, *Command Missions*, 236–40.
22. Hewitt, "Action Report," 15; La Monte and Lewis, *The Sicilian Campaign*, 145.
23. Truscott, *Command Missions*, 236–40.

Chapter 15. Capturing a Town, Losing a Commander

1. Eisenhower, *Crusade in Europe*, 176.
2. James Pence, "Operations of Company A, 16th Infantry, 1st Infantry Division, near Nicosia in northeast Sicily, 28–29 July 1943," Infantry School, Fort Benning, GA, 1948–49.
3. Richard Tregaskis, *Invasion Diary* (New York: Random House, 1944), 48–52.
4. Towne, *Doctor Danger Forward*, 75.
5. Pence, "Operations of Company A."
6. Mitcham and Stauffenberg, *The Battle of Sicily*, 132.
7. Woislaw, "The 1st Infantry Division in Sicily."
8. D'Este, *Bitter Victory*, 462–63.
9. Towne, *Doctor Danger Forward*, 74.
10. Astor, *Terrible Terry Allen*, 216–17; Baumgartner et al., *The 16th Infantry*, 57–58; Paul Gaujac, *L'Armée de la Victoire*, vol. 3 (Paris: Charles Lavauzelle, 1985), 58.
11. Astor, *Terrible Terry Allen*, 216–17.
12. Jack Belden, "The Battle for Troina," *Life*, 30 July 1943.
13. Towne, *Doctor Danger Forward*, 75–76.
14. Baumgartner et al., *The 16th Infantry*, 57–58.
15. "Gerry Kisters," www.cmohs.org/recipients/gerry-h-kisters.
16. Astor, *Terrible Terry Allen*, 216–17.
17. Baumgartner et al., *The 16th Infantry*, 64.
18. Eisenhower, *Crusade in Europe*, 176.
19. Astor, *Terrible Terry Allen*, 216–19; Baumgartner et al., *The 16th Infantry*, 59–60.
20. "James Reese," www.cmohs.org/james-w-reese, www.ww2fallen100.blogspot.com/reese.
21. Mitcham and Stauffenberg, *The Battle of Sicily*, 250; Pond, *Sicily*, 199.
22. Baumgartner et al., *The 16th Infantry*, 64; Morison, *Sicily-Salerno-Anzio*, 200.
23. Baumgartner et al.; Astor, *Terrible Terry Allen*, 216–19; Miller, *The Complete History of World War II*, 681.
24. Bradley, *A Soldier's Story*, 155–56.
25. Blumenson, *The Patton Papers*, 309.
26. Astor, *Terrible Terry Allen*, 219.

27. Astor, 223–24.
28. Baumgartner et al., *The 16th Infantry*, 65.
29. Joe Dawson, interview by John Votaw, First Infantry Division Museum and Archives, Cantigny Park, Col. Robert R. McCormick Research Center, Wheaton, IL, 19 April 1991.
30. Terry Allen papers, First Infantry Division Museum and Archives, Cantigny Park, Col. Robert R. McCormick Research Center, Wheaton, IL.
31. Quentin Reynolds, letter to Mrs. Allen, 20 June 1944, U.S. Army Military History Institute Research Center, Carlisle, PA.
32. Dawson interview.
33. Baumgartner et al., *The 16th Infantry*, 67.

Chapter 16. Fall From Grace

1. Patton, diary entry, 3 August 1943; Hirshson, *General Patton: A Soldier's Life*, 389.
2. Bradley, *A Soldier's Story*, 160–61.
3. Blumenson, *The Patton Papers*, 331–32; Korda, *Ike: An American Hero*, 408; Axelrod, *Patton: A Biography*, 118.
4. Axelrod, *Patton: A Biography*, 118.
5. Patton, diary entry, 10 August 1943.
6. Axelrod, *Patton: A Biography*, 118.
7. Bradley, *A Soldier's Story*, 162.
8. Garland and Smyth, *Mediterranean Theater of Operations*, 427.
9. Joseph Couch, "The Day Gen. Patton Slapped a Soldier," *Washington Post*, 3 June 1979.
10. Patton, letter to Beatrice Patton, 11 August 1943.
11. Whitman, *"Scouts Out!"* 30–31.
12. D'Este, *Bitter Victory*, 504–16.
13. Truscott, *Command Missions*, 241–42.
14. Ernie Pyle, *Brave Men* (New York: Grosset & Dunlap, 1944), 40.
15. Garland and Smyth, *Mediterranean Theater of Operations*, 408–9.
16. Pyle, *Brave Men*, 48–49.
17. Truscott, *Command Missions*, 242.
18. Whitman, *"Scouts Out!"* 32.
19. Eisenhower, *Crusade in Europe*, 177.
20. Butcher, *My Three Years with Eisenhower*, 407.
21. Pond, *Sicily*, 215.
22. Bradley, *A Soldier's Story*, 159.
23. Jack Belden, "World Battlefront: Battle of Italy: Finis and Prologue," *Time*, 30 August 1943.
24. Truscott, *Command Missions*, 242; Black, *The Ranger Force*, 169.
25. Truscott, *Command Missions*, 243.

26. Patton, letter to Beatrice Patton, 17 August 1943.
27. Truscott, *Command Missions*, 243.
28. Patton, diary entry, 17 August 1943.
29. Mitcham and von Stauffenberg, *The Battle of Sicily*, 294.
30. Darby and Baumer, *Darby's Rangers*, 109.
31. Belden, "World Battlefront."
32. Blumenson, *The Patton Papers*, 326–27; Follain, *Mussolini's Island*, 294–95.
33. Butcher, *My Three Years with Eisenhower*, 390–91.
34. Eisenhower, *Crusade in Europe*, 181.
35. Blumenson, *The Patton Papers*, 338.
36. Patton, letter to Eisenhower, 28 August 1943.
37. Couch, "The Day Gen. Patton Slapped a Soldier."
38. Patton, diary entry, 21 August 1943.
39. Patton, diary entry, 23 August 1943.
40. D'Este, *Bitter Victory*, 543–44.
41. Patton, letter to Davidson, 22 August 1943.
42. Patton, Seventh Army General Order 18.
43. Blumenson, *The Patton Papers*, 379.
44. Patton "apology script," Patton Papers collection.
45. Hoyt, *The GI's War*, 245; Patton, letter to Beatrice Patton, 11 August 1943.
46. Towne, *Doctor Danger Forward*, 81.
47. John Votaw and Steven Weingartner, *Blue Spaders: The 26th Infantry Regiment, 1916–1967* (Wheaton, IL: Cantigny First Division Foundation, 1996), 47.
48. Towne, *Doctor Danger Forward*, 81.
49. Vignette 149 from oral history interview with Gen. Theodore S. Conway, in Richard J. Sommers, ed., *Vignettes of Military History*, vol. 3 (Carlisle Barracks, PA: U.S. Army Military History Institute, 1982).
50. Lang, "Lucian King Truscott, Jr."
51. Belden, "World Battlefront."

Chapter 17. The Slaps Heard 'Round the World

1. Liddell Hart, *History of the Second World War*, 446; Holland, *Sicily '43*, 587.
2. Patton, diary entry, 14 September 1943.
3. Patton, letter to Beatrice Patton, 30 August 1943.
4. Patton, diary entry, 3 September 1943.
5. Blumenson, *The Patton Papers*, 346–49; Patton diary entry, 14 September 1943.
6. Towne, *Doctor Danger Forward*, 80, 82.
7. Eisenhower, *Crusade in Europe*, 183.
8. Darby and Baumer, *Darby's Rangers*, 115–23.
9. Whitlock, *The Rock of Anzio*, 314.
10. Blumenson, *The Patton Papers*, 345, 346, 354.

11. Patton, diary entry, 17 September 1943.
12. Patton, *War As I Knew It*, 72-82.
13. Patton, diary entry, 6 October 1943.
14. Towne, *Doctor Danger Forward*, 80–83.
15. Stanhope Mason, *Memoirs* (Wheaton, IL: First Infantry Division Museum and Archives, Cantigny Park, Col. Robert R. McCormick Research Center, 1988).
16. Patton, diary entry, 27 October 1943.
17. Patton, diary entry, 17 November 1943.
18. "Patton in Bad with Ike, Pearson Alleges on Air," *New York Daily News*, 22 November 1943.
19. Patton, diary entry, 24 November 1943.
20. "Patton and Truth," *Time*, 6 December 1943; "Drew Pearson," WWIIMemorial-Friends/posts/on-this-day-in-1943-commentator-drew-pearson-broke-the-story-that-lt-gen-george-/2293071804050685.
21. Eisenhower, *Crusade in Europe*, 182.
22. Charles Summerall, letter to Patton, 26 November 1943.
23. Patton, diary entry, 1 December 1943.
24. Blumenson, *The Patton Papers*, 379.
25. Patton, diary entry, 1 December 1943.
26. Patton, diary entry, 30 November 1943.
27. Blumenson, *The Patton Papers*, 385.
28. Patton, diary entry, 18 January 1944.
29. D'Este, *Patton: A Genius for War*, 593–94, 609–730.
30. D'Este, *Patton: A Genius for War*, 784–94.
31. Holsinger, James W. Jr., ed., *Patton's Tactician: The War Diary of Lieutenant General Geoffrey Keyes*. (Lexington: University Press of Kentucky, 2024), 222–23.

Epilogue

1. Pack, *Operation Husky*, 172.
2. Morison, *Sicily-Salerno-Anzio*, 20.
3. Pack, *Operation Husky*, 299–300.
4. Holland, *Sicily '43*, 579.
5. Black, *The Ranger Force*, 170.
6. Bidwell, 278–79.
7. Whitman, *"Scouts Out!"* 33–34.
8. Mitcham and von Stauffenberg, *The Battle of Sicily*, 299.
9. Mitcham and von Stauffenberg, 298–302.
10. Kesselring, *The Memoirs of Field Marshal Kesselring*, 165.
11. Pond, *Sicily*, 214. Pond exaggerated, but the numbers are still horrendous: British Empire troops during the eleven-month siege amounted to 31,389 killed, 87,749 wounded, 9,708 missing or captured, and 78,494 evacuated because of sickness.

See Edward J. Erickson, *Gallipoli: The Ottoman Campaign* (Barnsley, UK: Pen & Sword, 2010).

12. Butcher, *My Three Years with Eisenhower*, 387.
13. Blumenson, *The Patton Papers*, 387.
14. Hewitt, "Action Report," 1.

BIBLIOGRAPHY

Books

Alexander of Tunis, Earl (Harold R. L. G.). *The Alexander Memoirs: 1940–1945*. New York: McGraw-Hill, 1962.

Alexander, Mark J., and John Sparry. *Jump Commander: In Combat with the 505th and 508th Parachute Infantry Regiments, 82nd Airborne Division in World War II*. Havertown, PA: Casemate, 2010.

Allen, Janis, ed. *We Shall Come Home Victorious: Stories of World War II Veterans*. Privately published, 2020.

Astor, Gerald. *Terrible Terry Allen: Combat General of World War II—The Life of an American Soldier*. New York: Ballantine, 2003.

Atkinson, Rick. *The Day of Battle: The War in Sicily and Italy, 1943–1944*. New York: Henry Holt, 2007.

Axelrod, Alan. *Patton: A Biography*. New York: Palgrave McMillan, 2006.

Baumer, Robert W., and Mark J. Reardon. *American Iliad: The 18th Infantry Regiment in World War II*. Bedford, PA: Aberjona Press, 2004.

Baumgartner, John W., Al De Poto, William Fraccio, and Sam Fuller. *The 16th Infantry: 1861–1946*. Du Quoin, IL: Cricket Press, 1999.

Bidwell, Shelford. "Kesselring." In *Hitler's Generals*, ed. Correlli Barnett. New York: Grove Weidenfeld, 1989.

Birtle, Andrew J. *Sicily: The U.S. Army Campaigns of World War II*. Washington, DC: U.S. Army Center for Military History, 1993.

Black, Robert W. *The Ranger Force: Darby's Rangers in World War II*. Mechanicsburg, PA: Stackpole, 2009.

Blumenson, Martin. *The Patton Papers*. Boston: Da Capo Press, 1974.

———. *Sicily: Whose Victory? Ballantine's Illustrated History of World War II, Campaign Book No. 3*. New York: Ballantine, 1969.

Bradley, Omar N. *A Soldier's Story*. Chicago: Rand McNally, 1951.

Breuer, William B. *Air Drop Sicily: Allied Airborne Strike, July 1943*. Novato, CA: Presidio Press, 1983.

Butcher, Harry C. *My Three Years with Eisenhower: The Personal Diary of Captain Harry C. Butcher, USNR, Naval Aide to General Eisenhower, 1942 to 1945*. New York: Simon and Schuster, 1946.

Clark, Mark W. "Address of 1 June 1970." In *The Heroic Memory: The Memorial Addresses to the Rt. Hon. Sir Winston Spencer Churchill Society, Edmonton, Alberta*, ed. Ronald I. Cohen. Edmonton: Churchill Statue and Oxford Scholarship Foundation, 2004.

Codman, Charles R. *Drive*. Boston: Little, Brown, 1957.

Costanzo, Ezio. *La Guerra in Sicilia 1943: Storia Fotografica*. Catania, Sicily: Le Nove Muse Editrice, 2009.

Craven, Wesley F., and James L. Cate, eds. *The Army Air Forces in World War II*, vol. 2, *Europe—Torch to Pointblank: August 1942 to December 1943*. Washington, DC: Office of Air Force History, 1983.

Cressman, Robert J. *The Official Chronology of the United States Navy in World War II*. Annapolis, MD: Naval Institute Press, 1999.

D'Este, Carlo. *Bitter Victory: The Battle for Sicily 1943*. New York: Harper, 1988.

———. *Patton: A Genius for War*. New York: HarperCollins, 1995.

Darby, William O., and William H. Baumer. *Darby's Rangers: We Led the Way*. San Raphael, CA: Presidio Press, 1980.

Devlin, Gerard M. *Paratrooper! The Saga of U.S. Army and Marine Parachute and Glider Combat Troops During World War II*. New York: St. Martin's Press, 1979.

Echohawk, Brummett, with Mark R. Ellenbarger. *Drawing Fire: A Pawnee, Artist, and Thunderbird in World War II*. Lawrence: University Press of Kansas, 2018.

Edwards, Harry W. *A Different War: Marines in Europe and North Africa*. Washington, DC: Marine Corps Historical Center, 1994.

Eisenhower, Dwight D. *Crusade in Europe*. Garden City, NY: Doubleday, 1948.

Ellis, John. *The Sharp End: The Fighting Man in World War II*. New York: Scribner's, 1980.

Erickson, Edward J. *Gallipoli: The Ottoman Campaign*. Barnsley, UK: Pen & Sword, 2010.

Essame, H. *Patton: A Study in Command*. New York: Scribner's, 1974.

Farago, Ladislas. *The Last Days of Patton*. New York: McGraw-Hill, 1981.

Fauntleroy, Barbara Gavin. *The General and His Daughter: The Wartime Letters of General James M. Gavin to His Daughter Barbara*. Edited by Gayle Wurst. New York: Fordham University Press, 2007.

Ferguson, Harvey. *The Last Cavalryman: The Life of General Lucian K. Truscott Jr.* Norman: University of Oklahoma Press, 2015.

Finke, Blythe Foote. *No Mission Too Difficult: Old Buddies of the 1st Division Tell All About World War II*. Chicago: Cantigny First Division Foundation, 1995.

Fisher, George A. *The Story of the 180th Infantry Regiment*. Privately published, 1947.

Follain, John. *Mussolini's Island*. London: Hodder & Stoughton, 2005.

Frank, Joseph. *Mussolini's War: Fascist Italy's Military Struggles from Africa and Western Europe to the Mediterranean and Soviet Union, 1935–45*. Solihull, UK: Helion, 2010.

Garland, Albert N., and Howard M. Smyth. *United States Army in World War II: Mediterranean Theater of Operations, Sicily, and the Surrender of Italy*. Washington, DC: U.S. Army Center for Military History, 1965.

Gaujac, Paul. *L'Armée de la Victoire*, vol. 3. Paris: Charles Lavauzelle, 1985.

Gavin, James M. *On to Berlin: Battles of an Airborne Commander*. New York: Viking, 1978.

Gioannini, Marco, and Giulio Massobrio. *Bombardate l'Italia: Storia della guerra di distruzione aerea 1940–1945*. Milan: Rizzoli Libri, 2007.

Grigg, John. *1943: The Victory That Never Was*. New York: Hill & Wang, 1980.

Heiber, Helmut, and David M. Glantz, eds. *Hiter's Generals: Military Conferences 1942–1945*. New York: Enigma, 2003.

Hewitt, H. Kent. *The Memoirs of Admiral H. Kent Hewitt*. Edited by Evelyn M. Cherpak. Newport, RI: Naval War College Press, 2004.

Hirshson, Stanley P. *General Patton: A Soldier's Life*. New York: HarperCollins, 2002.

Hogg, Ian V., and John Weeks. *The Illustrated Encyclopedia of Military Vehicles*. London: New Burlington Books, 1988.

Holland, James. *Sicily '43: The First Assault on Fortress Europe*. New York: Penguin/Random House, 2020.

Holsinger, James W. Jr., ed., *Patton's Tactician: The War Diary of Lieutenant General Geoffrey Keyes*. Lexington: University Press of Kentucky, 2024.

Hoyt, Edwin P. *The GI's War: The Story of American Soldiers in Europe in World War II*. New York: McGraw-Hill, 1988.

Huston, James A. *Out of the Blue: U.S. Army Airborne Operations in World War II*. Nashville: Battery Press, 1972.

Hymel, Kevin M. *Patton's Photographs: War as He Saw It*. Washington, DC: Potomac Books, 2006.

———. *Patton's War: An American General's Combat Leadership*. Vol. 1, *November 1942–July 1944*. Columbia: University of Missouri Press, 2021.

Ingrisano, Michael N. *Valor Without Arms: A History of the 316th Troop Carrier Group, 1942–1945*. Hoosick, NY: Merriam Press, 1991.

Israel, David. *The Day the Thunderbird Cried: Untold Stories of World War II*. Privately published, 2005.

Katz, Robert. *The Battle for Rome: The Germans, the Allies, the Partisans, and the Pope*. New York: Simon & Schuster, 2003.

Kesselring, Albert. *The Memoirs of Field-Marshal Kesselring*. New York: Skyhorse, 2016.

Koch, George J. *First to Warn: My Combat Experiences in the 1st Reconnaissance Troop, 1st Infantry Division, in North Africa and Sicily in World War II*. Chicago: Cantigny First Infantry Division Foundation, 2004.

Korda, Michael. *Ike: An American Hero*. New York: HarperCollins, 2007.

Kurzman, Dan. *The Race for Rome: How the Eternal City Was Saved from Nazi Destruction*. Garden City, NY: Doubleday, 1975.

La Monte, John L., and Winston B. Lewis. *The Sicilian Campaign: 10 July–17 August 1943*. Washington, DC: Naval Historical Center, 1993.

Liddell Hart, Basil H. *History of the Second World War*. New York: G. P. Putnam's Sons, 1970.

Lowery, Robert G. *Letters from the Front: A Year in the Life of an Infantryman*. Bennington, VT: Merriam Press, 2006.

Macintyre, Ben. *Operation Mincemeat: How a Dead Man and a Bizarre Plan Fooled the Nazis and Assured an Allied Victory*. New York: Harmony, 2010.

Mauldin, Bill. *Sicily Sketch Book*. Palermo, Sicily: I.R.E.S., 1943.

McGaugh, Scott. *Brotherhood of the Flying Coffin: The Glider Pilots of World War II*. Dublin, Ireland: Osprey, 2023.

Miller, Francis T. *The Complete History of World War II*. New York: Home Education Guild, 1945.

Mitcham Jr., Samuel W., and Friedrich von Stauffenberg. *The Battle of Sicily: How the Allies Lost Their Chance for Total Victory*. New York: Orion Books, 1991.

Morison, Samuel E. *History of United States Naval Operations in World War II*. Vol. 2, *Operations in North African Waters*. Boston: Little, Brown, 1975.

———. *History of United States Naval Operations in World War II*. Vol. 9, *Sicily-Salerno-Anzio, January 1943–June 1944*. Boston: Little, Brown and Co., 1953.

Murphy, Audie. *To Hell and Back*. New York: Henry Holt, 1949, reprint 2002.

Nicolson, Nigel. *Alex: The Life of Field Marshal Earl Alexander of Tunis*. London: Weidenfeld and Nicolson, 1973.

Nordyke, Phil. F. *Four Stars of Valor: The Combat History of the 505th Parachute Infantry Regiment in World War I*. Minneapolis: Zenith Press, 2006.

North, Oliver. *War Stories III: The Heroes Who Defeated Hitler*. Washington, DC: Regnery Publishing, 2005.

O'Hara, Vincent P. *Struggle for the Middle Sea: The Great Navies at War in the Mediterranean Theater, 1940–1945*. Annapolis, MD: Naval Institute Press, 2009.

Otte, Alfred. *The HG Panzer Division*. West Chester, PA: Schiffer, 1989.

Pack, S. W. C. *Operation Husky: The Allied Invasion of Sicily*. New York: Hippocrene Books, 1977.

Patton Jr., George S. *War as I Knew It*. Boston: Houghton Mifflin, 1947.

Pond, Hugh. *Sicily*. London: William Kimber, 1962.

Province, Charles M. *The Unknown Patton*. New York: Random House, 1988.

Pyle, Ernie. *Brave Men*. New York: Grosset & Dunlap, 1944.

———. "Sicily Landing." In *The Army Reader*, ed. Karl Detzer. Indianapolis: Bobbs-Merrill, 1943.

Ready, J. Lee. *World War Two: Nation by Nation*. London: Arms & Armour Press, 1995.

Reynolds, Harley. *How I Survived Three First Wave Invasions*. Minneapolis: Mill City Press, 2008.

Robinson, Don. *News of the 45th*. New York: Grosset & Dunlap, 1944.
Sampson, Otis L. *Time Out for Combat*. Privately published, 2005.
Saunders, Anthony. *Hitler's Atlantic Wall*. Gloucestershire, UK: Sutton, 2001.
Scheffel, Charles, and Barry Basden. *Crack! and Thump: With a Combat Infantry Officer in World War II*. Llano, TX: Camroc Press, 2007.
Schilirò, Gaetano. *Pantelleria: More Bombs than Stones*. Ebook, 2016.
Schorer, Avis D. *A Half Acre of Hell: A Combat Nurse in World War II*. Lakeville, MN: Galde Press, 2002.
Shirer, William L. *The Rise and Fall of the Third Reich: A History of Nazi Germany*. New York: Simon & Schuster, 1960.
Showalter, Dennis, ed. *Patton in His Own Words*. Leesburg, VA: Weider History Group, 2010.
Sommers, Richard J., ed. *Vignettes of Military History*. Vol. 3. Carlisle Barracks, PA: U.S. Army Military History Institute, 1982.
Stanton, Shelby L. *World War II Order of Battle*. New York: Galahad, 1984.
Steinhoff, Johannes. *Messerschmitts over Sicily: Diary of a Luftwaffe Fighter Commander*. Mechanicsburg, PA: Stackpole Books, 2004.
Towne, Allen N. *Doctor Danger Forward: A World War II Memoir of a Combat Medical Aidman, First Infantry Division*. Jefferson, NC: McFarland, 2000.
Tregaskis, Richard. *Invasion Diary*. New York: Random House, 1944.
Truscott Jr., Lucian K. *Command Missions*. Novato, CA: Presidio Press, 1990.
———. *The Twilight of the U.S. Cavalry: Life in the Old Army, 1917–1942*. Lawrence: University Press of Kansas, 1989.
U.S. Army. Field Manual 7–37. *Cannon Company, Infantry Regiment*. Washington, DC: War Department, 28 March 1944.
Votaw, John, and Steven Weingartner. *Blue Spaders: The 26th Infantry Regiment, 1916–1967*. Wheaton, IL: Cantigny First Division Foundation, 1996.
Walling, Michael G. *Bloodstained Sands: U.S. Amphibious Operations in World War II*. London: Bloomsbury Publishing, 2017.
Warren, John C. *Airborne Missions in the Mediterranean 1942–1945*. USAF Historical Studies no. 47. Maxwell Air Force Base, AL: U.S. Air Force Historical Research Agency, 1955.
Westwell, Ian. *Spearhead: U.S. Rangers Leading the Way*. Hersham, Surrey, UK: Ian Allan Publishing, 2003.
Whiting, Charles. *Patton*. New York: Ballantine, 1970.
Whitlock, Flint. *If Chaos Reigns: The Near-Disaster and Ultimate Triumph of the Allied Airborne Forces on D-Day, June 6, 1944*. Philadelphia: Casemate, 2011.
———. *The Fighting First: The Untold Story of the Big Red One on D-Day*. Boulder, CO: Westview, 2004.
———. *The Rock of Anzio: From Sicily to Dachau—A History of the 45th Infantry Division*. Boulder, CO: Westview Press, 1998.

Whitman, William. *"Scouts Out!"* Los Angeles: Authors Unlimited, 1990.

Williamson, Kenneth D. *Tales of a Thunderbird in World War II*. Privately published, 1994.

Wurst, Spencer F., and Gayle Wurst. *Descending from the Clouds: A Memoir of Combat in the 505 Parachute Infantry Regiment, 82nd Airborne Division*. Drexel Hill, PA: Casemate, 2007.

Young, Peter, ed. *The Illustrated World War II Encyclopedia*. Westport, CT: H. S. Stuttman, 1978.

Interviews and Speeches

Argentino, Robert P. Interviewed by James Zanella, Heinz History Center, Pittsburgh, PA, 8 October 2004. https://www.heinzhistorycenter.org/wp-content/uploads/2022/08/Argentine-Robert.pdf.

Ballacchino, Francesca, Rosaria Castiglione, Pino La Rosa, and Mario Turco. Interviewed by Montclair State University (New Jersey) for the project "Food, Hunger, Migration and the American Myth in Sicily at the Time of the WWII Allied Landing." www.montclair/edu/inserra-chair/events/2018–19-events/events-2018–19-events-food-hunger-migration-and-the-american-myth-in-sicily-at-the-time-of-the-wwii-allies-landing.

Best, Wayne R. Interviewed by David Dean Barrett, Denver, CO, 3 June 2012.

Dawson, Joe. Interview by John Votaw. First Infantry Division Museum and Archives. Cantigny Park, Col. Robert R. McCormick Research Center. Wheaton, IL, 16 April 1991.

"Gertrude A. Lynn talks about her experiences serving in the U.S. Army Nurse Corps with the 59th Evacuation Hospital during World War II." Women's Overseas Service Oral History Project, Michigan State University. www.d.lib.msu.edu/wosl/103.

Heath, Bernice. Interview by Hermann J. Trojanowski. University of North Carolina at Greensboro, 2001. www.gateway.uncg.edu/islandora/object/wvhp%3A20835.

Merz, George, Lt. Col., USAF (Ret.). "A Very Special Report from Operation Husky." Interviewed by 1st Lt. Lewis E. Johnston, AUS (Ret.). https://amcmuseum.org/history/a-very-special-report-from-operation-husky/.

Morgan Jr., Fred B. Interview, Digital Collections of the National WWII Museum, 2015.

Patton Jr., George S. August 1943. Patton Papers Collection, 1940–1945, Library of Congress, Washington, DC.

Speairs, Ed. Interview by Flint Whitlock, 19 January 1995.

Periodicals, Scholarly and Academic Papers, Diaries, and Memoirs

Allen, Terry. Papers. First Infantry Division Museum and Archives. Cantigny Park, Col. Robert R. McCormick Research Center, Wheaton, IL.

Allmon, William B. "USS *Murphy*: Long Service in Wartime." *WWII History*, July 2011.

"Audie Murphy and 5 Killed in Plane Crash." *Los Angeles Times*, 1 June 1971.

Barnhart, Barton V. "The Great Escape: An Analysis of Allied Actions leading to the Axis Evacuation of Sicily in World War II." Master's thesis, U.S. Army Command and Staff College, Fort Leavenworth, KS, 2003.

"The Beginning of the End, Part 1: The Sicilian Phase—The Plan. June 1943–January 1944." First Infantry Division Museum and Archives. Cantigny Park, Col. Robert R. McCormick Research Center, Wheaton, IL.

Belden, Jack. "The Battle for Troina." *Life*, 30 July 1943.

———. "World Battlefronts: Battle of Italy: Finis and Prologue." *Time*, 30 August 1943.

Blazich Jr., Frank A. "Bridging the Gap from Ship to Shore." *Naval History* 35, no. 4, August 2021.

Bonta, James C. "The Invasion of Pantelleria, 11 June 1943: Personal Experience of a Company Executive Officer, Company A, 907th Air Base Security Battalion." Infantry School, Fort Benning, GA, 1949–50. https://mcoecbamcoepwprd01.blob.core.usgovcloudapi.net/library/DonovanPapers/wwii/STUP2/A-F/Bonta%20James%20C.%20CPT.pdf.

"British 8th Army Lands on Sicily." *Life*, 2 August 1943.

Couch, Joseph. "The Day Gen. Patton Slapped a Soldier." *Washington Post*, 3 June 1979.

"Doolittle Tells How Planes Took Pantelleria." *Denver Post*, 12 June 1943.

Dorr, Robert F. "Friendly Fire's Deadliest Day." *America in WWII*, February 2010.

Faust, William E. *Memoir.* Carlisle Barracks, PA: U.S. Army Heritage Center Foundation, 1982.

"Few Scattered Axis Units Yet to Be Corralled." *Denver Post*, 13 May 1943.

"First Pictures of Sicily Invasion." *Life*, 2 August 1943.

"White Flag Run Up Following Heaviest Air Attack of War; Eisenhower's Forces Move in Immediately and Gain Complete Control of Italian Island After 22-Minute Skirmish." *Denver Post*, 12 June 1943.

Gavin, James. "The Jump into Sicily." *American Heritage*, April/May 1978.

Gordon IV, John. "Joint Power Projection: Operation Torch." *Joint Force Quarterly*, Spring 1994.

"The Hand that Held the Dagger." *Time*, 22 June 1943.

Haskew, Michael. "How George S. Patton Vanquished Pancho Villa's Lieutenants." *Military Heritage*, May 2015.

"Heroic Spotter Pilot." *Shipmate*, July/August 1983.

Hewitt, H. Kent. "Action Report—Western Naval Task Force: The Sicilian Campaign; Operation Husky, July-August, 1943." *United States Naval Administrative Histories of World War II*, https://www.history.navy.mil/content/history/nhhc/research/library/online-reading-room/title-list-alphabetically/s/the-sicilian-campaign-operation-husky.html.

———. "Naval Aspects of the Sicilian Campaign." *Proceedings*, July 1953.

Hymel, Kevin. "Patton's War for Sicily's Beaches." *WWII Quarterly*, Winter 2022.

Jost, Harry. "Airborne Operations in Sicily, July 1943." Infantry School, Fort Benning, GA, 1948–49.

Kelly, Tom H. "War Criminal Paroled: Horace T. West and the Final Chapter of the Biscari Massacre." *Army Lawyer*, no. 5, 2020.

Lang Jr., Will, "Lucian King Truscott Jr." *Life*, 2 October 1944.

Lyle, James B. "The Operations of Companies A and B, 1st Ranger Battalion, at Gela, Sicily, 10–11 July 1943." Advanced Infantry Officers School, Fort Benning, GA, 1948–49.

"*Mare Nostrum*? Mussolini Looks out on the Mediterranean." *New York Times*, 27 April 1930.

Martin, Ralph G. "Invasion of Sicily." *Yank*, 13 August 1943.

Mason, Stanhope. *Memoirs.* First Infantry Division Museum and Archives. Cantigny Park, Col. Robert R. McCormick Research Center, Wheaton, IL, 1988.

McEniry, Robert F. "The WWII Bombing of Pantelleria Island: A Test of Air Power." *WWII History*, November 2009.

"Patton and Truth." *Time*, 6 December 1943.

Patton, Jeff. "Victory in the Mediterranean." *WWII History*, Fall 2015.

Pence, James. "Operations of Company A, 16th Infantry, 1st Infantry Division, near Nicosia in northeast Sicily, 28–29 July 1943." Infantry School, Fort Benning, GA, 1948–49.

Prefer, Nathan. "The Greek Holocaust." *WWII History*, Spring 2024.

Rogers, Edith C. "The Reduction of Pantelleria and Adjacent Islands—8 May–14 June 1943." Army Air Forces Historical Studies No. 52. Maxwell Air Force Base, AL, 1947.

"Rome Claims Pope Deplored Bombing in Letter to Vicar." *Denver Post*, 22 July 1943.

Rossi, Guido. "Italian Fellas in Olive Drab: Exploring the Experiences of Italian American Servicemen in Sicily and Italy, 1943–1945." Master's thesis, University of Southern Mississippi, 2017.

Sayre, Edwin. "The Operations of Company A, 505th Parachute Infantry (82nd Airborne Division), Airborne Landings in Sicily, 9–24 July 1943 (Sicily Campaign), Personal Experiences of a Company Commander." Academic Department, Advanced Infantry Officers Course, Fort Benning, GA, 10 November 1947.

Schultz, Duane. "George S. Patton Jr.'s Upbringing: The Making of the Legend." *WWII History*, February 2019.

Thompson, John "Jack." "Thompson Tells How Chutists Fought in Sicily." *Chicago Tribune*, 16 July 1943.

Uhrig, Robert. Diary. Author's collection.

Warren, John C. "Airborne Missions in the Mediterranean 1942–1945." USAF Historical Studies no. 74, Maxwell Air Force Base, AL, 1955.

Weller, Donald M. "Naval Gunfire Support of Amphibious Operations: Past, Present, and Future." Naval Sea Systems Command, Naval Surface Warfare Center, Headquarters U.S. Marine Corps, Dahlgren, VA, 1977.

Whitlock, Flint. "Sicilian Slugfest." *WWII Quarterly*, Summer 2018.

Wise Jr., James E. "To Sicily with Alec Guinness." *Naval History* 16, no. 3, June 2002.

Woislaw, Jonathan A. "The 1st Infantry Division in Sicily: A Case Study in Tactical Intelligence." Master's thesis, U.S. Army Command and General Staff College, Fort Leavenworth, KS, 2021.

Websites

"443rd Anti-Aircraft Artillery Automatic Weapons Battalion." www.texasmilitary forcesmuseum.org/36division/archives/443/44344.

"456th Parachute Field Artillery Battalion." ww2airborne.net/the-battalion-1/africa-and -sicily-1.html.

"Alexander Pete Suer." https://www.uswarmemorials.org/html/people_details.php ?PeopleID=10744.

"Armistice with Italy; September 3, 1943." The Avalon Project, Yale Law School. https:// avalon.law.yale.edu/wwii/italy01.asp.

"Arthur Royall—Operation Ladbroke." https://war-experience.org/index.php/?s=Arthur %20Royall.

"Biazzo Ridge." www.tiger1.info/Biazzo-ridge.

"Casablanca Conference." history.state.gov/milestones/1937–1945/Casablanca.

"Charles H. Kuhl: The George S. Patton Slapping Incident." https://www.alexautographs .com/auction-lot/the-george-s-patton-slapping-incident-charles-h-k_FA24C55823.

The Churchill Project. "Were 'Soft Underbelly' and 'Fortress Europe' Churchill Phrases?" 1 April 2016. www.winstonchurchill.hillsdale.edu/soft-underbelly-fortress-europe.

"Crimes of the Allies in Sicily and Naples in the Second World War." Interview of Giovanni Bartolone by Federico Dal Cortivo. www.leccecronaca.it/ index.php/ 2012/10/29/i-crimini-degli-alleati-in-sicilia-e-a-napoli-nella-seconda-guerra-mondiale-il-ruolo-della-mafia-e-quello-della-massoneria.

"Dan McIlvoy." www.ww2-airborne.us/units/505/505_memories.html.

"Death of Charles Kuhl." militaryhallofhonor.com/honoree-record.php?id= 2725.

"Douglas M. Bailey, 463rd Parachute FA Bn.: The Landing in Sicily," www.secondworldwar .nl/douglas-m-bailey-landing-in-sicily.php.

"Drew Pearson." www.WWIIMemorialFriends/posts/on-this-day-in-1943-commentator-drew-pearson-broke-the-story-that-lt-gen-george-/2293071804050685.

Edwards, Harry. "A Different War: Marines in Europe and North Africa." www.nps .gov/parkhistory/ online_books/npswapa/extcontent/ usmc/pcn-190–003125–00/ sec5b.htm.

"Gela Beachhead Counterattack of 1943." www.comandosupremo.com/gela-1943.

"George S. Patton in World War I." www.historyonthenet.com/patton-ww1.

"Gerry H. Kisters." https://www.cmohs.org/recipients/gerry-h-kisters.

"H-021–2: Operation Husky, the Invasion of Sicily, and Operation Avalanche, the Invasion of Italy." www.history.navy.mil/about-us/leadership/director/directors-corner /h-grams/h-gram-021/h-021–2.html.

"Historical Record of the 2nd Armored Division, 22 April–25 July 1943." https://mcoecbamcoepwprd01.blob.core.usgovcloudapi.net/library/Documents/Hardcopy/paper/802AD_403.pdf.

"Informal Announcement of the Attack on Sicily at a State Dinner in Honor of General Giraud." July 9, 1943. www.Originalsources.Com/Document.Aspx?Docid=Zz4fpgtigrx7tu&H=1.

King, Amy. "Artifact Spotlight: Capt. R. Conolly's DESRON 6 Pennant." 26 January 2012. www.navalwarcollegemuseum.blogspot.com/2012/01artifact-spotlight-capt-r-conolly.

Long, Perrin H., Lt. Col., Medical Corps. Letter on the subject of "Mistreatment of Patients in Receiving Tents." 16 August 1943. https://members.tripod.com/msg_fisher/93evac-9.html.

McLain, Raymond S. "Diary of the Sicilian Campaign." https://www.45thdivision.org/Veterans/McLain_Sicily.htm.

Mills, Megan. "Remembering Operation Husky." 30 July 2021. www.dvidshub.net/news/402282/remembering-operation-husky.

"Operation Husky: The Invasion of Sicily, 9 July–17 August 1943." https://www.history.navy.mil/browse-by-topic/wars-conflicts-and-operations/world-war-ii/1943/sicilian-campaign.html.

"Operation Ladbroke." www.operation-ladbroke.com.

"Prince Philip and the Invasion of Sicily." www.history.co.uk/article/prince-philip-and-the-invasion-of-sicily.

"Remembering a Veteran: Colonel Troy H. Middleton, 4th Division, AEF." roadstothegreatwar-ww1.blogspot.com/2021/05/remembering-veteran-colonel-troy-h.

"USS LST 393." www.lst.393.org.

"USS Philadelphia V (CL-41)." www.history.navy.mil/content/history/ nhhc/research/histories/ship-histories/danfs/p/philadelphia-v.html.

"USS Philadelphia—CL-41—Handwritten Notes, Saturday, July 10, 1943." www.brigs.us/Phila/Handwritten-notes-7–10–43.

"William O. Darby." https://encyclopediaofarkansas.net/entries/william-orlando-darby-2414/.

INDEX

ABOUT THE AUTHOR

Flint Whitlock, a former U.S. Army officer and Vietnam War veteran, is the award-winning author of seventeen books, the majority dealing with World War II. He has also appeared on the History Channel and in numerous documentaries, leads battlefield tours, and was editor of *WWII Quarterly* magazine for twelve years. Notable titles include *Desperate Valor: Triumph at Anzio* (2018); *Given Up for Dead: American POWs in the Nazi Concentration Camp at Berga* (2005); *The Fighting First: The Untold Story of the Big Red One on D-Day* (2004); and *The Rock of Anzio: From Sicily to Dachau—A History of the 45th Infantry Division* (1998). In 2021 he became the first author inducted into the Colorado Authors Hall of Fame. Whitlock lives in Denver, Colorado, with his wife, Dr. Mary Ann Watson.

The Naval Institute Press is the book-publishing arm of the U.S. Naval Institute, a private, nonprofit, membership society for sea service professionals and others who share an interest in naval and maritime affairs. Established in 1873 at the U.S. Naval Academy in Annapolis, Maryland, where its offices remain today, the Naval Institute has members worldwide.

Members of the Naval Institute support the education programs of the society and receive the influential monthly magazine *Proceedings* or the colorful bimonthly magazine *Naval History* and discounts on fine nautical prints and on ship and aircraft photos. They also have access to the transcripts of the Institute's Oral History Program and get discounted admission to any of the Institute-sponsored seminars offered around the country.

The Naval Institute's book-publishing program, begun in 1898 with basic guides to naval practices, has broadened its scope to include books of more general interest. Now the Naval Institute Press publishes about seventy titles each year, ranging from how-to books on boating and navigation to battle histories, biographies, ship and aircraft guides, and novels. Institute members receive significant discounts on the Press' more than eight hundred books in print.

Full-time students are eligible for special half-price membership rates. Life memberships are also available.

For more information about Naval Institute Press books that are currently available, visit www.usni.org/press/books. To learn about joining the U.S. Naval Institute, please write to:

Member Services
U.S. Naval Institute
291 Wood Road
Annapolis, MD 21402-5034
Telephone: (800) 233-8764
Fax: (410) 571-1703
Web address: www.usni.org